2/17/7X - 3/14/14

The
BILLIE HOLIDAY
Companion

APR   1997

The
BILLIE HOLIDAY
Companion

Seven
Decades of
Commentary

Edited by
LESLIE GOURSE

SCHIRMER BOOKS
An Imprint of
Simon & Schuster Macmillan
New York

Prentice Hall International
London Mexico City New Delhi Singapore Sydney
Toronto

Schirmer Books
An Imprint of Simon & Schuster Macmillan
1633 Broadway
New York, NY 10019

Library of Congress Catalog Card Number: 96-31528

Printed in the United States of America

Printing number
1 2 3 4 5 6 7 8 9 10

Library of Congress Cataloging-in-Publication Data

The Billie Holiday companion : seven decades of commentary / edited by Leslie
   Gourse.
      p.   cm.
   Discography: p. 195
   Includes index.
   ISBN 0-02-864613-4 (alk. Paper)
   1. Holiday, Billie, 1915–1959—Criticism and intepretation. 3. Singers—
United States—Biography. I. Gourse, Leslie.
ML420.H58B45   1997
782.42165'092—dc20
   [B]   96-31528
                                                               CIP
                                                               MN
This paper meets the requirements of ANSI/MOSP 739.48-1992 {Permanence of Paper}.

Contents

Preface

"This month there has been a real find in the person of a singer named Billie Halliday. Although only eighteen she weighs over two hundred pounds, is incredibly beautiful, and sings as well as anybody I ever heard," John Hammond wrote for the London magazine *Melody Maker*, in the April 1933 issue.

Those were probably the first words ever published about Billie Holiday—certainly the first in a magazine with international distribution. John Hammond, working as a journalist, a talent scout for jazz and blues musicians for Columbia Records, and record producer, discovered Billie singing in a Harlem club. She was using the last name "Halliday." Either she felt reluctant to capitalize on her relationship to her father, Clarence Holiday, then a popular big band, rhythm guitarist, or else she preferred to rely upon her own merits, because her father did nothing to encourage her at the start of her career. Today, however, the legend of Billie Holiday has generated more books, films, stage productions, and articles than the life story of any other jazz singer in history, with the possible exception of singer and trumpeter Louis Armstrong. Even the composer Ned Rorem has peppered his memoirs with vignettes of Billie, who influenced the way he composes songs. I took special pleasure in compiling this book, because it distills many of the best articles and excerpts from books about Billie by some of the greatest jazz historians and critics. They present a variety of memories and points of view. Please note that, with minor exceptions, pieces are reprinted as they appeared, with stylistic inconsistencies, British spellings, and grammatical idiosyncrasies retained.

Most aficionados of Lady Day agree that the best, albeit the most depressing, book to appear so far is Donald Clarke's *Wishing on the Moon*, published in 1994. For all its faults and fabrications, Billie

Holiday's own book, *Lady Sings the Blues*, ranks as the most intriguing. Excerpts from these books are included. Whitney Balliett's article on Billie's later recordings, which appeared in his collection *Dinosaurs in the Morning*, comes as close to making Billie's voice and style audible as any printed document about her. The late Leonard Feather's personal memories of Billie both early and late in her career are invaluable. Max Jones captured Billie's essence on paper brilliantly and lovingly, and Willis Conover presented her speaking for herself on the Voice of America. I want to thank all the writers and journalists for their cooperation and good will. They did her justice, as nothing else but her recordings can do.

· · ·

The stories of all the artistically great, financially successful, half-happy jazz singers have many similarities. It's Billie Holiday's often pathetic odyssey that is profoundly offbeat. For that reason, more than for her extraordinarily affecting sound and eccentric style, this beautiful, brawling outlaw, who also, by the way, loved to laugh, has become the most written about woman jazz singer in history.

Billie started to become an icon a few years after her death at age forty-four in 1959, when her recordings were first reissued and sold well. Then, for a while, because her heroin arrests were out of the headlines, she became a shadowy figure. In the 1970s, Diana Ross starred in a film, *Lady Sings the Blues*, which gave new impetus to the legend of Lady Day outside of jazz circles. The screenplay took great liberties with Billie's autobiography of the same name and distressed her close associates so much that many of them winced and walked out of theaters. Billie herself had improvised many of the facts in her book for her cowriter, journalist William Dufty, because she wanted to produce a commercial property and cover up some of the seamier, more unfortunate aspects of her life. Her experience had been far worse than she allowed and about as savory as survival tales of street urchins in wartime Saigon. Perhaps an even better comparison could be made between Billie and the legendary French diva, Edith Piaf, the Sparrow, who started singing in the streets as a child in the impoverished Belleville neighborhood of Paris.

Published in 1956, the original *Lady Sings the Blues* turned out to be the first of many attempts to tell Billie's true story. Each has borrowed facts from the others and tried to unmask previous inaccuracies or supply missing details. Several, beginning with John Chilton's book, *Billie's Blues*, published first in England, have been major works. Robert O'Meally's *Lady Day: The Many Faces of Billie Holiday* won the Ralph J. Gleason award in 1991; O'Meally was the first to *analyze*, not simply admire, the many photographs of Billie. She never looked the same twice. His observation is both astounding and true. Bud Kliment's book for young adults is a good introduction to Billie for general-interest readers. Most of these books are more accurate than her own, though none has been as readable, graphic, emotionally stirring, and accurate as *Wishing on the Moon* by Donald Clarke.

The illegitimate daughter of an illegitimate daughter, Billie was born on April 7, 1915, in Philadelphia, where her mother, Sadie Fagan, worked as a maid. When they went back to Baltimore, Sadie's hometown, their relatives looked down on them. Billie's father, Clarence Holiday, a big-band guitar player and occasional singer, rarely visited them. Billie began her own book with a completely fallacious paragraph, "Mom and Dad were just a couple of kids when they got married. He was 18, she was 15, and I was 3." Actually Sadie and Clarence never married, and Mom was older than Dad. But Billie's grandfather, Sadie's father, was affectionate, and so was his mother, Billie's ancient great-grandmother.

Sadie often sojourned in the north, where salaries for maids were higher than in Baltimore, and left Billie—whose real name was Eleonora Fagan—with relatives and friends. They insulted and hit her. Billie even spent some time in a Catholic institution, the House of the Good Shepherd for Colored Girls, possibly for truancy and other mischief, until her mother secured her release through the help of a white family. (Louis Armstrong had a similar experience in New Orleans.)

As a child, Billie fell in love with recordings by Bessie Smith and Louis Armstrong. Dreaming of a better life for herself, she took her first name from an actress she admired, Billie Dove. A precocious adolescent, Billie Holiday began singing in little joints and whorehouses in Baltimore. Nowadays writers believe that Sadie working in New York learned about her daughter's wildness and sent for Billie a little before 1930. Billie went north, where she refused to become a maid, headed for Harlem, and started working as a prostitute. She gravitated to singing, drawn to clubs by her talent and love for music.

Because of the unusual pitch of her voice, its eerie sound, and her technique of lagging behind—laying back on the beat, as jazz musicians say—to make her singing a lazy drawl, she found commercial success elusive. But fearlessly, she threw anything that came to hand—including large pieces of furniture—at club owners who told her how to sing. And she had the courage to set out as one of the first black singers to tour with a white band, Artie Shaw's, in 1939.

Billie's survival from her earliest days depended on how well she kept up her guard at all times, for she was usually surrounded by abusers, narcissists, hustlers, and ignoramuses. Many of them she never even met; they were in her audiences. By 1941, during her first marriage to a hustler and drug user named Jimmy Monroe, brother of an important Harlem club owner, Clark Monroe, she became addicted to heroin. She went to jail for possession in the mid-1940s, and on the day that she was released after serving nine months of her sentence, she started using drugs again. Her accompanist Bobby Tucker met the train bringing her home to his family's house in New Jersey. He and Billie were going to begin rehearsals for a concert. Right away he noticed the damage she had already done to herself. He was flabbergasted and disconsolate. Nevertheless, with him leading the group behind her, she performed for a sold-out, critically acclaimed concert at Carnegie Hall—one of the best moments of her life.

Unable to break away from all kinds of drugs and alcohol except for short periods, she fought the inevitable breakdown of her body, performing despite cirrhosis of the liver and other ailments until two months before her death. She was arrested on her deathbed for possessing heroin in a hospital. That alone is the stuff that legends are made of.

It's unlikely that all the truth will ever come out in one book or article—or perhaps at all. Clarke's *Wishing on the Moon* on balance constitutes the longest and best attempt so far. He based much of his book about her on countless taped interviews with musicians and friends of Billie's. The tapes were made during the 1970s by a remarkable woman, Linda Lipnack Kuehl, who was preparing to write her own book about Billie. But Linda committed suicide before it was finished.

Since Billie chose to send up a smoke screen to obfuscate so much of her experience, Kuehl's legacy constitutes the biggest and most valuable source material about Lady Day's life. Musicians and friends corroborate and extend each other's perceptions and observations with exquisite candor, even when some of them are forced to reveal their own crazy periods as heroin addicts. Kuehl's tapes were used by Robert O'Meally, too, though he didn't mine the riches as thoroughly as Clarke did. Clarke's portrait, molded from a plethora of directly quoted tapes, brings her to life.

In the aggregate, these books and articles constitute a vivid, sometimes seamy and depressing account of her ups and downs as a heroin addict and even a bisexual. By turns she was a selfish, temperamental star and a generous friend, a cunning politician in the netherworld in which she dwelled, a self-protective fighter who could knock out two sailors when they harassed her at a bar, and a dependent fool ripe for parasites. All sources about Billie say that her men—husbands and managers—beat her up and took far more than their share of her money. (Clarke is the only one who has revealed that she invited these men to beat her up before her performances so she could sing with authentic feeling, and if the men weren't available, she recruited her accompanists to stand in for them.)

It's a wonderful idea to read a wide variety of pieces about Billie. Not even the most authoritative book, Clarke's, has all the best information. Some writers, including Clarke, have had their own pet theories that have little to do with the reality of Billie's life. Clarke indulges in some debatable social philosophizing; for example, he claimed that Billie's problems stemmed from the absence of a father in the house. However, Louis Armstrong, Ella Fitzgerald, and Ethel Waters, along with countless other great American success stories, were brought up by their mothers, aunts, and grandmothers. Billie's insecure circumstances, not simply her fatherless homes, if they can be called homes, gave her a wretched start—and finish.

Then there have been writers, such as Leonard Feather, who have tended toward idealizing Sadie Fagan as a doting mother, and writers who have tried to choose which of her boyfriends and husbands Billie loved most. Clarke, for example, tries to make a case that her first husband, Jimmy Monroe, a pimp, was a better, more loyal fellow than her last husband, Louis McKay. The opposite may have been the truth, according to many people who knew her. McKay, like all her men, was also a hustler, and he, too, hit her. As her manager, he took a great deal of money, and after her death, he inherited substantial royalties from her reissued records. He bided his time before putting a marker on her grave and may have been pushed to take action when his oversight came to light. But for all his faults, he tried mightily at times to preserve what was left of her health and career in the last years of her life. McKay even pulled strings to keep her out of jail on a drug charge, and in so doing put himself in a position where he might have gone to jail himself. Only his connections with politicians and the police saved him.

Billie herself mentioned another man, a married pianist whom she never named, as the one man in her life who made her feel loved. She mentioned him early in her own book, at a point in her life when she was still struggling in Harlem. She set people speculating forever about whom she meant. The most likely candidate, Bobby Henderson, lived with his mother and had a weakness for alcohol. He himself said that he couldn't stand the ferocity of Billie's fights with her mother. Despite her mother's possessiveness, the pianist seemed to blame Billie. That turned out to be his excuse for not marrying her.

The truth may actually be the many facets of Billie that emerge in the variety of writings in this book. The general consensus is that none of her men were sterling characters. Clarke and other writers can be forgiven for jumbling or groping with the facts, such as they were, about one of the most myth-prone aspects of Lady Day's legend. Each article and excerpt is a milestone, a building block in the emerging approximation of the story of Billie Holiday.

More than any other portion of her life, her childhood may never be illuminated. John Chilton, Robert O'Meally, and many article writers accepted Billie's story that she took a nap with her great-grandmother and woke up to find the old woman's arm wrapped tightly around her. Her great-grandmother was dead, and rigor mortis had set in. Donald Clarke disputes the tale, claiming that Billie never knew her great-grandmother. (It is odd that rigor mortis set in so quickly; it must have been a long nap.) Clarke rightly notes that the politics of her scrappy family were complex. But according to him, she was brought up by virtually a wholly new cast of characters—not her relatives, as previous books claim. Clarke opined that white friends, her mother's former employers, may have raised Billie for a time.

Clarke bases his distrust of Billie's version of the story on the testimony of one of her uncles. Yet Clarke doesn't reveal much about that uncle or his relationship to Billie. In fact, the uncle seems to have had a cool, even cold, attitude toward her. And Billie knew the details of her great-grandmother's life and death. In her family no one would have bothered to tell Billie so much about the woman. To his credit, Clarke recognizes that his material on her early life is shaky, and he doesn't wholly trust the testimony of his sources.

There are even conflicting opinions about Billie's early days in New York. Billie contended that she went out on a cold night to audition for a job as a dancer at Pod's and Jerry's, a popular Harlem speakeasy. Billie claimed she was hired as singer that night, because the club's pianist encouraged her to sing once he saw she couldn't dance. She needed that job so she could support her mother, Billie wrote. This anecdote from her autobiography lent pathos to her tale and incidentally shed light on Billie's relationship with her rather parasitic mother. Billie did support her far beyond the call of duty at times and neglected her at other times, much in the same way that Sadie Fagan had treated Billie as a child.

But Clarke and other writers have discovered that Billie had been singing all over Harlem before she worked at Pod's and Jerry's to support herself and to indulge her own love for music. Clarke claims that she was singing at another club, where she invited Pod's and Jerry's pianist, Bobby Henderson, to sit in; that's how they started working together. At that time, she seemed far older than her years, a connoisseur of marijuana, which she had learned to love even before she had arrived in New York. There was nothing of the Little Match Girl in her character.

John Hammond also recalls hearing her first at another club, Monette's, before she went to work at Pod's and Jerry's. He was believed to have been embarrassed by a suggestive song he heard her sing, but not by the way she sang. (Billie recalled Hammond first hearing her at the Log Cabin.) And a few other writers and quite a number of musicians recall Billie singing in many places in Harlem, Queens, and Brooklyn before she worked at Pod's and Jerry's. Some entertainers also have a strong memory of her as a prostitute first and a singer second.

Unique among the writers who did not meet her, Donald Clarke made it unequivocally clear that despite her personality weaknesses, she had the wit and courage to live the part of a pioneering black woman. That assessment might have surprised Billie. She did go so far as to call herself "a race woman," club owner Barney Josephson recalled of her as a young star. But Billie herself probably never cast herself in the role—and certainly not consciously—of a social revolutionary, activist, agitator, or pioneer. She did carry on affairs and friendships with white men and women, some of them socially prominent or famous, whenever she pleased. She judged each situation and person on his or her own merits to the best of her ability and took the risks she thought could further her ambitions. She knew she was an enchantress, able to hold people rapt whether she was sitting naked in a dressing room in front of her sidemen or standing center stage with only one spotlight illuminating her face. As a singer Billie tried to demand her due, even if it meant doing battle with racists or people with tin ears. She trusted her great physical strength to get her through her risky battles with people, drugs, and the law.

Donald Clarke ends his book with a hilarious and bittersweet narrative from pianist Jimmy Rowles, who accompanied her many times. That memoir seemed to me a most fitting way to end this companion. Rowles finished his commentary on Billie by saying, "With Lady Day, you thought permanent." And so do writers and publishers. Books and articles keep coming out about her. They tend to take advantage of the contemporary freedom to bare all sides of a celebrity and make Billie into more and more of a cause celebre and social anomaly. Undoubtedly more books will appear, with claims and counterclaims. Billie may not have been a more commercial singer than Ella Fitzgerald, but "Lady," as her friends called her, is certainly one of the most commercially viable and fascinating jazz musicians as a subject for biographies, sketches, and memoirs. Now there is a fairly large body of engrossing work to enlarge upon. And the treasure chest of the gritty, touching Kuehl tapes has still not been fully explored and revealed.

· · ·

One of the few films of Billie in performance offers perhaps the greatest insight into her life and career. Nat Hentoff wrote about it from his invaluable personal experience, and his article is included in this book. Every jazz lover feels the magnetic pull of this revelatory jazz film.

In December 1957, the Columbia Broadcasting System presented this film as part of a series called "The Seven Lively Arts." Jazz was then slowly coming to be recognized in the United States as one of the great arts and an original American art form. Many of the early jazz players and singers had suffered through hardships and insults because they performed emotionally stirring music that had gotten its start in some of the nation's poorest neighborhoods. In case there is somebody who still doesn't know, early jazz musicians often played in after-hours clubs, gambling houses, and brothels, primarily in African American neighborhoods. Early jazz was also played in gamy white neighborhoods, such as the white section of Storyville in New Orleans. White and African American jazz musicians were discriminated against throughout the first half of the twentieth century wherever they played. But the African Americans, who had created jazz, suffered most of all. The social prejudice and legal strictures against them carried over to their new, free-spirited music. To say the least, it was not accorded the respect it should have gotten.

The civil rights movement—to try to correct the injustices against African Americans, including musicians, of course, and to lift their lives— was just beginning to take effect when CBS presented "The Seven Lively Arts," a television series to showcase the best in American arts and culture. It would be another decade before well-known jazz musicians began teaching in considerable numbers in schools. Not until 1968 would the National Endowment for the Arts start awarding financial grants to jazz musicians for study, composition, and performances.

All along, some white people loved and respected jazz. They became fans and champions of jazz musicians and helped them finally achieve recognition as great creative artists. Nat Hentoff, who became renowned as a civil libertarian, was one of the champions. Some people at CBS recognized how important jazz was; so they decided to include jazz performed by remarkable, pioneering players as part of the arts and culture series in 1957.

At the time, Billie Holiday was one of the most famous jazz singers—a tall, statuesque woman with the most distinctive sound and style in jazz singing history. No one ever mistook her sweet, plaintive, dreamy sound for anyone else's. She made sudden octave jumps and landed true on high notes that other singers would have missed by a mile and sung out of tune. She had a lazy way of improvising melodies—changing and embellishing the tunes and giving them a bluesy feeling whether they were essentially melancholy or bright. She accented her ideas with unusual pauses, rhythmic emphases, and even pretty, musical whines. And she punctuated her songs with surprising chirps. Whitney Balliett called them "laughlike staccato notes," describing one of her most endearing and unique techniques.

It almost didn't matter what words she was singing. The quality of her voice really told her stories. Walt Whitman once wrote about himself, "I contain multitudes"; so did Lady's sound. Especially when her voice became raspy from the wear and tear of her life's experiences, she could manipulate it to dramatize that her heart was breaking from disappointment, though she managed to salvage her passion for singing out of the wreckage.

In 1956, Billie had signed a contract to record for CBS, so she was a natural choice to sing with the group of prominent, male instrumentalists who were asked to play for the TV special. One of the men performing with her was her old friend, tenor saxophonist Lester Young. They had become buddies over twenty years earlier in Harlem, where they discovered that they always performed together with exceptional beauty and sweet communion. Very close friends, but never sweethearts, they had gone to clubs in Harlem and listened to music together. And for the love of music, without pay, they had performed in jam sessions long before they ever recorded together. Music poured from them as slowly as honey can drip. Lester had the smoothest, most mellow sound of all the saxophonists; often Billie sounded exactly like him. Both had small, quiet voices. It was uncanny how much emotion they could communicate with their intimate styles. Neither of them ever belted or screeched a song.

Eventually they drifted apart. Nobody knew exactly what quarrel or difference of opinion may have alienated the friends for a while. Billie may have hurt his feelings in some way; Lester was extremely sensitive. In any case, they lost touch with each other. For most of their adult lives, both suffered from deep-seated personal problems. Lester's weakness was alcohol. It maimed and destroyed him. When the taping of the CBS show brought them together, they were both very sick. But they became radiant with the power of their musical gifts and kinship.

For the show, which was taped in black and white, all the musicians dressed in casual clothes. Lester wore his trademark porkpie hat. Billie pulled her lustrous hair straight back from her temples. The ponytail style called attention to the fine bones and shape of her oval face, which was much thinner than it had been in her heyday. She had a pretty little nose and an exquisite, regal-looking profile. As usual by that time, she brought a bottle of gin and cans of Coca Cola to the studio. She drank and smoked continuously when she wasn't singing. The audience didn't see her do that. Strangers rarely had a view of anything but her charm during a performance.

Singing her own composition, "Fine and Mellow," which she had first recorded with her own orchestra in 1939, she and Lester performed with languid, plaintive sounds. With her eyes shining, she watched him raptly and joyfully as he played. A slight smile curved her lips. Her head swayed slowly to signify that she was mesmerized by his smooth, fluid style. Her dreamy expression may have been abetted, too, by the alcohol she had been drinking. The audience for this television special had no idea of her personal troubles at that moment, because her performance was so touching and seductive to see and hear.

Still photographs of Billie taken at that taping have been used extensively ever since for books, albums, advertisements, posters, T-shirts, and every type of jazz-related enterprise. Billie's face alone has become symbolic of the mystery and magic of jazz.

If her voice was no longer as clear and fresh as it had been at the start of her career, her star quality, her singing style, and her passion for music had endured. What she had lost in animation, she replaced with feeling and the aura of experience. And the film she helped make that day—"The Sound of Jazz"—became one of the most famous films in jazz history. Other contributions to the CBS series are never seen these days, to my knowledge. But "The Sound of Jazz" endured because it was high art—an easily understood testimonial to the hypnotic power of jazz and the artistry of the pioneering musicians, with Billie as the main attraction.

She died a year and a half later.

WHITNEY BALLIETT

Whitney Balliett, who began writing about jazz for the *New Yorker* in 1957, ranks unquestionably as one of the greatest jazz critics of the century; some people choose him as their favorite jazz critic. He is a master of *le mot juste*. In part because of his ability to pick the perfectly appropriate adjective, he can effect the miracle of writing a pithy piece that encompasses a musician's entire career accurately and with uncanny vividness. His overview of Billie's life and art serves to introduce this entire companion so well that all the other articles seem to flow from his precis.

His pieces for the *New Yorker* have been collected into at least a dozen books. He was born in New York on April 17, 1926, graduated from Cornell University with a bachelor's degree, and first contributed to the *Saturday Review of Literature* and the *New Yorker* in the early 1950s.

In June of 1937, Billie Holiday, backed lustrously by Buck Clayton, Lester Young, and Jo Jones, made an extraordinary recording of an inconsequential Tin Pan Alley tune called "Me, Myself and I." The lyric ends, "Me, myself and I are all in love with you." The song could be a description of Holiday herself, for she was at least three different people. The most famous was the tortured tabloid figure, who desiccated and dying, was arrested in her hospital bed by the New York police for possession of drugs. (This Holiday, now largely legendary, is very much with us—in movies, on the stage, and in novels, poems, biographies, and autobiographies, including her own hocus-pocus *Lady Sings the Blues*.) The second Holiday was the singer, the statuesque presence, standing on the stage with a gardenia in her hair, her elbows bent at her sides, her left hand snapping silently on the afterbeat, her head tilted back, almost visible music is pouring out of her. (This Holiday can be heard, at various removes, in the singing of Frank Sinatra, Julie Wilson, Nancy Harrow, Peggy Lee, and Susannah McCorkle.) The third Billie Holiday was almost invisible. She was the insecure child who, less than twenty years younger than her ineffectual parents, never had the chance to grow up. Battered by racism, by hoody music-business people, and by a succession of manipulative lovers (she married twice), she hid behind a violent temper and a foul mouth, and searched most of her life for solace in drugs and drink. (This Holiday remains as elusive as ever.)

Billie Holiday was born in Philadelphia in April of 1915 to Sadie Fagan and Clarence Holiday, unmarried teenagers. She was raised in Baltimore, and she was a wild one. At ten, she was sent to a Catholic reformatory, the House of the Good Shepherd for Colored Girls, and at twelve she was a prostitute. When she was fourteen or fifteen, she moved to New York. She had been singing since she was thirteen, and several years after she moved north she was discovered in a Harlem club by Mildred Bailey and Red Norvo. Billie made her first important recordings in 1935, when she sang "I Wished On the Moon," "What a Little Moonlight Can Do," "Miss Brown to You," and "A Sunbonnet Blue" with a small pickup band that included Benny Goodman, Roy Eldridge, Ben Webster, Teddy Wilson, and Cozy Cole. She was already scratching out a living in such Harlem clubs as the Yeah Man, the Hot-Cha, Pod's and Jerry's, the Alhambra Grill, and Dickie Wells's Clam House. Her career was never smooth. She took her first downtown job at the Famous Door, on Fifty-second Street. Working opposite the roughneck white New Orleans trombonist George Brunies, she was told not to sit with the customers between sets—to stay out of sight. She lasted four days. Then she joined Fletcher Henderson at the Grand Terrace in Chicago; the manager, Ed Fox, shouted at her, told her she sang "too slow," and fired her after a single evening. She went back to Fifty-second Street, alternating at the Onyx Club with the violinist Stuff Smith. Smith became jealous of all the applause she got, and she was fired again. She retreated to Monroe's Uptown House, in Harlem, and, in 1937, joined Count Basie, leaving under mysterious circumstances after less than a year. Then, putting her head in the lion's mouth, she went with Artie Shaw, who fended off the bigots until Maria Kramer, the owner of the Hotel Lincoln, in New York, where Shaw had landed an important job, made her use the service entrance and the freight elevator, and she quit.

She was given a reprieve in 1939. Barney Josephson, the owner of the new and completely integrated Café Society Downtown, hired her, and she stayed for a (more or less) peaceable year. Josephson did not allow his performers to use marijuana at the club, and between shows Billie would sometimes get in a cab and go up to Central Park and smoke pot. "One night she came back and I could tell by her eyes that she was really high," Josephson once said. "She finished her first number and I guess she didn't like the way the audience reacted. Performers often wear just gowns and slippers, no underwear, and at the end of the song Billie turned her back to the audience, bent over, flipped up her gown, and walked off the floor." Billie worked on Fifty-second Street in the forties, and it was there that she began wearing her famous gardenia. The singer Sylvia Syms claims that she was responsible for Billie's first putting the flower in her hair. She used to hang around Billie on the Street, and one night, at Kelly's Stable, Billie burned her hair with a curling iron just before she was to go onstage. Syms ran down the street to the Three Deuces and bought a gardenia from the hat-check girl, and Billie fastened it on the burned place. "I can remember her . . . at the Onyx Club," Syms has said, "coming down those little stairs in the back and the lights softening and the room becoming silent and her moving onto the stage and looking just like a panther."

In 1947, she was arrested for the possession of drugs, and her life began going downhill. She spent nine months in the federal women's reformatory in Alderson, West Virginia. The New York police revoked her cabaret card, and she was never again able to work legally in a New York night club. (Without a cabaret card, entertainers could not appear in any place where liquor was sold. The police supervised this cruel, archaic practice until the late sixties, when it finally ended.) She was allowed to give concerts in New York, and, of course, she could work in clubs elsewhere. She earned a considerable amount of money, but it slipped through her fingers or was stolen by hangers-on and dishonest managers. Drugs, then heavy drinking began to affect her voice. But the old lightsome Holiday would surface occasionally. She sang, startlingly, like the bluebird of 1937 on a European tour she made in 1954. She also sang well on the CBS television show "The Sound of Jazz" in 1957, and her sequence—she sat on a high stool, her hair in a ponytail—has been shown so often on television that it has become the image most people have of her. She died in 1959, at the age of forty-four. She had fifteen fifty-dollar bills strapped to one of her legs and seventy cents in the bank.

No one had ever sung like Billie Holiday when she first appeared. She was deceptive. She made her voice sound smaller, more little-girlish, than it actually was; it gave the impression of being completely homemade. (She took her rhythmic ideas from Louis Armstrong and her poise from Bessie Smith.) Her articulation was so clear that she seemed to speak her lyrics, and her vibrato let out just enough emotion. She had the uncanny ability to digest new songs at a recording session and sing them—improvise on them, really—as if she had known them for years. Billie was a rhythm machine. No jazz instrumentalist has had a more flexible sense of time, and it was infallible. In such recordings as "It's Too Hot for Words," "Foolin' Myself," "I Can't Pretend," "I Don't Know If I'm Coming or Going," "You're Just a No Account," and "A Sailboat in the Moonlight" she disconnects each song from its chump-chump-chump rhythm, and, for the two minutes or so that her vocal lasts, makes the song float along somewhere behind the beat, thereby setting up an irresistible, swinging tug-of-war between the original tempo and her version of it. This freeing effect was doubled when Lester Young accompanied her. They were twins rhythmically and tonally, and while she sang he would improvise a soft countermelody behind her—applauding her, caressing her, welding their voices. (Young died just four months before Billie; their voices in decline, faltering and bare, had remained much alike.) These passages—in "I'll Never Be the Same," "A Sailboat in the Moonlight," "Born to Love"—are incomparable lullabies.

In the late thirties, Billie began to take herself seriously. Her morose, indelible recording of "Strange Fruit," a devastating song about lynching, became something of an event, and she began to be courted by liberals and lefties. Her voice grew heavier, she used dramatic dying notes, and her larking, daring quality diminished. She lost some of her rhythmic agility. She still sang very well—better, indeed, than anyone else—but the joy and the quickstepping intensity were less apparent. This new seriousness persisted through the forties and was underlined by the strings and bouncy big bands she was given as accompaniment. Then around 1950, her voice took on a subtly dismaying hue. Her undertones and low notes began to sound almost burnt; they took on an acrid quality. By the mid-fifties, only the outlines of her original style were in place. Her voice came and went, just as Mabel Mercer's did in her last years, and she often used a gravelly parlando. She refused to let on that anything had changed, and this bravery gave her a confusing majesty.

PART ONE

God Bless the Child: Memoirs

Leonard Feather was one of the most prolific writers about jazz. He was also involved in the jazz world as a composer, a concert and record producer, a member of many organizations affiliated with jazz, and a talent scout and a career promoter. Because of all his activities, Leonard Feather knew many musicians very well, including Billie Holiday. The following is one of the most intimate views of Lady Day over the long haul of her life. Feather met her soon after she left Count Basie's band in 1938; he toured in Europe with her under living conditions that would have crushed a less spirited woman, and he was one of the people who witnessed her deterioration and worried about her during the final months of her life. Her entire odyssey is recounted here in a very gentle but graphic way. The article testifies to Feather's talent as a chronicler of the jazz world in which he thrived.

Leonard Feather was born in London, England, on September 13, 1914, where he attended the University College. He studied piano and arranging, and he began his myriad activities in the jazz world even before he arrived in New York City in 1935. In the early 1940s, he wrote criticism for *Metronome* and *Esquire* magazines, and increasingly he established himself primarily as a critic. By the 1960s, he became the jazz critic at the *Los Angeles Times*, a post he held until the end of his life on September 11, 1994.

He was always associated with many great singers and musicians, producing recordings and writing songs—"Evil Gal Blues" for

Dinah Washington being one example. British jazz pianist George Shearing has said that Leonard was pivotal in helping him build a performing and recording career in the United States. Leonard produced Sarah Vaughan's first recordings. He became world renowned for his jazz encyclopedias done with the help of critic/writer Ira Gitler. In 1949, Leonard published his first book, *Inside Bebop* (later reprinted as *Inside Jazz*), which introduced the world to the art of bebop and the great bebop players.

For *Metronome* magazine he created an entertaining and engrossing column, "The Blindfold Test," challenging prominent musicians to identify by ear whom they were listening to. Later *Down Beat* magazine continued the column. His 1950 test with Billie published in *Metronome* appears in this collection.

A complex and extremely influential critic, who was madly in love with jazz, he irritated some people, and he also made great friends in the jazz world; sometimes they were the same people at different junctures of their careers. According to critic Gary Giddins, the legendary saxophonist, trumpeter, arranger, composer, and bandleader Benny Carter sat at Leonard's bedside, when Leonard lay moribund in a coma in a hospital. Day after day, Benny played recordings for Leonard. His commitment to jazz was complete and profound.

In 1935, at a studio on Long Island, Duke Ellington and his orchestra made one of their rare motion-picture appearances in an all-musical two-reeler, *Symphony in Black*. It incorporated, for a few incandescent moments, the totally unfamiliar and unidentified sight and sound of Billie Holiday. She sang just twelve bars of blues. The picture was made shortly before Billie's twentieth birthday; later that year her career was launched in earnest when the first records in which she was vocalist with Teddy Wilson's small band were released. They made a profound impact on the jazz audience.

Billie was a second-generation jazz artist; her father, Clarence Holiday, had played guitar with Fletcher Henderson and Benny Carter. She and Ella Fitzgerald became prominent at the same time. Both came from broken homes; both had suffered years of poverty and Jim Crow before achieving recognition as jazz singers; yet there the resemblance ends. Their subsequent attitudes, styles, and careers contrasted as sharply as those of Charlie Parker and Dizzy Gillespie a decade later: one an emotionally unstable, supremely innovative artist destined to die young, a victim of narcotics and of social pressures; the other a greatly gifted performer, who would ultimately be acknowledged as a major jazz influence, and live to enjoy the financial rewards and professional security that should have been achieved by both.

Although some critics believe (wrongly, in my opinion) that Ella Fitzgerald is no more than an exceptionally capable popular singer, no such assessment was ever made about Billie Holiday. Every note of every lyric she sang proved her to be the complete, untrained, unadulterated, definitive jazz singer.

To the public, of course, the front-page headline, freak-show aspect of her life was uppermost; ever since her death there has been talk of a motion picture or stage show about her. Ironically the artist most often suggested as best suited for the role of Billie Holiday used to be Dorothy Dandridge, whose own tragic life ended a few years after Billie's. After Billie's posthumous admission to the *Down Beat* Hall of Fame in 1962, I wrote: "It is easy to imagine how *The Billie Holiday Story* would shape up on Broadway or in Hollywood. Who will they get to sing the sound track? Mabel Mercer? Chris Connor? Who will score the music? Lawrence Welk?" Yet in 1971 fantasy became reality: It was announced that a multi-million-dollar motion picture was to be made in which the statuesque, jazz-rooted Billie Holiday would be portrayed by the diminutive, soul-soaked Diana Ross. As if this were not enough, Miss Ross would do her own sound track. If, God forbid, our grandchildren had to base the knowledge of musical history on the biographical distortions of the motion picture industry, they would be hard put to understand the high esteem in which we held some of our idols.

There are those who listen to Billie Holiday as they would read a Scott Fitzgerald novel. Too far separated from Billie's era to feel any direct sense of communication, they can nevertheless penetrate the veil of time drawing from her gifts-and-caviar tones some understanding of what she brought to music.

Then there are those who can hear Billie more subjectively, as part of a world they once knew, and remember a unique segment of musical history that returns fleetingly to life when they listen to her records.

I once wrote:

Billie Holiday's voice is one of the incomparable sounds that jazz has produced . . . the timbre, despite its gradual deepening through the years, has remained unique. The coarse yet warmly emotional quality of this sound, and the exquisite delicacy of her phrasing and dynamic nuances, were often given added luster by the support she gained from her long association with Lester Young and other members of the Basie band on her earlier records.

If you find no message here or in her records, perhaps the only thing you can do is take a backward journey through time and be born in the twenties, so that the arrival of Billie's glorious four years of regular sessions with the Teddy Wilson combos (Brunswick-Vocalion-Columbia) will coincide with your high school or college days. And by the time she spends a full year at the Onyx on Fifty-second Street, reducing audiences of noisy drunks to silence with her gracious, dignified, gardenia-embellished beauty as she sings her brand-new hit "Lover Man," you will be in your twenties, and part of a warm and wonderful new jazz era that is growing with Billie. By the time you are in your thirties you will have been so conditioned to a love of the Holiday sound that you will excuse the little flaws, the gradual withdrawal of assurance, the fading of the gardenia. By now you are in love with Lady Day and every thing she does; each tortured lyric she sings about the men who have laid waste her life will have meaning for you whether she hits the note or misses it, holds it or lets it falter.

But chances are you weren't born in the twenties, and so you must listen to the early Holiday records as you might read *Tender Is The Night*, trying to assimilate the mood of the era. Perhaps it will bring her a little closer if you know something of the young woman who was the maker of so much that we found beautiful.

Billie died at forty-four. Like many people who led turbulent, stimulant-governed lives, she was unpredictable, moody, impassioned, paradoxical. With the possible exception of her mother, there was not a single person among those she was fond of, or who were fond of her, with whom she was not at one time or another violently at odds. But Billie could not stay angry long with anyone, nor could any of us who loved her and quarreled with her hold onto our grievances. As her close friend Maely Dufty, wife of her biographer, once said, "Billie's not a woman—she's a habit."

It would be a gigantic oversimplification to pretend that social conditions alone shaped her life, formed her vocal style, led to her death. Ella Fitzgerald's family background was at least partly comparable to Billie's, yet Ella's career, untouched by scandal, brought her undreamed-of success. For Billie it was marijuana at fourteen, a jail term for prostitution at fifteen, and heroin addiction from her late twenties to her death.

What made the two singers' lives so different from one another? What caused the self-destructiveness in Billie that ultimately proved fatal?

For anyone who knew her, it is impossible to listen to Billie's records today and not be engulfed by a wave of nostalgia. With one of her early 78s on the turntable, I flash back to a small, dimly lit Harlem apartment in 1938, where I first interviewed Lady Day.

A door opened on the first floor up; a huge woman emerged, glancing down the stairs with mixed curiosity and suspicion. "You the feller wants to see Billie?"

There was no need to ask who was addressing me. The round face and full mouth; the whole impression of Billie multiplied by three, pound for pound, told me that this was Mrs. Holiday, the patient and aggrieved mother whose life was vainly dedicated to achieving communication with her daughter.

The little living room was in almost complete darkness. Four or five men sat intently absorbed in *Lights Out*, a weekly radio thriller. Closest to the radio, and wallowing in an aural orgy of murder and gunfire, was the woman who, as always, was the focal point of the room. Sleek-haired, smartly dressed, elaborately made up, Billie to me was the epitome of glamour, a young woman by whose side I was neither a visiting London journalist nor a guest but simply a naive and nervous cipher in the presence of royalty.

As *Lights Out* ended, the party came to life, and Billie brought out a big stack of records, her own, Teddy Wilson's, and dozens more. On the mantelpiece were signed photographs of Teddy, Maxine Sullivan, Pha Terrell (a popular black ballad singer with Andy Kirk's band) and one of Billie herself in an ingenious frame composed of 5,000 matchsticks—she told me proudly that it had been painstakingly assembled and sent to her from jail by an admirer who was serving a twenty-year sentence. "He sent me a song along with it that he wrote and wants me to use. Maybe I'll do it on my next session."

Nothing about Billie during that evening presaged misfortune or doom. Instead, an unselfconscious camaraderie was immediately discernible in her warm, friendly manner. I asked her to play "Billie's Blues," which had a special meaning for me: as John Hammond's guest, I had first met her during the session at which it was cut. It was doubly significant to me because I had been as much in love with the blues as with Billie.

Asked where she had found the unusual lyrics, she replied, "I've been singing them same blues as long as I can remember. I made up those words myself. That's how I made my whole income as a composer. A couple of months ago I got a royalty check for the record—just eleven bucks!" but she said it without a trace of the rancor that twenty years later was to run through the pages of her *Lady Sings the Blues*.

Sadie Fagan Holiday interrupted us with the story of how her daughter used to annoy an aunt with whom she lived by singing those same blues about "my man this and my man that." Billie was a child, she was told, and had no business singing about such things. "But the first song she ever sang was 'My Mammy,' and she used to sing that to me all the time!"

During my first visit to Billie's apartment, I found her to be poised and gracious. I knew no more about her private indulgences than Mrs. Holiday did, but had I known I'm sure I would have justified them with elaborate rationalizations. I have a theory about Billie that conflicts with the conventional explanations of her life and times. I believe that if she had been taken out of the environment that was slowly beginning to swallow her up, the end would not have come when it did and her vivid patterns of gently twisted melody might still be part of our lives. Had she accepted an offer to go to England, for example, and found there a group of admirers who could give her personal and economic security, the agony and the squalor might have been avoided.

On that first evening I had tried to convince her that she and the overseas audience were ready for one another. "Well, I had one offer last year, 50 pounds a week," she said. (That was $250, and in those days, for Billie, it was a very substantial temptation.) "But those musicians over there they can just about read and that's all, huh? I'd have to bring my own musicians with me."

I tried to reassure her by playing a few of Benny Carter's new recordings with a British band. She hadn't suspected until that moment that British musicians had even heard of swing music. When a particular passage moved her, she would say, "Man, that sure sends me!" and rock in gentle rhythm around the room. But when a passage displeased her, she would murmur, "No, I ain't comin'!"

It did indeed seem to me, even then, that Billie preferred balling to taking care of business. But this may have been the effect rather than the cause of her misfortunes; none of us knew then the frightening story of her childhood.

Billie's career at the time of our 1938 encounter was in one of its first states of temporary collapse. She had been on the road for some months as Count Basie's band vocalist; now Basie had let her go. It seemed apparent to me and to others close to the scene that many of her white audiences did not probe far enough beneath the tonal eccentricity of her style to appreciate her fully. She had refused to change her style, ignoring those who urged her to commercialize it.

All the might-have-beens of Lady Day's life cannot alter one central fact: from 1935 (the year when her long series of collaborations with Teddy Wilson was inaugurated) until her death, Billie Holiday put on record a timbre like that of no other woman, a manner of phrasing evocative at times of Bessie Smith or Louis Armstrong, and a casual air that lent gaily rhythmic meaning to the most trivial of tunes.

Of the hundreds of records she cut between her debut with Benny Goodman in 1933 and her last, stumbling effort for MGM in 1959, less than a dozen were blues. She was always referred to in the lay press as a blues or torch singer, yet essentially she was neither. There is a tendency on the part of latecomers to the art of Holiday-analysis to draw everything in terms of gloom and doom, to equate with her private life the quality she gave to her songs. This posturing was aggravated as early as 1938, when suddenly she became an object of social significance. There is a measure of truth to John Hammond's observation that "artistically, the worst thing that ever happened to her was the overwhelming success of her singing of the Lewis Allen poem 'Strange Fruit,' which amassed a host of fans among the intelligentsia and the left." I disagree, however, with John's implication that Billie's career, as a consequence, moved steadily downhill from 1939, when she introduced that song. He and I shared enough evenings at Cafe Society in the 1940's, and I spent enough unforgettable nights on tour with her in Europe in 1954, to know that her magic never quite left her, not until very close to the end, when her physical equipment itself collapsed.

But there is another and highly relevant reason for refuting the theory that Billie was a messenger of misery. It is to be found in one of the most durable compilations of her records: *Billie Holiday: The Golden Years*, Vol II. Checking the lyrical and melodic character of the material, the happy songs and the sad, I found, not much to my surprise, that the former outnumber the latter by about two to one. That she sang twice as many salutes to love and light as odes to missing men and gloomy Sundays will come as a surprise only to those who did not know Billie during those years.

"Yes," you may say, "but she can convert the happiest rhythm songs into blues." On the contrary, the fact is that Billie often turned a melancholy refrain into something with a light, bouncing air, as is immediately demonstrated in *I'm Painting the Town Red*. When she tells us that she is painting the town red to hide a heart that is blue, you are not, if you understand Billie, listening to those corny lyrics. You are reacting to what she does with the melody, and this, it seems to me, was her chief purpose in many of her songs.

Billie's spectrum ranged from a light treatment of mediocre tunes to a deep probing of first-rate lyrics, as in "Solitude" and the magnificent "My Last Affair," a too-long forgotten song by Haven Johnson. Given the kind of songs that often constituted her material, one can only be thankful for her "Tain't watcha do, it's the way thatcha do it" attitude.

It has been said often that Billie rose above her surroundings, that in later years she was saddled with batteries of pretentious strings and indifferent rhythm sections. Yet one must remember that her musical accompaniment from the very start ranged from superb to fair to downright mediocre.

It is impossible to describe Billie's voice: the tart, gritty timbre, the special way of bending a note downward, the capacity for reducing a melody to its bare bones or, when it seemed appropriate, for retaining all its original qualities. But it is worth noting that although her actual vocal range was limited, her emotional range was not; nevertheless during the early years her sound broadened rapidly beyond the high-pitched, teen-aged hollering of the two tunes ("Your Mother's Son-in-Law" and "Riffin' the Scotch") in which she appeared as guest vocalist with a pickup recording band led by Benny Goodman. John Hammond produced this early session, as well as many others during her evolutionary phase. His tireless, unpaid efforts in her behalf changed the pattern of her career. From an aimless round of obscure uptown nightclubs she was set on a course that could lead to success, despite the restrictions of being black. But just as surely as Jim Crow, she herself was responsible for many lost opportunities.

Little by little, Billie's relationship with Hammond deteriorated. His dedication to the lustrous warmth of her voice was not matched by her dedication to work. Hammond, for one thing, would not allow a recording session to be interrupted while its star participant lounged around smoking pot in the hall. Whatever the conditions, the recording dates from 1935 to 1942 produced a series of masterpieces; for many who knew her then, her talents were crystallized during this seven-year span. She wrote "God Bless the Child," with Arthur Herzog, after a quarrel with her mother, although that kindly, unsophisticated woman probably never fully grasped the sardonic import of Billie's lyrics. An argument between Billie and her husband, Jimmy Monroe (he had arrived home "with lipstick on his collar"), led to "Don't Explain," another song written with Herzog.

During this time Billie changed physically and emotionally from a chubby, pretty girl into an exquisitely beautiful woman, tall and slender, always impeccably gowned when she worked. Her innate sexuality informed the slightest movement of her body, every snap of her fingers, every twist of her lips. But this was also the time when Billie was victimized by the cruelest, ugliest humiliations of racial discrimination. I remember particularly traveling one day from New York to Boston for her debut with Artie Shaw's orchestra at the Roseland Ballroom. As the first black vocalist ever to join a white orchestra, she was more than a mere token; for Shaw himself she was a dangerous experiment, a calculated risk.

Billie did not simply wear a mask to cover her apprehension; she sensed how self-defeating it would be to nourish any resentment toward those who felt only empathy and affection for her. Her grievances and animosities were selective. Here unwillingness to strike out indiscriminately at the whole white world, tempting though that may have been, is poignantly expressed in the chapter of her book dealing with the Shaw ordeal. Amplifying her statement that "most of the cats in the band were wonderful to me," she relates painful incidents in which Shaw, Tony Pastor, Georgie Auld, and others fought actively to protect her against the outright crackers, the well-meaning but ignorant whites who hurt her unwittingly, and all the other hassles that were a daily part of the obstacle course of living black.

Professionally, the years after she renounced touring as a big-band vocalist ("I swear I'll never sing with a band again," she told me after leaving Shaw) were those in which her life seemed most stable. She played better nightclubs for bigger money, and received an award each year the *Esquire* jazz poll was held (1944–47).

Yet it is important to bear in mind that in 1942 the jazz fans who voted for their favorite singers in the *Down Beat* poll elected Helen Forrest (who, ironically, had been the white "protection" second vocalist with Shaw during Billie's incumbency). In 1943 they chose Jo Stafford, and in 1944, probably Billie's peak year musically and commercially, the winner was Dinah Shore. Such were the patterns of American life, and it would be naive to think that this did not affect Lady Day's view of the world.

After her first victory in the *Esquire* poll, Billie was invited, along with a dozen other winners, to take part in a concert I had been deputized to assemble. It was not only the first jazz concert ever held at the Metropolitan Opera House, but the first gala occasion at which Billie was treated as a major artist. The following year she made the long train haul to California, for a celebration at the Los Angeles Philharmonic Auditorium. This time Hollywood celebrities presented the "Esky" statuettes. Billie, in superb vocal form, was genuinely moved when the award was presented to her by Jerome Kern. This sort of treatment, of course, would have been accorded her more regularly if the projected European tour had actually come about; but there was always some delay, some interruption, professional or personal.

In 1946, recognized at long last by the motion-picture industry, Billie was assigned a role in a feature film, a ridiculous pseudo-jazz history called *New Orleans*. True to the pattern of Hollywood, she played a servant. I recall her attempt to cover her frustration when she broke the news to me. "I'll be playing a maid," she said, "but she's really a cute maid."

Billie sang well in the picture and had some effective scenes with Louis Armstrong. But it was the last event of any consequence before her habit and the law finally tangled. In May 1947 she was arrested in Philadelphia for narcotics violations. The district attorney observed: "She has had following her the worst type of parasites and leeches you can think of. . . . in the past three years she has earned a quarter of a million dollars; last year it was $56,000 and she doesn't have any of the money."

After kicking cold turkey, Lady spent a year and a day at the Federal rehabilitation establishment for women at Alderson, West Virginia. Soon after her release she appeared in a triumphant concert at Carnegie Hall. She looked healthy to the point of overweight but she was still beautiful.

Those who knew her only through the lurid headlines may find it hard to understand that at heart Billie might have liked to be an average, well-adjusted housewife. She was a capable cook; she liked neatness and order; she yearned for "straight" social relationships. But once she was in the grip of heroin, she saw her dream disappear. After the breakup of her marriage and several turbulent relationships with men who encouraged her dependence on drugs, she became involved with a man named John Levy; in 1949 the two of them were arrested in San Francisco. (Levy died many years ago.)*

---

*This John Levy is no relation to the bassist John Levy, who played for Billie at her Carnegie Hall concert and later became the Los Angeles-based manager of many great jazz artists [Editor].

Down Beat reported Billie's situation following a masterful defense by her lawyer, Jake Ehrlich: "Broke and alone after her manager John Levy left her to face trial here . . . Billie Holiday decided to go back to work . . . But despite the fact that the jury said they believed Billie had been framed by Levy, she said, 'If he was to walk into the room this minute, I'd melt. He's my man and I love him.' The trial appeared to confirm that a package of opium had been planted on Billie just before the raid. Billie came to trial with a black eye she said Levy had given her. 'You should see my back,' she added. 'And he even took my silver blue mink—18 grand worth of coat . . . I got nothing now, and I'm scared.'"

During the 1950s some of her fears were alleviated through the help of Norman Granz, who signed her up for his record company and got her concert dates. Then at last, in January of 1954, the dream we had talked about sixteen years earlier became a reality. Billie was to star in a show I had been asked to package for Nils Hellstrom, the Swedish concert promoter. The tour would take us all over the Continent, and Billie would then play a couple of dates on her own in England.

The man in Billie's life now was Louis McKay, later her widower. He accompanied her on the tour and seemed able to keep her in good mental and physical shape. The other musicians were her pianist, Carl Drinkard; the Buddy DeFranco quartet; the Red Norvo trio; and an all-girl instrumental trio led by Beryl Booker, a talented pianist.

By 1954 Lady Day's reputation preceded and predamned her at every step. Although the Billie Holiday who traveled through Scandinavia, Germany, Holland, Belgium, France and Switzerland was not the same woman who had put fear into the hearts of nightclub owners and of musicians who worked for her, nevertheless such were the misgivings about becoming involved with her that none of the three bass players and two drummers wanted to work with Billie and Drinkard. Finally Red Mitchell and the drummer Elaine Leighton agreed to do the job—but the agreement was arrived at too late for rehearsal.

We were supposed to open in Stockholm, but the airport there was snowed under. We were all dumped off the plane in Copenhagen to straggle in by train a few hours before the first show. The critics, knowing nothing of this, gave everyone including Billie a cold reception. Morale was not improved when it was reported next day that a hypodermic needle had been found in Billie's dressing room. Later it was learned that her visitors had included a Swedish musician who was a notorious junkie, but to this day I am uncertain whether Billie was at fault that night. During the rest of the tour (except for one night when she drank before the show instead of afterward) her behavior was impeccable, whether she was using or not.

The working conditions on a tour of this kind would tax the patience and the voice of any artist. Photographers were a constant problem. They jumped up on the bandstand while she was singing, and in Cologne, during her poignant ending to "I Cover the Waterfront," one leapt forward and exploded a flash gun within inches of her face. The audience reacted with a barrage of titters, whistles, and derisive applause for the intruder, yet Billie behaved as though she had noticed nothing and went on with her performance.

Often, if we went to a nightclub after the show, everyone would beg her for "just one song," and weary though she might be, Billie usually obliged. One evening, after the concert in Nuremberg, Billie and Beryl Booker were invited by some officers to a U.S. Army hotel, which for years had been frequented by Hitler and the Nazi hierarchy. In the big salon where the Fuhrer had once roared and raved, the dry-ice tones of Billie rang smooth and clear across the room.

I was not surprised by her cooperation and comportment throughout the tour. Everything contrasted sharply with her life in America. Instead of the second-rate ghetto theaters, tacky dressing rooms, and half-empty minor-league nightclubs in Detroit and Pittsburgh that typified her directionless career, she found audiences teeming with fans who had dreamed for years of seeing her, bouquets presented to her onstage and backstage, autograph hunters, deferential treatment—and never a glimpse of racism. When treated like a lady, she acted accordingly. Her morale was never better. Only once, when a newspaperman asked about narcotics, did she bridle. "I didn't come 3,000 miles to talk about that. That's past and forgotten. I don't even want to think about it."

My most vivid memory of the tour is of her indomitable pride and firmness under pressure. One morning in Brussels we missed the musicians' bus that was to take us to Frankfurt, West Germany. With Hellstrom and McKay, we chased clear across Belgium in a taxi to the German border, then had to change there for a German cab all the way to Dusseldorf—and arrived shivering at the airport to find the last plane to Frankfurt had just left. A small plane was hastily chartered. It seated only four; since I was required to appear as the show's master of ceremonies, Louis McKay had to proceed by train. With the pilot and Hellstrom up front in the freezing cold plane, Billie and I huddled in the back seat and killed a small bottle of Steinhaegen, a remedy that did little to allay our incipient frostbite. We reached Frankfurt barely in time for the show. To Hellstrom's amazement, Billie gave two magnificent performances that night, showing not a trace of the ordeal.

This incident, however, reveals one side of the Billie Holiday paradox. Two days later, after a particularly gruelling day's travel, she announced that she was calling Joe Glaser in New York to arrange for her immediate return home in mid-tour. Louis McKay assured us that she was "just talking," and he was right.

Back in the United States after that generally heartening interlude, Billie found herself surrounded once again by her usual crowd of pushers and hangers-on. Significantly the very next event reported in her biography after the European tour is her arrest in Philadelphia in 1956. It was as though nothing of consequence had happened in the interim.

Later that year Billie's self-esteem was helped by the publication of *Lady Sings the Blues*. Written in collaboration with William Dufty, it is a mixture of half-truths, untruths, and events seen by Billie through a haze of wishful thinking. John Hammond, Teddy Wilson, and others close to her were quick to point out the inaccuracies, as was I; yet the overall impression of the impact of racism on the life of a gifted black American woman compensates for many of the flaws and distortions.

For anyone who knows the circumstances of Billie's death, the final chapter contains two passages that cannot be forgotten: "There isn't a soul on earth who can say that their fight with dope is over until they're dead." And the concluding paragraph: "Tired? You bet. But all that I'll soon forget with my man."

By 1958 her man was gone: Louis McKay took off for California. Her voice half-shot, the rich timbre lost except on an occasional good night when she pulled herself together, Billie continued the round of clubs and theaters, her asking price down and her morale even lower.

In September she agreed to make guest appearances at two history-of-jazz concerts I was staging. Several of her old friends took part: Mal Waldron, her pianist; Georgie Auld, a friend from the Shaw band days; and Buck Clayton, whose delicate, sensitive trumpet had been so important to Billie when she sang with Basie.

One of the shows, at a theater in Wallingford, Connecticut, was recorded. Billie sang "I Wished on the Moon," the first tune she had recorded during the first Teddy Wilson small-band session inaugurating the classic series of Wilson-Holiday collaborations; she followed it with "Lover Man." The record confirms that her voice had regained its old timbre and assurance. But backstage over a drink before the show, she told my wife: "I'm so goddamn lonely. Since Louis and I broke up I got nobody—nothing." Her misery was the inevitable result of an impossible situation: Billie's basic urge simply to love and be loved, so long frustrated, by now had become hopelessly mired in a desperation that made her impossible to live with, hard to reason with, and pathetically easy to sympathize with.

A few months later she astonished us by refusing a drink and asking instead for a cup of tea. "The doctor says I have cirrhosis of the liver and I can't drink." Needless to say, the doctor's warning was soon ignored.

In mid-March, when I called at her small, ground-floor apartment on West Eighty-seventh Street to escort her to the funeral of Lester Young, her close friend in the Basie days, I saw her slip a small bottle of gin into her purse. After the services she talked dejectedly, drawing an ominous parallel between herself and Lester. "I'll be the next one to go."

Our next meeting was a few weeks later, on her birthday. Billie had decided: "I ain't celebrated my birthday in fifteen years and this time I'm going to throw me a party." Among the well-wishers were Ed Lewis and Jo Jones of the old Basie band, Annie Ross, Elaine Lorillard, the Duftys, and Tony Scott. The party lasted all night, winding up at Birdland, and Lady never stopped toasting herself; bottles were emptied with alarming speed. Many of us wondered whether there would be any more birthdays to celebrate. She had already become skinny rather than slender. Those of us who watched her follow the Prez pattern begged her, vainly, to stop. Thinner and paler with each passing day, she continued to argue that she had cut down on her drinking and was taking care of herself.

Soon after the birthday party there was an incident typical of her stubbornness, pride, and confusion. She woke me at 2 A.M. and in a passionately angry tone of voice insisted that I come to her apartment immediately. I rushed over and found her sitting at a table nursing a bottle. It seemed that she had been told I was spreading a rumor that she had been drunk all through her engagement the previous week in Boston. "What's all this shit going on? I don't want people putting my fucking business in the street. I made every show and you can ask anybody."

I didn't have to ask; I knew what a successful week it had been, and that was the story I had been spreading. Within a half hour Billie's rage had shifted to the person who had indicted me.

It was agonizing to observe how uncertain she felt that anybody really cared for her, how intensely anxious that nobody derogate her. Worse, she knew that now only disparaging talk could help her at the box office. "They're not coming to hear me," she said, "they're coming to see me fall off the damn bandstand."

Not long afterward, on May 25, Billie was to appear in a benefit concert at the Phoenix Theatre for which Steve Allen and I were the emcees.

I looked into her dressing room to say hello, and saw her seated at the makeup table coughing, spittle running unchecked down her chin. Looking at her, I was on the verge of tears and she knew it.

"What's the matter, Leonard? You seen a ghost or something?"

Indeed I had; a ghost so emaciated, so weak and sick, that it was impossible for me to hide my feelings. She had lost at least twenty pounds in the few weeks since I had seen her.

Steve Allen helped Billie to her feet, walking her a short distance to a microphone, which had been deliberately placed at the near corner of the stage. She managed to get through "'Tain't Nobody's Business If I Do," the song of defiance that had become a staple of her repertoire in these fading days; she sang one other tune. It was the last time she was ever to sing.

The next morning I called Joe Glaser and Allan Morrison, then the New York editor of *Ebony*, with the suggestion that the three of us as a delegation might be able to break down her long resistance to hospitalization. As we sat in her apartment Glaser did most of the talking, guaranteeing all her hospital expenses and begging her to call off an opening scheduled for Montreal the next week. "Give me another week," she said. "The doctor said these shots he's giving me will do it." We left in a mood of frustration and despair.

Billie never got to Montreal. Five days after we saw her she collapsed, and the inevitable hospitalization followed. Then came the obscenely gruesome headlines in the sensation-hungry press: Billie, part of a society in which addiction was still a crime rather than a sickness, was arrested on her deathbed. Police were posted outside her hospital room. She lingered, rallied long enough to give us hope, then on July 17 it was over.

To the end Billie was uncertain about who her true friends were and who was trying to make money out of her. Notwithstanding possible selfish interests, many people close to her felt sincere love, regard, and pity for her right up to the end, but Billie was unable to accept any of the love offered her during those last days.

It was probably too much to hope that she would survive any longer than she did the kind of life she had led for so many years. Whether the final abandonment was from Louis McKay (who flew in from California soon after her hospitalization), or with Lester's death, or with the arrest in the hospital, nobody will ever know.

Billie Holiday's voice was the voice of living intensity, or soul in the true sense of that greatly abused word. As a human being she was sweet, sour, kind, mean, generous, profane, lovable, and impossible, and nobody who knew her expects to see anyone quite like her ever again.

British musician and writer John Chilton asked his friend, trumpeter Buck Clayton, to write the introduction to his biography of Billie Holiday, *Billie's Blues*. Buck was an ideal choice; he had been one of Billie's good friends from the early days of their careers. His recordings with her became classics of the late 1930s. And Buck had the uncanny ability to discuss her life accurately without detracting from her image as a glamorous, talented Lady. Summing up the gritty side of her life and personality, he simply called her "tough."

He was a man of a few words and gentle expression. No matter how many interviews he gave about Billie after her death, he always approached them with enthusiasm, as if he was enjoying the happy opportunity to talk about a subject dear to his heart. He exhibited the same refreshing, natural attitude in his own autobiography, *Buck Clayton's Jazz World*, published in 1986.

Wilbur Dorsey (Buck) Clayton was born in Parsons, Kansas, on November 12, 1911. He led a big band in China, then distinguished himself as a soloist in Count Basie's band in the 1930s, and became known as an arranger, too. After he could no longer play trumpet because of illness and dental problems, he continued his eminent career as an arranger. Slender and frail but still distinguished-looking, perched on a stool, he had no trouble commanding his own big band in the last years of his life. He died on December 8, 1991.

When I first met Billie Holiday she lit up, but I must say that it was her face that lit up. John Hammond first introduced me to Billie, at the first recording date of my life, and I was surprised to see that she was such a young, healthy, robust and pleasant girl, the kind that I grew up with when I was a boy in Kansas.

That first recording date was in January 1937, and I was so surprised when I walked into the studio and saw for the first time Benny Goodman. Previously, I had only heard Benny, and his great band of the 1930s, on records and radio. I knew Teddy Wilson would be on the date as he made practically all of Billie's first records. Freddie Green I didn't know at all. He was just a New York guy sitting on a tall stool holding his guitar. Little did I know that he was one of the world's greatest guitar players.

Billie was running over a song at the piano with Teddy Wilson. After getting an introduction together we proceeded to start what was my first recording (I had not yet recorded with Count Basie). Billie sang just beautifully on this date and after several coffee breaks and a few visits to the nearest bar I began to get a little closer to Billie and found her to be a very warm person.

Before coming to New York, when I was in Los Angeles, I heard Billie's first recordings. After meeting her and getting to know her I liked her singing even more than I had in California. I'll never forget the mornings I would awake to 'If You Were Mine' in my hotel-room on Central Avenue in Los Angeles. I'd never heard Roy Eldridge and Benny Morton in person, and to hear them together with Billie was a perfect combination.

After making several more recording dates with Billie we began to be great friends, and she would take me to all of the 'joints' in Harlem; well-known to Billie, but unknown to me. At the time of my first meeting with Billie she also met up with Lester Young—and there was one of the greatest companionships that I've ever seen, and that is all it was, and ever would be. They were so close that many believed them to be in love, but that never was the case. If you've ever seen two guys become great pals, then you can see the companionship of Billie and Lester. I know this, because I was one of the 'Unholy Three', as we used to call ourselves when we were together in some pad in Harlem. Lester had his girl friends, and Billie had her boy friends and there was never any confusion. However, I do believe that if they had to, they would have given up all the girl friends and all the boy friends, and still they would have remained no more than great friends. Billie admired Lester's playing, and he obviously admired her singing and they complimented each other. 'Lady Day' and 'Pres' made one of the greatest combinations together that I've seen in my life, but were never in any way more than just great buddies.

I think that during those days I may have been in Billie's company a bit more than Lester was, even though we were all together quite often. Sometimes, Billie and I would cover as many as ten or twelve Harlem pads in a matter of a few hours, because she didn't like to stay in one place too long. She was always anticipating going to the next one. Pads with soft lights, pot, incense and good jazz records—mostly by Louis Armstrong, Duke Ellington and Billie Holiday. Billie knew every corner of Harlem, and I got the best introduction to Harlem that anyone could possibly get. It seems that everyone in Harlem knew Billie personally, and there were always little stories that would circulate through Harlem about some episode that involved Billie, but Billie never gave a damn what people might say and she retained that attitude all through her life. Some of the tales were probably true, some of them false, Billie became one of the most talked-of personalities of Harlem. Good or bad.

Later, when she joined Count Basie's band it was one of the joys of our lives. To have the great Billie Holiday singing with our band was something we never thought possible—a pleasure we never thought we would have. It was through John Hammond, and her acquaintanceship with me and Lester, that Billie joined Basie. I think she was as happy to join as we were to have her. She asked me to make a big band arrangement, as she had no music for a band the size of Basie's, and the first one she wanted was 'I Can't Get Started With You'. She made her debut in Pennsylvania, and I was pretty proud, the arrangement was good and she sounded marvellous. During her stay with Basie, I must say that like the rest of us, she lived in a bus on 'one nighters'. She would, like all of us, shoot craps, sing and drink to get over the rigours of the one-nighters.

Many mornings about five o'clock, when everyone else was asleep on the bus, Billie and I would talk of the highlights of our lives. I'd tell her of some of my experiences in Shanghai, which especially interested her. Later on, whilst visiting her home, I noticed in her room a picture that was painted for her by an artist friend, of the head of a Chinaman lying in a Shanghai street—after a battle with the Japanese. It seemed pretty gruesome to me, but it was a favourite with Billie. She would tell me all of her experiences, and believe me there were many.

During Billie's whole time with Count Basie she only became involved with one musician, and that was Freddie Green. Many think it impossible that this was all that happened with Billie but it's true. Freddie was the only one, and sometimes they would fight all over the bus—but only as people fight when they care for each other. Freddie was always an admirable guy, and the only one that Billie admired.

Billie remained with Count Basie for some time and then, for a reason that I never knew, she left the band. I suppose it was the politics that occurred in big bands during those days, but I never knew for sure. A few months later she was singing with Artie Shaw's Band.

I saw and worked with Billie periodically after that. During the 1940s she worked and lived in California quite a bit. One afternoon, while I was with the 'Jazz At The Philharmonic' group, under Norman Granz, I was among several musicians who were having a jam-session at Billy Berg's Club in Hollywood when Billie showed up. She didn't sing that Sunday afternoon, but she told me that the night before she had been introduced to heroin by an artist who lived in Hollywood. She went on to tell me how good it was, and that it wasn't as harmful as people had led her to believe. 'Come on Bucket,' she said, 'it will make you feel like you've never felt before.' I listened to her, but then I told her 'No, Lady, that's not for me.'

After that, she became more deeply involved with narcotics, and it began to take its toll. Gradually she became very thin, gone was the plump girlish Billie that I first met. She always had trouble with narcotic agents, and she was an easy mark for the many unscrupulous men in her life. She was preyed on by so many hangers-on, who were out for either a fix or some money, and being always big-hearted and sympathetic she was taken advantage of numerous times.

During the latter part of the 1950s we played the Art Ford Jazz Show, a television show out of Newark, New Jersey, and I noticed that Billie was more and more in a bad way. She was very thin, her skin was sallow, and her voice cracked—which was something I never thought I'd hear. Shortly afterwards, she entered hospital for the last time. Even though Billie is gone now, every time I play or hear a Billie Holiday record it brings back many memories of the wonderful, kind, tough, and sympathetic person that I was very proud, or rather, that I am very proud to have known.

BILLIE AT CAFE SOCIETY
JOHN CHILTON

In November, *Down Beat* magazine remarked Billie Holiday appeared with Artie Shaw's band; a month later, England's *Melody Maker* reported that Billie left the band. A great deal of controversy surrounded the end of Billie's days with the Shaw band. Shaw was broadcasting regularly on radio, and his sponsors preferred that he use his other band singer, Helen Forrest, a young white girl, for the broadcasts instead of Billie. Or perhaps it wasn't his sponsors or not only his sponsors; it might have been the song pluggers for the music publishers, who didn't want to hear Billie's improvisations on the written songs. And Shaw's management wanted Shaw to use Helen, who had a more commercial sound and style at that time.

Billie didn't quit the band right away. She later said she reached her level of tolerance when the band went into New York's Lincoln Hotel. Its owners refused to let her go to the bar or the restaurant to socialize with customers and made her wait upstairs in a little dark room until she was called downstairs to sing with the band. And then she wasn't called downstairs at all, because she wasn't being used for the radio broadcasts, or remotes, from the ballroom.

Billie blamed Artie Shaw for giving in to the pressures of businesspeople around him. A great deal more emphasis was put on her acrimonious relations with Artie Shaw at that time than on her opening at a new little Greenwich Village club, Cafe Society, at Sheridan Square, in February 1939. With hindsight, everyone would realize her engagement at Cafe Society had a longer-lived, more salubrious effect on her career than her essentially frustrating stints as a bandsinger with Count Basie and Artie Shaw.

Cafe Society's owner Barney Josephson took John Hammond's advice to hire Billie for the club's opening. Billie began to attract the hip, socially prominent, white, quintessentially New York clientele who happily shared the intimate club's space with African American customers at a time when an integrated club was a novelty. And the New York audiences loved her offbeat style.

As usual, Billie retained a degree of turmoil and cynicism in her relations with other people. Audience acceptance could hardly obliterate her earlier, negative personal and professional experiences. But she gained in exposure—always a deciding factor about who will become famous and who will remain on the sidelines. British writer and musician John Chilton, in his remarkably canny book, *Billie's Blues*, wrote about her emergence at Cafe Society from the isolating cocoon of her relentless struggle.

Cafe Society (Downtown) was the first club venture for Barney Josephson, then a thirty-six-year-old ex-shoe manufacturer whose parents had been immigrants from Latvia. The club was later to have a twin—Cafe Society (Uptown). The Downtown branch had room for 220 customers, its slogan was 'The wrong place for the right people'. Admission charges were $2.00 for weeknights and $2.50 at weekends, beer was sixty-five cents a glass and hard liquor seventy cents—you could, if needs be, nurse one drink all night without the staff having apoplexy. More novel than the tariff was the rule that black and white customers could sit together anywhere within the club.

Whitney Balliett, in his book *Ecstasy at the Onion*, eloquently summed up Josephson's modus operandi: 'His intent was simple and revolutionary;

to present first-rate but generally unknown Negro and white talent to integrated audiences in honest attractive surroundings.'

Once again, John Hammond had been the instigator of a new phase of Billie's career; it was Hammond who recommended Billie to Josephson, who admits the debt. 'Whatever I learned, I learned from Hammond.'

In general Billie and Josephson enjoyed an easy-going relationship. The club-owner told writer Derek Jewell, 'Don't misunderstand me. We had our rows. To her I was a white man boss—and no white man was to be trusted. She wasn't a bad girl. She had to stand so much she got molded wrong. She was good-looking but never a beauty. She never had a really big voice—it was small, like a bell that rang and went a mile.'

After a few minor setbacks, the club became fully operational in January 1939. The opening bill featured Billie Holiday, trumpeter Frankie Newton and his Band, and the boogie-woogie pianists, Albert Ammons and Meade Lux Lewis (who were later joined by Pete Johnson). Billie was accompanied by 'Sonny' White, the pianist in Newton's Band. Ellerton 'Sonny' White from Panama, was then just twenty-one years old, he enjoyed working with Billie and the professional relationship between the two soon developed into personal closeness.

Frank Newton's Band enjoyed working at the Cafe Society, there was a good group spirit, and excellent rapport with Billie. John Williams, bassist with the band, said 'Billie and Newton would kid each other about the Band. It was Frankie's band but Billie would say, "this is my band," and would go to Barney the owner and say, "Newton don't need a raise but give my band one." Her dressing room door was always open to us and I've never known her to hurt anyone but herself. She had the "World on a String," being beautiful, having a hell of a figure, personality plus, and a style of her own that no one could steal. She was always the same and would never say "you fellows didn't play my music right, so that's why I didn't go over big." Lady Day was a beautiful woman and it's a shame Hot Pants were not in style, for the Boys really missed something.'

Occasionally the band and Billie did 'outside gigs', working at private parties and receptions away from the Cafe Society. Kenneth Hollon, who played tenor-sax in the band told writer Johnny Simmen of one such booking—'We had a society date to play in the Sixties street area, and Billie and I went by car. Since we arrived at the address too early we stayed in the car until it would be the time to get to the place. Billie was smoking pot, I didn't know too much about reefers at that time. Billie said, "This stuff is good. It comes from Dakar, Senegal, Africa. Try one." Billie showed me how to inhale, hold it in and then exhale what was left. I followed all her instructions to the last detail. When we arrived at the place where we were to play I got out of the car but could hardly pick up my heels. We went inside and everything was going round and round including my head. I made an attempt to set up my stand for the music, but somehow I couldn't do it. All this time, Frankie Newton was watching me, noticing how strangely I was acting. Finally, I was ready to play the first tune. I felt so good that I just tried to play the tune from memory. I thought I was knocking everybody out (I sure was knocking myself out) but when we finished our first number Frankie came over to me and said: "What the hell did you think you were doing?" I replied, "Playing my horn man, what else?" Frankie said, "You think you're raising hell?" I answered, "Yeah man that's what I'm doing," but he didn't think so. "Well you ain't," he said. When he said this, right then I got tickled and all I could do was laugh! I couldn't play another thing. I stayed high for four or five days. I ate like a pig, drank gallons of water, but nothing helped. Never since that night have I ever touched another reefer. There's no doubt that the stuff Billie gave that night was the real McCoy.' Hollon, like others who knew Billie at this time, said, 'I never saw her drink or shoot dope, all she did was smoke weed.'

Barney Josephson's strictly enforced rule was that there must be no smoking of marijuana in his clubs. He told Whitney Balliett, 'When Billie Holiday was with me, she'd get in a cab between shows and drive through Central Park smoking. One night she came back and I could tell by her eyes that she was really high. She finished her next number and I guess she didn't like the way the audience reacted.' Because of the heat from the spotlights, Billie like many other female night-club artistes wore no underwear on stage. She didn't criticise the audience verbally for their indifference; instead, she turned her back on them, bent over, and flipped up her gown to give the crowd a full view of her rear, she then hustled back to her dressing-room. This was an isolated incident; usually, Billie's performances were received in rapt silence.

But appreciation from a dedicated audience, and stimulation from marijuana were not enough to dispel the bouts of melancholia that Billie got. An inkling of occasional despair can be felt in a letter that she wrote in June 1939 to English bass-player Jack Surridge: 'Nothing anyone would say could make me feel any worse than I do, but I guess it will all come out alright in the end.'

Besides reading comics, Billie also played cards during her spare time at Cafe Society—the club had three shows a night, at 9 pm, midnight and

2 am. She would often visit the bandroom and play hearts or blackjack with the musicians. Overall, Cafe Society was probably the happiest booking of Billie's life, it did wonders for her confidence on-stage, enabling her to project a more sophisticated act. Barney Josephson encouraged and advised Billie; later he was to do the same thing for Lena Horne, who said, 'It was Barney who encouraged us, as artists, to express our individuality in our performances. It was Barney who decided that all guests were to be seated and served without discrimination.' (*Lena*, p. 192.)

It was at the Cafe Society that Billie began to feature 'Strange Fruit', the song that was to become irrevocably linked with her. The liberal atmosphere of the club, with its clientele of 'New Dealers', and the humanitarian principles of its owner made it a receptive setting for the presentation of the song's dramatic anti-lynching lyrics.

Poet Lewis Allen, then working as a schoolteacher, approached Barney Josephson and Robert Gordon (who helped organise floor-shows) with a set of lyrics that he had adapted from his own poetry; they recommended that Allen should meet Billie and offer the song to her. At first, Lady was slow to understand the song's imagery, but her bewilderment decreased as Allen patiently emphasised the cadences, and their significance. After a few readings, Billie was 'into' the song, but was unconvinced that the material was suitable for her. Her incredibly gifted interpretations of lyrics had enhanced many songs, but these songs, for all the varying skills of their composers and lyricists, had only dealt with the problems of love, unrequited or otherwise, skies blue and June moons. Here, Billie was being asked to provide a musical commentary on an issue raw enough to be unmentionable in urban New York.

Billie's hesitancy showed that although she often proudly said, 'I'm a race woman,' she was uncertain about accepting the onus of delivering this early protest song. She told Lewis Allen that she would have to think it over. Within minutes of his leaving the club she had made up her mind; as Frankie Newton's Band came off stage she greeted them with the words, 'Some guy's brought me hell of a damn song that I'm going to do.'

Her decision to feature 'Strange Fruit' was to be the factor that changed her career. The overt brandishing of an anti-racialism banner was certainly not the sole reason for Billie's choice; being the great artist that she was, her intuition told her that here was a lyric into which she could pour much of the pent-up dramatic feelings that sometimes engulfed her. The material and the message were powerful enough to allow her to project the qualities of a great actress without appearing absurd. Overnight, she changed from being a marvellously talented club singer to a 'La

Grande Chanteuse'—fortunately, this change in presentation didn't diminish the jazz content of her work.

Leonard Feather visited the Cafe Society in April 1939, just before Billie first recorded 'Strange Fruit'; he described the night to *Melody Maker* readers: 'Frankie Newton leads the regular band in this pleasant room which had modern decorations, and many brilliant murals to help the atmosphere. During the show the M.C. announced Billie Holiday who stood in a small jet of light, turned on her most wistful expression for the mike, and sang a number written specially for her, "Strange Fruit", a grim and moving piece about lynching down South. To-day she is recording this for a special Commodore Music Shop session.'

The Commodore Music Shop that Feather mentioned was owned by Milt Gabler. From there Gabler ran his own record label which catered exclusively for jazz fans. He had known Billie ever since she visited his original shop on 42nd Street in 1936; in 1938, he opened a branch at 45 West 52nd Street, and from there he would often go downtown to hear Billie at Cafe Society; he had said 'There was no sense in going home without hearing Lady. When she was out of town it was no town to me. Billie was my constant love, I don't mean the physical kind, we had a great thing for each other, and she respected me. When she was on stage in the spotlight she was absolutely regal. It was something, the way she held her head up high, the way she phrased each word, and got to the heart of the story in a song, and to top it all, she knew where the beat was.'

It was through Gabler's admiration and enterprise that Billie managed to record 'Strange Fruit'. Her guarded acceptance of the song was soon followed by a spate of passionate fervour for every stanza in the song, she felt that everyone in the world should hear the words. The big drawback to this was that the Columbia Record Company, to whom she was contracted, weren't willing to issue a recording of the song. However, they were not against its message and gave their permission when Billie and Milt Gabler asked if they could record the song for Commodore. This decision surprised and delighted Gabler, he said 'Billie and I were grateful to Columbia for allowing her to record this important song for my label.'

On Billie's first session for Commodore she recorded four tunes: 'Strange Fruit', 'Yesterdays', 'I Got a Right to Sing the Blues' and a twelve-bar blues, 'Fine and Mellow'.

In a 1973 *Down Beat* interview Gabler explained why he particularly wanted Billie to record a twelve-bar blues: 'Her 1936 "Billie's Blues" was (and still is) a favorite of mine. Billie didn't sing the blues like Bessie Smith or Ma Rainey. She was more like *today*.

'The night before the session, I went down to Cafe Society to get things set with the band and Billie. I told her I wanted a blues, so we sat down at a little "deuce" table just outside her dressing-room door and started to write down blues verses for the still untitled song.' In this extemporised lyric session Milt Gabler came up with a line that provided the title for the composition: 'Fine and Mellow'.

Everything went well at the recording, both for Billie and the accompanying band led by Frankie Newton, with Sonny White on piano. After the session Billie felt on top of the world and impetuously told the *Melody Maker* correspondent an item of news that was dutifully printed in the 20 May issue: 'Billie Holiday, still singing at Cafe Society, announces that she will shortly be married to her piano accompanist, Sonny White.'

The marriage never took place, Sonny was supporting his widowed mother, and Billie was doing likewise; the economic and domestic problems of setting up an instant home for four were insuperable—the romance ended in a fairly fast-burning fizzle.

Billie was still a long way from being 'in the money', she was one of life's spenders and rarely saved any of her earnings. In the late 1930s, when she was averaging seventy-five dollars a week she always bought Coty perfumes and expensive bath oils; once she splashed two weeks' salary on matching shoes and handbag made in green crocodile. Her wage at Cafe Society was not colossal but the booking brought her into contact with promoters, film stars, agents, show-bookers, and news columnists. She loved the feel of hob-nobbing, but never let it interfere with, or affect, her own social circle. Many of her old friends dropped into the club, including Lester Young. One dawn in the summer of 1939, after deciding that there was still time for more fun, she accompanied Lester up to Puss Johnson's Tavern on St Nicholas Avenue in Harlem, where a big after-hours jam session had been planned. This was the era of the jam session— the informal assemblies where jazz musicians could improvise for as long as they liked on any material they chose.

The gathering planned for Johnson's bar was something special. Coleman Hawkins, then the undisputed champion of jazz tenor-saxophone playing, had recently returned to the U.S.A. after five years in Europe. During his absence, several younger men were put forward as contenders for his crown, principally Lester Young, Leon 'Chu' Berry, Ben Webster and Dick Wilson. It seems significant that Hawkins, after looking down the short list, arranged that one of his first tasks was to be blowing in the same place and at the same time as Lester Young. He let it be known that he would attend the jam session at Puss Johnson's Tavern; Lester

Young, who had planned to go before receiving the news, was undeterred.

The meeting of the twin colussi of jazz tenor playing had all the drama of a gun-fighting duel, the result however, was less conclusive. There could scarcely be any winning or losing, since both men played in such dissimilar styles. Nowadays, with hundreds of recorded examples of both men's work readily available there is still dispute as to which man was the greater jazz player.

In a summary of the session, *Down Beat* passed on the views of the Fats Waller Band (who were at the Tavern as listeners); they thought that Hawkins came out on top, and they also reported that Lester had said he'd had enough after an hour's blowing.

Billie was working in Chicago by the time the magazine appeared, and after reading the report her reaction was swift and decisive. She immediately contacted the main *Down Beat* office in Chicago and emphatically refuted the suggestion that Coleman Hawkins had 'carved' Lester. *Down Beat* published her comments that the report was 'unfair', and that 'Young really cut the Hawk, and most everyone there who saw them tangle agrees on that.'

By this time, 'Strange Fruit', and its coupling 'Fine and Mellow', had been released. None of the reviewers was ecstatic, however 'Gordon Wright' (a nom-de-plume for George T. Simon) wrote in *Metronome*: 'A record that's going to cause tremendous controversy is Billie's "Strange Fruit", an anti-lynching song, which she sings with immense feeling, and which also has effective passages by trumpeter Frankie Newton and pianist Sonny White. Its reverse "Fine and Mellow" is good blues.' 'Barrelhouse Dan' in *Down Beat* was much less enthusiastic: 'Perhaps I expected too much of "Strange Fruit", the ballyhooed Allen-Sacher tune, which, via gory wordage, and hardly any melody, expounds an anti-lynching campaign [sic]. At least I'm sure it's not for Billie, as for example, "Fine and Mellow" is.'

Considering the record was issued by a small company, at the relatively high price of one dollar, it sold very well indeed. Its release gained enormous publicity for Billie, but despite the wide press coverage she still felt that she was no nearer receiving acceptance from the general public. As soon as the tumult of acclaim had subsided she felt that she was as far as ever from the glamorous fame for which she was striving. Late in 1939, she told Dave Dexter (then associate editor of *Down Beat*), that she would quit the singing game if she failed to gain national prominence—'with the public as well as musicians and jazz fans,' by the time she was 26 (1941). She admitted that she was aware of the great respect that musicians had for her, but said that she was discouraged 'after nine years of hard work' and felt 'at a loss as to why the public at large had failed to respond to her.'

The publication of this interview was the first inkling of one dilemma that was to shadow the rest of Billie's life. She was worshipped by jazz musicians of every school, she was envied and copied by almost every girl vocalist of the day, writers showered her with praise, but to the masses she was practically a nobody. She yearned to see the glint of recognition in everyone's eyes, she longed to be pestered by autograph hunters, instead, she was virtually ignored.

Ella Fitzgerald, who had shyly asked Billie for her autograph a few years before, was, by 1939, well on her way to international stardom, her record of 'Tisket a Tasket' having sold a quarter of a million. Billie's first real talks with Ella had taken place in 1938; then, Ella had often visited the Roseland State Ballroom in Boston to hear Billie sing with Artie Shaw's band. At that time, Ella was the featured singer with the band led by drummer Chick Webb. She too, had had a very hard childhood; the change in her fortunes had occurred after her successes at amateur nights, first at the Harlem Opera House and then at the Apollo. As a result, she signed with Chick Webb's Band, remaining with that leader until his untimely death in June 1939. Billie did not feel jealous of Ella's success and her subsequent popular adulation; she learned to shrug off any comparisons and poll-placings. However, she felt keen disappointment in 1939 when the leading journalists of the Associated Negro Press voted Ella their favourite female vocalist and chose Maxine Sullivan in second place.

Billie's initial run at Cafe Society lasted for almost nine months. Long after it had ended, Billie saw how important it had been in terms of publicity and prestige, but in August 1939 she could merely reflect that she was getting little more than she was at the beginning of the residency. However, Milt Gabler said in 1973, 'I never heard of Barney Josephson retiring with a bundle, in fact he is back in the business running "The Cookery" in Greenwich Village.'

A CRUCIAL ENGAGEMENT
BUD KLIMENT

This excerpt is from a biography of Billie Holiday written for young readers. Kliment, though not a jazz critic, has written books about jazz artists for young adults, and he has had notable success for several reasons. He is a fine researcher. Although he doesn't mince words about Billie—that is, he doesn't cover up the troubles in her life—he protects both Billie and his intended audience from the effects of an excessively maudlin and seamy account. Too often, writers have stressed Billie's miseries and neglected her happier moments. Her success by itself was a great joy and a triumph. She knew how good she was and what her just desserts should have been. And sometimes she was able to demand them.

The first chapter of Kliment's book on Billie focuses effectively and warmly on one of the highlights of her career—her triumphant concert at Carnegie Hall shortly after her release from prison. Kliment does not mention she was already using heroin again. Billie herself might have been relieved to have read his balanced work about her strengths. He tried to portray her as a woman who did the best she could and who, despite all her handicaps, achieved immortality. And so, his book is inspiring.

As the hour approached midnight on March 27, 1948, thousands of music lovers converged on 57th Street in New York and filed into Carnegie Hall, one of the city's most prestigious concert halls. The men and women who made up this large group of ticket holders came from all walks of life. "Platinum mink rubbed shoulders with worn tweed," noted one observer. "Music critics smiled at young, poorly clad kids, Harlem sat next to Park Avenue."

The audience had come to hear an Easter eve concert that had first been announced two weeks earlier in the *New York Daily News*. A small notice in the paper had served as the show's lone advertisement. It read: "One night stand. Carnegie Hall. Billie Holiday. March 27." Yet that tiny message, which ran just eight times, had been enough to cause the show to sell out.

Many people considered the 32-year-old Holiday to be the world's most distinctive jazz vocalist. For almost 17 years, she had performed regularly in New York City, garnering a large following wherever her bittersweet voice filled the air: in Harlem night spots, Greenwich Village cafés, and clubs on the midtown block known as Swing Street. But then she left the music scene. By March 1948, when her late-night show at Carnegie Hall was announced, she had been absent from the stage for almost a year. Accordingly, her fans thrilled at the prospect of hearing her perform again in New York City. Lady Day, as they called her, was coming home at last.

By the night of the concert, anticipation over Holiday's return had swelled to an electrifying pitch. Because the demand for tickets to her comeback engagement was so overwhelming, extra chairs were placed onstage so that 300 additional fans could attend the show. Nevertheless, this added measure failed to accommodate thousands more of her admirers who came to the theater's box office only to be turned away, disappointed.

Holiday was among those who understood that the show had become more than a jazz concert—it had turned into an event. Seated in her backstage dressing room before the start of the concert, she sensed the air of expectation that surrounded her return. She was aware, too, of the irony of the situation. There she sat, preparing to sing to a capacity crowd at one of the leading concert halls in the world, when only 11 days earlier she had been a lonely inmate in prison.

Holiday had not performed in public for almost a year because she had been serving time for possession of narcotics. In 1941, she had begun using heroin, and she had quickly become hooked on the drug. By the mid-1940s, she had become a full-fledged addict with a habit that required her to spend $500 a week on the narcotic. (An equivalent habit today would cost almost four times as much.)

Then, in the spring of 1947, Holiday got caught. Agents of the U.S. Bureau of Narcotics arrested her and charged her with drug possession. She stood trial on May 27, and the presiding judge sentenced her to serve a year and a day at the Federal Reformatory for Women at Alderson, West Virginia.

To Holiday, who had grown accustomed to expensive gowns, lively nights, and loud applause, Alderson seemed to belong to another world. The reformatory was a desolate place consisting of 6 small houses, with 50 to 60 women quartered in each building. Nearly half the prisoners were black, and they were forced to eat, sleep, and worship separately from the white inmates because Alderson, like virtually all southern institutions in the late 1940s, was racially segregated.

Even though Holiday had experienced great hardship on account of racial inequality many times before, Alderson's policy of segregation was not easy to bear. Moreover, it was not the only difficulty she had to face in prison. She also had to go through drug withdrawal because the authorities would not allow her to use the narcotics to which she had become addicted.

Forced to end her heroin addiction cold turkey, Holiday spent the first month of her sentence in quarantine. For 19 days, her body seemed to revolt against itself as she attempted a complete and abrupt withdrawal from the drug. She shook violently, suffered chills, and barely slept or ate. "The first nights I was ready to quit," she said of the experience. "I thought I'd just explode."

Nevertheless, Holiday managed to make it through the agonizing withdrawal period. She then settled into the dull routine of prison life. Initially, she was assigned to work on the prison farm, picking vegetables and taking care of the pigs. Yet her body was still ravaged from her years of drug addiction, and she was unaccustomed to strenuous labor. On one excruciatingly hot day, she collapsed from sunstroke.

Deciding that Holiday was not at all suited to work outdoors, the prison authorities ordered her to cook and clean in one of the prison houses. She prepared the meals and did the dishes, washed the windows and scrubbed the floors, and brought buckets of coal up from the cellar. Apart from carrying the coal, which was used to keep the stove lit and the house heated, she did not mind her new duties very much.

The sense of isolation that accompanied prison life was an entirely different matter. Alderson cut Holiday off from her friends and fans, from everyone she knew and loved. Being alone wore heavily on her, and prison regulations did not make the situation any easier.

The rules at Alderson dictated that inmates could receive only letters sent by their immediate families. Because both of Holiday's parents were dead and she knew of no other living relatives, she was not permitted to read any of her mail, even though her friends and thousands of her fans from around the world had written to her, offering their support and love. The warden, sympathetic to Holiday's situation, eventually intervened on her behalf and allowed her to receive three letters a week.

But Holiday's mood barely improved. Many of the inmates, aware of her talent and reputation, asked her to sing for them, but she refused. The warden requested that she take part in the amateur talent shows held regularly by the prisoners. Holiday said no. Lonely, separated from the world, she argued that she had nothing to sing about. "The whole basis of my singing is feeling," she said later. "In the whole time I was there I didn't feel a thing."

But Holiday somehow persevered, making up her mind to stay in line and perhaps win an early release for good behavior. After 8 months of being a model inmate, she was told that the prison review board had decided to reduce her sentence by 72 days. When March 16, 1948, arrived, she would be released on parole.

Upon hearing this good news, Holiday's manager, Joe Glaser, immediately booked her to play Carnegie Hall. He scheduled her return to the professional ranks for March 27—an arrangement that left her only 11 days to prepare for the show. Bobby Tucker, a pianist who was a close friend of Holiday's, offered to help her get ready.

As soon as Holiday was released from Alderson, she took a northbound train and met Tucker at the station in Newark, New Jersey. They got in his car and drove to his mother's house in nearby Morristown, hoping that Holiday would be able to rehearse undisturbed and unwind more easily if she was away from the New York limelight. When they entered the house, Holiday's eyes filled with tears. She saw that Tucker's family had kept its Christmas tree lit for her even though it was well past the holiday season.

The scene at Holiday's first rehearsal was nearly as emotional. As they got under way, she told Tucker that she had not sung in prison and was not sure how well her voice would sound. All the same, she asked him to play "Night and Day," a popular Cole Porter tune that had always given her trouble. Tucker played the opening chords slowly, then Holiday joined in. "I'll never forget that first note, or the second," she said later. "Or especially the third one, when I had to hit 'day' and hold it. I hit it and held it and it sounded better than ever. Bobby almost fell off the stool, he was so happy. And his mother came running out . . . and took me in her arms."

Holiday replayed this happy scene in her head as she sat backstage at Carnegie Hall a week later. If only starting over could be that simple. A year was a long time to be away from the stage, and she had not exactly been on vacation. Moreover, many people disapproved of ex-convicts and drug addicts, whether they had reformed or not. One radio station even went so far as to ban her records from the airwaves.

Even though Holiday knew her voice was as powerful as ever, she remained filled with doubt. Had the concert sold out because the public really wanted to hear her sing, or was the house full simply because she had become a curiosity? This engagement would provide the answer. She got up from her seat and walked tentatively to the wings of the stage, where she waited with Bobby Tucker and three other backup musicians as the houselights dimmed and the audience grew quiet. Reflexively, she smoothed down the sides of her dress.

Fred Robbins, a New York disc jockey, stepped onto the stage and strode to the microphone to introduce Holiday. A deafening roar went up from the crowd as she walked slowly into the spotlight. According to the jazz periodical *Down Beat*, it was "one of the most thunderous ovations ever given a performer in this or any other concert hall." Holiday waited for the cheering to die down, then launched into her first number, "I Cover the Waterfront." By the time the song was over, it had become clear to the entire audience that the singer's stay in prison had not affected her ability to perform.

The set continued with Holiday tackling several of her most popular songs with consummate ease. At the end of each tune, the audience's response seemed to grow louder. Time magazine later reported that the "hysterical applause gave the event the quality of a revival meeting."

There was a brief intermission after 15 songs. Backstage, Holiday said that she felt "elated." She changed into a black dress, then spotted some gardenias that a fan had sent her. Touched that "somebody had remembered" that the flowers were her trademark, she placed them in her hair without realizing that a hat pin lay hidden beneath the blossoms. Her head began to bleed because of the sharp pin. Bobby Tucker took one look at her and grew alarmed. "Lady, you can't go on," he said. "You must be dying." But Lady Day, bent on finishing this crucial performance, washed off the blood and returned to the stage, hiding her discomfort from the crowd.

Holiday began the second set with "Don't Explain." More tunes followed, including "All of Me," "My Man," and "Solitude." As the set drew to a close, she began to feel weak. She motioned to Tucker to skip "Night and Day" and move on to the last song, "Strange Fruit," which had become her signature number. When she finished, the crowd was on its feet, asking for more. Now that Lady Day had finally come home, they did not want to let her go. She took two curtain calls before collapsing backstage.

Holiday's midnight show at Carnegie Hall—described by Tucker as "the musical treat of my life"—lasted more than two and a half hours. It was one of the milestones of her career. She had never performed more brilliantly, not to a more appreciative audience. But, as was so often the case for her, good fortune did not hold out. In the years that followed her Easter concert, she met repeatedly with trouble, both privately and professionally, at times creating the difficulties herself.

As though following some erratic inner rhythm, Billie Holiday's life constantly alternated between triumph and tragedy. Hardship was always mixed in with success—even from the beginning.

BILLIE HOLIDAY IN ENGLAND: 1953
MAX JONES

American jazz writers have long admired their British colleague, Max Jones, for his perceptive and knowledgeable writings about jazz. He combines a connoisseur's taste in jazz with a sensitivity to people, a knowledge of American cultural history, and an exemplary prose style. Add to that his special affection for Billie Holiday that predated his meeting her by about fifteen years, and the resultant story is a gem.

From this piece, we come to understand that he charmed a world-weary Billie into trusting him, confiding in him, befriending him, and teasing him gently. He traveled around England with her, went out on the town with his wife, Billie, and her last husband, Louis McKay, and penetrated to the heart of her concerns and perceived the level of her mentality.

This intimate visit with Billie is a longer and more languid one than most writers have provided. Jones depicts Billie in chronologically continuous action for her stay in England. Therefore the piece is really a very generous gift from Lady via Max Jones to "Holiday freaks," as Jones called people like himself.

Someone should write a musical play, "Lady Day in London," based on the chronicle of Jones's friendship with Lady. The one drawback to its commercial appeal would be that she was happy in London; or at least she wasn't unhappy. And so far all the dramatizations of her life have concentrated on its tragic aspects.

Max Jones was born in London on February 28, 1917. He played saxophone and clarinet beginning in the 1930s, when he and his friends fell in love with American jazz recordings, and by the 1940s he established himself as an editor and writer for jazz publications. He is best known in the United States for his long association with England's *Melody Maker* magazine. He died on August 1, 1993, in Chichester, England.

One day, late in 1953, I received news from Leonard Feather that Billie would hit Britain in February 1954 at the close of a European tour of his 'Jazz Club USA' package, in which she was the star.

The rest of the company couldn't play here, because of the policy of the musicians' unions involved, but concerts were fixed for Billie and she was able to use pianist Carl Drinkard.

Billie was due to arrive at London Airport from Paris on Monday, February 8, following three weeks in Scandinavia, Germany, Switzerland, Holland and France. I made arrangements with *Melody Maker* to drive out to Heathrow to greet her and to 'cover' her in general, as chance permitted. Reports of the tour had been favourable. Need I say that I looked impatiently to meeting, at last, the Princess of Harlem, as they were calling her in France?

The red-letter day came and I drove to the airport well before mid-day, armed with a photographer and half a bottle of whisky. Both could be useful, I knew, as a means of breaking the ice, and both were to come in handy. Stories of Lady Day's uncertain temper and 'unreasonable behaviour' crossed my mind as I drove. Parking near the Arrivals lounge, I felt the *frisson* of an imminent adventure—eager anticipation tinged with apprehension.

I had not long to wait. A commanding figure, recognisable on first glimpse, emerged from the Customs Hall. She was clad almost from neck to foot in a luxurious, blonde fur coat topped by a tight-fitting woolly hat, and was following through the barrier by three men. It transpired that they were—in priority order—husband-manager Louis McKay, her pianist Carl Drinkard and dancer Taps Miller who chanced to share the same plane from Paris.

The singer looked tired, cold and resentful, as though she had suffered many fools in the recent past. Not wanting to be added to the total, I greeted her with measured warmth, politeness and degree of reserve I was far from feeling. I was honoured, I said, to make her acquaintance. It was no lie. First impressions? They were all I had expected and more—quite apart from the amount of mink. I saw an imposing woman of average height (she was 5 ft 5 in, I believe)—an inch or two taller than I had guessed—with handsome, well-boned features and an intolerant, faintly mocking expression. She seemed to me less lean in the face than I had gathered from the New Orleans screen image. Her speaking voice was slurry, a little cracked in tone, and 'meanly attractive'. What she said inclined to the brief, hip and pithy. She had dignity and natural magnetism and I thought I perceived in her an odd amalgamation of naïvety and experience.

She was moderately friendly, though understandably detached, and her manner thawed when I referred to mutual acquaintances such as Marie Bryant, Helen and Stanley Dance and Mary Lou Williams. Everyone who warranted it was introduced to everyone else and we secured a few photographs.

I got off to a poor start by suggesting a shot with Drinkard and Taps (the latter had caused a hold-up at French customs by being checked for drugs, which had infuriated Billie). In addition, this delayed her progress to the waiting limousine. She signalled her impatience to be moving but something guarded me that morning and she agreed to the picture with a resigned lift of the eyebrows. Her glance clearly warned me: 'You're taking chances, buster; let's get it over and blow.'

Now, it isn't the simplest act in the world to present a half of Scotch to a proud-looking woman who is at once your jazz heroine and a virtual stranger—and, by now, also shut away in the rear of a hired car. Worse, she was refusing to look in my direction. But faint heart never won fur-coated lady.

Opening the door gingerly I proffered the bottle, asking whether it was too early for a taste and apologising for the lack of glasses. The look of menace was replaced by a smile. I don't think she spoke but she slid forward and the bottle vanished into the mink, just as her retinue entered the limo. Then the car was driven away in the direction of London.

A press reception had been fixed for early afternoon at the Piccadilly Hotel, where Billie was staying, and the questioning was under way when I arrived. Already the star was looking harassed. The lay-press agents—minimally concerned with her musical accomplishments—wished to know about her drug habit and prison sentence. As I entered she smiled across the room and told Louis McKay: 'There's the man who saved my life at the airfield.'

The reporters knew she had been imprisoned on narcotics charges, and that she was not allowed to sing in any New York 'cabarets' because the Police Department had withdrawn her cabaret card. They questioned her closely, and exclusively so far as I recall the occasion, about her troubles. 'Are you still on dope, Miss Holiday?' asked one pressman pointedly.

Billie ignored the question, but explained that she had served her time for the offence and expected to be able to start off again with a clean slate. 'I can't work in any places in New York that sell whisky', she said. 'Why whisky? It's a city ordinance or something. I guess they're stuck with it. I'm trying to get my police card back. You know, I'm not the only one: some kids have been in trouble two, three times . . .' [here she named a well-known girl singer who was not, as it happened, black] '. . . and are still working. So why pick on me? Somebody's got a hand in it somewhere; some kind of politics. That's what I'm squawking about'.

Interrupting another question, she answered: 'No, I don't think it's because I'm a Negro. I just don't dig it. I guess somebody has to be the goof.'

I should cut in on the story here to say that Billie, to judge by what I knew of her, was not obsessed by race relations and colour bias. She was, I think, a 'race woman' in the sense that she refused to imitate 'white' manners, modes of speech and standards of conduct, and ridiculed those that did. But she was in no way a 'professional Negro' or, for that matter, a professional personality of any kind. What she believed, she said: and what she believed was most likely to be the result of her personal experience. In Billie's experience, the police were part of a system which was subject to bribery, political pressure, gangster pressure, moral prejudice and all the weaknesses of mankind. She thought the withholding of a police card was unfair, but she wasn't prepared to attribute it to Jim Crowism on the part of the cops. Perhaps it was due to Billie's intransigent nature, more than anything. As Josh White once said of her: 'She'd had to fight all her life, and most people hate fighters, I can tell you.'

Whatever the Police Department's motives may have been, Billie didn't want to talk about them this first afternoon in London. Her face often bore an expression of deep sadness and, as often, one of dissatisfaction tinged with a smouldering kind of explosiveness; at this early stage in our acquaintance I thought I could detect danger signals. Billie's answers were becoming briefer now.

'I suppose your friends are still fighting for you', said one Daily.

'You know, we don't talk about it, we *forget* it', she told him meaningfully.

Rescue was urgently called for and I told the company at large that I didn't suppose Miss Holiday had travelled all this way to give a lecture on narcotics. I asked how she had come by her nickname, Lady Day (though I knew the answer), and she shone upon me a real smile and expression of gratitude. Would she be singing *Strange Fruit* at her concerts? I followed up. Then, whenever a drugs question began to rear its head, I interposed a query about her programme or records or accompanists.

Billie saw what I was up to and seemed appreciative. Though able to look after herself, physically and verbally, she felt uncertain in strange surroundings, among alien accents. She told us how Lester Young named her Lady (Day) and her mother Duchess. 'I named him the President, and actually I was also Vice President . . . of the Vipers Society, you know. We were the Royal Family of Harlem.'

As the conversation warmed up, with assorted references to ofays and spooks, Pres and Pops, Bessie and the Queen (Dinah Washington), a few pressmen left. 'Who the hell was that guy?' she asked about the prinicipal inquisitor. 'He couldn't say nothing but "dope"'.

When I told her he was the *Daily Blank*, she did a bit of swearing. 'Well', she said with an air of finality, 'I was just about ready to run his *Daily Blank* ass out of here'.

She laughed at this, drank a little Scotch and looked offended. 'I hate it without ice,' she said.

While somebody ran down for ice-water, Lady Day mused over Lester:

'Now that's been going on since around 1938,' she told us. 'I was given that title by Lester Young, the President. I was with Basie's band for a time, and Lester used to live at home with my mother and me. I used to be crazy about his tenor playing, wouldn't make a record unless he was on it. He played music I like, didn't try to drown the singer. Teddy Wilson was the same, and trumpet player Buck Clayton. But Lester's always been the President to me; he's my boy—and with him I have to mention Louis Armstrong and Bessie Smith. Many's the whipping I got for listening to their records when I was a child.

'I used to run errands for a madam on the corner. I wouldn't run errands for anybody, still won't carry a case across the street today, but I ran around for this woman because she'd let me listen to all Bessie's records . . . and Pops's record of *West End Blues*.

'I loved that *West End Blues*, and always wondered why Pops didn't sing any words to it. I reckoned he must have been feeling awful bad. When I got to New York, I went to hear him at the Lafayette Theatre. He didn't play my blues, and I went backstage and told him about it. I guess I was nine years old then. Been listening to Pops and Bessie ever since that time. Of course, my mother considered that kind of music sinful; she'd whip me in a minute if she caught me listening to it. Those days we were supposed to listen to hymns or something like that.'

By this time, most of the daily Press had stolen out. Billie didn't seem worried by their departure. 'Some of those guys were getting me a little salty,' she explained to us. 'I didn't come three thousand miles to talk about that shit. It's ended.'

Before leaving, we asked Billie when her British visit would be over.

'I'll be here until Tuesday, I reckon, after that I'm not sure,' she said. 'We've been offered so many jobs—Paris, Africa, even some Variety in England. Daddy'—here she looked across at husband Louis—'hasn't made our plans yet, but we have a good offer back home.'

Louis McKay added that getting back into New York cabaret could mean upward of $75,000 a year. Billie said: 'It's not just the dough, it's the principle of the thing. To me, it's unfair.'

On the way out of the hotel, we said goodbye to Billie's accompanist, Carl Drinkard. He joined Billie in Washington in 1949, his first recording with her being *Crazy He Calls Me*. Said Carl: 'I've been with Lady nearly five years. You know something? Her singing still amazes me.'

That evening, at her invitation, I returned to the hotel with Betsy, a Decca record player and a bunch of new and old Holiday recordings. She and Louis were in bed but not sleepy. For a few hours we played music, smoked and drank a little, and chewed the fat. Billie loved hearing the old sides, and reflected in outspoken terms a spontaneous stream of thoughts about songs and musicians she had worked with. All fascinating to us, of course, and rewarding to someone who had hoped fervently to strike up a sympathetic relationship with the prime enchantress of his first jazz decade.

Of Lester Young, Teddy Wilson, Freddie Green, Louis, Bobby Tucker, Annie Ross, and Ben Webster she spoke fondly, ladling out praise to instrumentalists who accompanied a singer unselfishly and helpfully. Now and then a bitter note intruded (she was contemptuous of phonies in any walk of life), and sometimes she allowed personal consideration to colour her assessments. At the sound of Buck Clayton she announced: 'Prettiest cat I ever saw.' When Roy Eldridge cropped up in the conversation, she surprised us by confiding: 'He stole my cherry, you know.' But she smiled appreciatively when Little Jazz's mean trumpet snaked from the grooves. Almost more abrupt was her confession on Sid Catlett: 'Honey,' she told me in solemn tones, as a Leavisite might deliver an important critical judgment. 'Big Sid . . . biggest dick I saw in my whole life.' I was certainly impressed.

Chatting with Billie, as you can guess, was a kick. I never heard her put down a really good singer, though she could be very cutting about the duds and those she supposed had slighted her. Some entertainers, Lena Horne and Ella Fitzgerald among them, she evidently loved as friends.

On the subject of people who are generally acknowledged to have copied aspects of her performing style, she was strikingly tolerant. She viewed the imitations as a form of fondness and admiration, and she spoke affectionately of Peggy Lee, though retelling some scurrilous remarks about Peggy's presentation made by a world-famous actress (Tallulah Bankhead in fact) who had sat next to her at a Peggy Lee performance.

In the course of the next few days, I travelled around with Billie and her husband, and got to know her quite well. I saw a good deal of Billie's 'temperament', but during that week she was more often happy than low, though the smallest upsets would soon get her storming. At first rehearsal, with Carl Drinkard and several British musicians in a Leicester Square club, she was angry about some mislaid music parts. She settled down grimly to the job of running through her programme, saying nothing except what was relevant to it, and singing only the minimum amount necessary to a productive rehearsal. Even so, it was my first 'live' audition and I was absorbed and moved by it.

As soon as it ended, I had to return to work. And I left without speaking to Billie, mainly because she was arguing with someone and looking thunderous. Maybe her pianist was having a hard time that day. He took me aside and explained: 'If Lady likes you, she'll do anything in the world for you; but if she don't—look out! I mean, when she's feeling evil, don't cross her. Because if you do, she's going to hit you . . .' He weighed me up in his mind before continuing: 'And if she hits you . . . let's face it, she's going to knock you down'.

It was a friendly warning, though I never needed it. Like most artists, Billie Holiday liked to be appreciated. Next time we met, she said: 'I saw you digging me'. And after her opening concert in Manchester, she remarked on the 'awareness' of the English audience. I realised she was gratified but nevertheless puzzled by the extent of our admiration and knowledge of her work.

For me it was the start of friendship I found as touching as it was surprising. I chauffeured her when needed, ran errands, took her out for food and drinks, and visited her and McKay at the hotel. I saw as much of her as I could—and hold on to my job—and as she had taken instantly to Betsy we were able to go on the town as a foursome—invariably augmented soon after the first few glasses had been emptied. Mostly we talked about music, booze, sex, drugs, politics, gangsters, film actors, club owners, writers and Café Society; also about dogs, or clothes and shopping. Billie nursed a belief that many of the mishaps and misfortunes befalling her were due to 'politics', by which she seemed to mean the machinations of nebulous forces connected with an underground fellowship of bookers, managers, cops, lawyers, taxmen, pushers and assorted authorities.

Her own life-style, probably responsible for much of the disorder swirling about her person, she defended stoutly as 'my own damn business'. Sadly, she accepted responsibility for her habits, while fully conscious of the fact that dope suppliers (at times husbands or lovers) had leeched most of her earnings, and continued to amuse herself in her chosen fashion. I say 'sadly' only because the immoderate use of stimulants shortened her life. This she foresaw, naturally, and accepted. She wasn't unhappy about it while we were with her in '54, and it is necessary to correct impressions of a tragic lady with morbid interests, very rough language, and a taste for bad husbands and depressing songs.

Some of these things, yes; however she enjoyed drinking and narcotics, and the men while they lasted, and smiled (inwardly at any rate) while singing *What A Little Moonlight Can Do, I Only Have Eyes For You, Them There Eyes* and one or two others. More wistful items like *Willow Weep* were uplifting, too. Her bearing on stage was something to see, and

God Bless the Child
41

in the street she also looked stunning. Her language could be savage, it's true, but usually to the point. She was bright, tough, realistic, stylish, transparently sincere most of the time and lovable for much of it.

She fitted comfortably into a quiet corner of the Studio Club in Swallow Street late one afternoon, looking swish in a ski suit newly purchased from Simpson's, plus the familiar knitted cap, and making cute faces for 'Daddy' as he popped off a few shots for the family album. Beryl Bryden, just in from France, tracked us down via a call to my home and joined the appreciation society. Billie took a sort of child-like pleasure in this open admiration she found in England, and accepted the compliments without demur. When my brother-in-law, alerted by telephone of this impromptu 'sundowner', came in and paid his heartfelt respects, he ended by asking if he could have the honour of getting her a drink. 'Yes, I'll have a treble brandy with a cointreau float,' she said.

Later that night we moved on to the Stork Club, almost next door, for food and drink 'on the McKays'. After some champagne-celebrating Beryl suggested that Billie sing, which I thought unwise as Lady had told me she hated 'sitting-in' at sessions. Billie reversed the request and Beryl—reluctantly for her—obliged with *Billie's Blues* in front of its now-legendary creator, who gave every sign of feeling overjoyed and flattered by the rendering. Eventually Billie was persuaded to sing two or three with pianist Danny Turner's trio—which she judged to be with-it. When we collected our coats in the small hours I heard her remonstrating with the captain to the effect that if those goddam people knew what she was paid to sing professionally, they'd have brought champagne on the house. Instead they had given Louis the whole bill. I never discovered the outcome of that dispute but Billie was accustomed to winning her fights, and I thought her to be in the right. In any event, the night was not over.

Most times, whatever we put forward in the way of outings was okay with the McKays; if he had something better to do, he opted out. We would very much like to have entertained them at Primrose Hill. When I invited her, however, for the second time, she explained that she never went to people's houses. Asked why, her reply was typically honest: 'Because the drinks don't come up fast enough, honey, and you can't leave when you want to.' Oddly enough, at the Stork we had met Dick Kravitz from *Esquire* mag; he knew Billie from somewhere and spoke about getting her on the Esky cover—a big deal to her. He twisted her arm, or McKay's, and it was agreed we'd all motor over to Regents Park and sink a bottle or two at the elegant home of Vasco Lazslo, the noted painter, who not unnaturally had to be prised from his bed in order to receive the unexpected revellers. I remember little of consequence about that conversazione except that soon after we were seated a plaintive voice demanded: 'Who's pouring the damn drinks here? They ain't comin' up very fast.' When Billie began carousing she wanted to carouse.

Another day, when Billie was pursuing an idea for an evening binge, I told her we were booked for a sort of dinner-convention laid on by a trade organisation known as the Jazz Record Retailers Association. It sounded a stiff affair, I warned, guessing she wouldn't want to know, but of course she would be welcome to accompany us. They were jazz people, after all, including several Holiday freaks: I knew that for a fact. To my astonishment she accepted on the spot. The JRAA committee, after initial consternation, readily agreed to lay on an extra place at the set dinner. Made a last-minute guest of honour, and treated with reverent courtesy by the record dealers, Billie exuded charm and patience during the business hocus pocus and established an easy rapport with the company on her own serene terms.

Seeing the photographs now I'm struck by the surreal nature of the occasion—worthy British collectors like me, Doug Dobell, Pete Payne, Stan Wilcox, Morris Hunting, Mike Butcher and Dave Carey politely fêting the greatest woman jazz singer alive at a formal feed in an upstairs room of a middle-class restaurant in Bloomsbury, London. Taking her there was, I guess, one of the most quietly spectacular achievements of my jazz-hacking years.

Lady Day's brief concert tour kicked off on 12 February. This is part of what I wrote in Melody Maker *of 20 Feburary 1954 under 'Max Jones Spends A Holiday with Billie'.*

When Billie Holiday stepped onto the stage of the Free Trade Hall last Friday, the applause must have frightened the porter in the Midland Hotel up the street. The almost unbelievable had happened. Lady Day was behind a Manchester microphone, wearing a black dress with a gold thread in it, diamond necklace and earrings, and a patch of silver-sprayed hair a little to one side—where the gardenias used to be pinned. She smiled slightly in acknowledgement and rocked into *Billie's Blues*, then a fastish *All Of Me*, a beautiful *Porgy, I Cried For You* (which began slowly, then whipped up), and a rather weird *Them There Eyes* on which she and pianist Carl Drinkard seemed to travel separate ways. This was really it—for me and, I'm sure, most of the 2,000 people there. I had gone into the hall with the conviction that Billie was the best lady singer still on the jazz scene. So the performance was a confirmation rather than a discovery. She looked calm and happy until the microphone gave up on *Blue Moon*, her eighth number. She then gave us *My Man* unaided by electricity, and retired before doing the encores, *I Only Have Eyes For You* and *Strange Fruit*. The band, with Drinkard, Tony Kinsey, Dick Hawdon, Don Rendell, Tommy Whittle and Ronnie Ross variously featured, provided what I thought was the best support she got on her short tour.

And Billie's own performance moved me more than any of her others—perhaps because it was my first Holiday concert; perhaps because the hall was good, the crowd dead silent, and I was positioned to catch every vocal inflection and every gesture of face, hand and shoulder.

Now and again she announced a song, looking surprised the first time when applause broke out before she had reached the title. Afterwards, she told me:

'I never speak on the stage, once did 36 songs at Carnegie Hall and didn't say a damn' word. I just felt happy with this English audience . . . diggin' everything I was doing. I guess they wanted to hear my talking voice as well as my singing.' The idea of this seemed completely new to Billie.

We went back to the hotel and celebrated Lady Day's first British concert. Carl Drinkard, Doug Tobutt (of the Harold Davison office) and the Flamingo's Jeff Kruger were there, and later Harold Pendleton came over from the hall, full of regrets for the faulty mike.

'Forget about it,' said Billie. 'That was such a sweet little guy who came out and apologised and brought me another mike . . .' (this one didn't work either) . . . 'he apologised so much I felt sort of as if I'd ruined his show. When you go back be sure to tell him I love him.'

Billie was in top form for the celebration, posing for innumerable pictures taken by husband Louis McKay (an almost non-stop photographer who even takes pictures out of the airplane windows), taking photos herself, and talking with relish about Basie band days.

Naturally, she spoke of Lester Young and of his battles with section-mate Herschel Evans. 'Normally I don't go for those saxophone battles,' she said, 'but those cats really hated each other, and it kept them both blowing all the time.

'They were for ever thinking up ways of cutting the other one. You'd find them in the band room hacking away at reeds, trying out all kinds of new ones, and anything to get ahead of the other.

'Of course, Herschel had the great big beautiful tone: Lester had less tone, but a whole lot of ideas. Once Herschel asked Lester: "Why don't you play alto, man? You got an alto tone." Lester tapped his head: "There's things going on up there, man," he told Herschel. "Some of you guys are all belly."'

On Saturday, soon after midday, we left for Nottingham, where Billie was appearing at the Astoria Ballroom.

Rehearsal was called for five, and Carl Drinkard—who, like the Aga Khan, is worth his weight in platinum on these occasions—went through the routines with the rhythm men from the resident Derek Sinclair orchestra.

They were Ken Pye (drums), Jimmy Luke (bass) and Don Sanford (guitar), and as things were going smoothly Billie slipped out to boost her spirits, with a tomato juice and several milk chocolates.

Like most performers, she never eats a meal for some hours before a concert.

Then she went off on a shopping expedition, via the local pubs, with wife Betty, and took considerable pleasure in buying pyjamas and other things for 'my Louis', as she called him. Presented with the bill at Marks and Spencer, Billie hauled up her skirt and produced a roll of notes from the top of her stocking (shades of Bessie Smith), observing that 'It's safer there.'

The two women had escaped while I watched rehearsal, so I started doing the round of local taverns. I had checked out only three before I found them in the far corner of a bar, laughing at life over two large drinks. 'I knew he'd track us down, honey,' she observed in her special voice which conveyed a kind of fond derision.

I called up liquid reinforcements and joined the table in the 'Horse and Groom', which Billie thought looked just like the pubs she had seen in films made in England. Soon we got onto her nickname, Billie.

'I was a real boy when I was young,' she explained, 'and my old man called me Bill. You see—he wanted a boy and Mama a girl, so they were both satisfied. My real name's Eleanor, but almost everyone calls me Billie, excepting Basie and Billy Eckstine. To this day they still call me William.

'Of course, if I go to my home town, Baltimore, someone will shout out "Eleanor". And nobody answers. I'm looking round and thinking "where the hell's Eleanor?"'

That evening Billie did two sets at the Astoria, one around nine and

God Bless the Child

the other about 10.45. Each was of five songs, and for the second spot she brought out two we hadn't heard at Manchester: *What A Little Moonlight Can Do* and *You're Too Marvellous*.

Being a ballroom, the place was noisy: too noisy for proper appreciation of Billie's subtleties. But the place was packed to capacity, the atmosphere was festive, and nobody got too upset when the mike played up through a couple of numbers. I think Billie was expecting it by now.

In Nottingham then there appeared to be a surfeit of girls and women (because of the lace industry, I was informed). Walking round the balcony between sets, Billie eyed the dancing throng with a sardonic expression. 'Hey! Look at those bitches dancing together,' she told Betsy with obvious enthusiasm. The scene added something to her knowledge of the Old Country, and you got the feeling these were the types of ordinary people she understood and felt to be square and not too corrupted.

I had offered the McKays and Dougie Tobutt a lift in my car back to their London hotel, wishing to save them time and trouble. I should not have done it.

With a Sunday rehearsal before them, she and Louis packed quickly and got into the car, expressing the hope that Jones would find the swiftest night route to London. 'You probably won't hear a word out of me until we get to that hotel,' Billie promised, and fell immediately to sleep.

She was awakened only too soon, in deep, dark country, to find the car stationary, bonnet up and wreathed in steam. In an effort to promote American standards of heating, I had shut the radiator blind for too long; the hose had blown off, and the last of the water was now gone with the wind.

As it happened, there was no garage open for 46 miles, the way we were going, and only the unstinted help of a Bingham policeman, who (clad in pyjamas, coat and slippers) brought up reserves of water and tools, got us mobile by one in the morning.

Lady Day, I could sense, was sorry she hadn't gone by train, even though she doesn't much care for trains. 'I like flying,' she'd told me earlier. 'I'd fly across the street if they ran a service for it.'

As we lumbered off, hissing like a Stanley Steamer from the leaks in the joint, I asked incautiously if Lady was all right.

'No, I ain't,' she said promptly. 'I'm cold and disgusted. Take me to an airstation, a railroad station, anywhere there's something goin'. Only get me out of this car.' After a resigned silence, she inquired: 'How much damn' farther we got to go?'

Before I could whisper the dreadful truth, Doug Tobutt—with fine managementship—said soothingly: 'We're nearly there, Lady, it's just a few miles. You go to sleep.' I dipped the headlights in time to miss a signpost. It read: 'London 110 miles.'

We stopped repeatedly to replenish the cooling system, and when the cans were empty I resorted to extreme measures in order to get us to a café on the Great North Road. Waking up again, Lady demanded suspiciously: 'What's he up to now?' Betsy admitted I was peeing into the radiator. Billie subsided with some profanity, but I believe she liked me for that. At the café, Doug, Louis and the Joneses slunk inside for refreshments, leaving the legendary body sleeping and dishevelled on the rear seat of the Ford. We looked up apprehensively every time the door swung open, McKay seeming to be as scared as the rest of us. But Billie slept on, and we resumed the stop-start progress.

We bade the McKays a brief goodbye at the Piccadilly Hotel at 5.30 a.m. on Sunday. That afternoon, Billie rehearsed hard with Jack Parnell's band, and in the evening gave a splendid performance of 15 songs at the Albert Hall, ending—as she likes to do—with *Strange Fruit*.

Despite bad lighting and the odd tricks of the hall that make drummers' offbeats hit your ears like bad on-beats, Billie gripped an audience of some 6,000.

Billie had discarded some of her underclothes during the long night ride (while feeling unwell), and these Betsy washed and pressed in time to return to their owner at the Albert Hall. Lady reacted with genuine gratitude and surprise, as though such little kindnesses were still unexpected. Feeling uneasy, I said nothing until offering her a whisky in the interval.

Once more, and again that night at the Flamingo Club, she proved that her relaxed, expressive singing brings freshness and added meaning to any worthwhile pop-song. Her style has outlived several 'new' vocal styles and will probably outlive many more. Dill Jones told me: 'Billie is one of the most poised women I've ever seen, and unquestionably the greatest jazz singer I have heard since Louis.'

Don Rendell, another admirer, rushed from work to the Flamingo to accompany Billie (at her invitation), got there just in time, but was unable to press through the crowd to get to the bandstand.

After the show, I found Billie and Don toasting each other in the band room. 'You know Don?' she said to me. 'He's my boy.' To Don she said: 'I still love Max in spite of that car ride.' I hope she means it.

She enjoyed the acclaim she received in Europe—later she said the crowd of 6,000 at London's Albert Hall gave her one of the greatest receptions of her life—and she worked as hard as her health would allow to earn it.

Saying goodbye to Billie was like saying goodbye to an old friend who values you despite your faults. She had said to Betsy one day: 'I know Max loves me, but can you stop him talking me to death?' I hoped she would forgive me for that and the car journey; and I believe she did because on November 11, 1958 I received a telegram from Paris at my Primrose Hill address. It read: 'AT HOTEL DE PARIS TILL THUR EVENING LOVE BILLIE HOLIDAY'. Next day I telephoned her there. She sounded dragged, said there was nobody who spoke the damn' language, and asked: 'Why aren't you here?' I should have gone at once, but the paper didn't want to release me or pay expenses and I was as usual strapped for cash. Betsy's advice was to draw out what savings I had, sod the MM, and do what I could for the dispirited singer. I have always regretted not taking her advice.

Soon Henry Kahn in Paris was telling me she wanted to come to London and stay here. Since separating from McKay she no longer wished to live in the United States. 'I want to settle in Britain because I love the people,' she declared. 'They do not just call me a singer; they call me an artist and I like that.' After a tour round France, Kahn reported, Billie would go to Italy, then probably prepare to come to London.

Without warning, late in February 1959, I heard from Harold Davison's office that Lady Day was scheduled to appear in a London TV show. I checked arrival time, hotel booking and so on, then drove out to meet her plane. It was the prelude to a few more hectic days in her extraordinary presence. And the lasting friendship I felt had been struck up in '54 resumed as if there had been no interruption. But this time Billie was separated from Louis and the mink coat, was showing signs of increased strain, and was clearly dissatisfied with her domestic and professional life. Nevertheless, she was an often diverting, always interesting, companion. I guessed she was ill but her defiant nature would not allow her to give in, just as it would not allow her to feel apologetic about her need for drugs. She spoke repeatedly of her desire to live over here and, at the time, she was serious. Back home again it might have been a different matter. I never really knew. I tried to arrange record dates but had no luck. It was a sort of tragedy she couldn't have got over here while there was a chance of regular work.

Again, I spent most of my waking hours with her, collecting her on the morning of the programme to take her to rehearsals (no one had laid on a car), shopping for vodka when we reached the studios (she was meticulous about paying for bottles, handing me the cash in dollar bills), and lending support through the day. Singers Beryl Bryden and Yolande Bavan, and the faithful Betsy, all turned up at Granada to lavish help and attention on their favourite. In fact, we formed an ad hoc Holiday Supporters Club, bent on giving her the best care we could. One event I cannot forget was taking Billie to the Downbeat, a musicians' hangout in Soho. She wanted to sing, and a spontaneously formed group accompanied her in several songs. The club telephone rang in mid-song, and when a Hooray Henry customer prolonged his 'phone conversation, an enraged Kenny Graham (bandleader, tenorman and Holiday worshipper) moved swiftly towards him and carried the protesting Hooray bodily away to enforced silence. The act somehow typified the hold Billie exercised on all *her* people. This is what I wrote about other aspects of that final visit (*Melody Maker*, 28 February 1959).

Billie Holiday looked almost as surprised to find herself in London on Sunday night as I felt at seeing her here.

'The whole thing was a rush. We only heard about this TV date two or three days ago,' she said when she was safely off the Jet Clipper. 'That's why I couldn't let you know in time. I knew damn well you'd be here anyway.'

The TV date was for 'Chelsea At Nine.' On Tuesday, Lady Day sang *Porgy, Please Don't Talk About Me* and *Strange Fruit* at the Granada Theatre in the King's Road.

The last was accompanied largely by her pianist, Mal Waldron. The others had the full support of Mal and Peter Knight's orchestra. The entire show was filmed, and viewers will see it in March.

On a song that measures up to her, she can communicate the mood with an almost painful intensity. Part of it is 'soul', part is expert timing. Then there is the troubled tone—Ethel Waters said she sings as though her shoes are too tight—and what Steve Race described last week as 'the curiously instrumental quality of her vibrato'.

The subject of vibrato came up spontaneously, while the Lady relaxed one evening at the Club Caribe in Leicester Square.

Proprietor Alex Graham maintained a flow of recorded music, and when one of the LPs got under way, Billie demanded to know: 'Who is that? Sounds as though she's crying. She reminds me of Judy Garland with the vibrato.'

It turned out that the owner of the vibrato was Roberta Sherwood, and Billie went on to tell us:

'When I got into show business you had to have that shake. If you didn't, you was dead. I didn't have that kind of vibrato, and when I sang people used to say: "What's she putting down?"'

'I always did try to sing like a tenor, or some horn. That big vibrato fits a few voices, but those that have it usually have too much. I just don't like it. You have to used it sparingly. You know, the hard thing is not to sing with that shake.'

I read Billie some of the things Miles Davis said about her to Nat Hentoff in 'An Afternoon with Miles Davis' in *The Jazz Review*, December 1958. Among them: 'I love the way she sings . . . like Lester Young and Louis Armstrong play . . . she doesn't need any horns. She sounds like one anyway.'

Billie smiled faintly and said: 'That's how I try to sound; I didn't know I succeeded.'

The record that brought Billie close to the gramophone was one called *Out There With Betty Carter*, on the Peacock label. Betty Carter used to be billed as 'Miss Bebop' when she sang with Lionel Hampton, is now known as 'Lady Cool'.

Billie listened a long while in silence before saying: 'I love her. She's really got something. On the slow tunes her diction's bad—that's the onliest fault I've got to find. I think she's crazy—she can scat like Leo Watson. You remember Leo?'

I did, of course, but Betty Carter was new to me. This didn't surprise Billie, who suffers from no delusions about the British public, though she likes working to it.

'Betty's five years ahead of her time,' Lady said, to clear up the situation. 'They don't dig her even in America, so you know they won't dig her here.'

The possibility of making Europe her headquarters is still much in Billie Holiday's' mind. I reported last November that she contemplated settling here, and she insists now that she will buy a house in London and work in Britain, France, Sweden . . . 'wherever the opportunity arises'.

The reason is simple. 'I can't get my police card to work New York, so how can I make it there?' she asks. 'America won't let me work, so I'm going to make it in Europe or somewhere.'

Billie argues that she's paid for any offences she's committed, and expiated the deeds. She wants a fair chance to go on earning her living. The withholding of a police card means she is unable to work in New York clubs.

On the face of it, her case sounds reasonable. 'I'm Billie Holiday,' she explains. 'Singing's the only thing I know how to do, and they won't let me do it. Do they expect me to go back to scrubbing steps—the way I started out?'

Anyway, she had no further opportunity of making the move. Soon reports were coming in regularly of her deteriorating condition. At the end of May she collapsed and was taken to hospital, suffering from liver and heart complaints.

Still harried by the authorities, she died in degrading circumstances at 3 a.m. on 17 July 1959, with 70 cents in the bank and 750 dollars in large notes strapped to her leg. She was, by her reckoning, only 44 years old. And I was halfway through a letter to her when friends telephoned to say she was dead. Though half expecting it, I was devastated by the news.

But still, we have those many lovely or disturbing recorded performances. They will pleasure my ears for the rest of my life and those of future generations for all time, I guess. On a personal note, again, I will always gladly and sadly remember that at her birthday party on April 7 that year, Lady asked the BBC's Barrie Thorne to pass on to me her 'undying love'.

And Maely Dufty, who said she contributed a large chunk to *Lady Sings the Blues* with her then husband Bill Dufty, wrote to Dave Carey in a letter of December 1962: 'Please tell Max Jones that Billie, during the two months at the hospital (and I was with her till the end), often spoke about him with much affection. Tell him to drop me a line.'

Later, while living in London, Maely called me to say how greatly Billie had felt wanted, and how there were 'Holiday freaks' who loved her, when she was in England. Max was high on the list of the constant lovers. I suppose I feel as gassed about that as any tribute received in a lengthy and misspent life on the jazz case.

PART TWO

What a Little Moonlight Can Do:

Billie Holiday in Performance and in Her Own Words

BILLIE HOLIDAY: STORYVILLE, BOSTON
DOM CERULLI

This excellent little review reveals Billie's mystique in a nightclub performance. It originally appeared in the jazz magazine, *Down Beat*, in its "Caught in the Act" column.

The old Billie Holiday, who owns dozens of ballads and many, many memories, held her audience spellbound at George Wein's Storyville with vocal excursions into the past.

From the first words of her first offering, "Willow Weep For Me," it was apparent that the Bostonians present had come to hear Billie and savor her songs. Throughout her four numbers and two encores, patrons didn't stir. Nothing disturbed the mood set by her songs except enthusiastic applause following each number.

Billie followed "Willow" with a jumpier "Nice Work If You Can Get It," and the lighting which had been shadowy during the ballad brightened and etched her against the black background of the stage. The spot dimmed down to a bare illumination of her head and shoulders, and she delivered "Easy Living."

The gardenia was missing, but that was about all. The lazy inflection, the languid phrasing were there, a bit darkened by the years, but plaintive as ever. Billie has an edge to her voice which she uses, along with her expressive hands, to accent a word or a phrase. It was particularly telling on her final encore, "I Cover the Waterfront."

Billie also sang "I Only Have Eyes For You" and "God Bless the Child." She spoke very little, only to introduce "Waterfront" and to acknowledge her accompanists.

Patrons included a healthy percentage of middle-aged couples and parties, for whom Holiday apparently was more than a name on older records. Judging by the buzz of conversation following her set, her old magic is still there.

JAZZ SINGING: PURE AND SIMPLE
JOHN S. WILSON

John S. Wilson, who retired as the *New York Times*'s chief jazz critic by the 1990s, was, in this compiler's opinion, the dean of the jazz critics. In a straightforward style, he delivered judgments that were invariably on the mark. He never fell prey to any kind of prejudice or predilection. He always knew exactly what he was hearing and the value of it for the short term and long run. He combined the best instincts of the journalist and tastemaker to set standards for the art of jazz criticism.

He never lamented that the style of music he was hearing wasn't more pleasing; he always accepted the music on its own terms. He always knew what he was talking about. He never superimposed his own temperament on a musician. He never used a piece of music or a performance as a chance to air his own views but always focused on the music presented to him. He never seized on an inconsequential detail or lost his sense of proportion. He was able to appraise a long piece of work in a single column or less. And he never, to my knowledge, used a column as a chance to damn a young artist; instead he ferreted out young talented people and gave them attention in the *New York Times*, which, rightly or wrongly, for better or worse, ranks as the most influential publication in the country. And he could actually instruct musicians or help them improve or correct themselves.

In this little review of about four hundred words, Wilson summed up the story of Billie's waning life and caught the essence of the beauty of her last recordings. Miles Davis and other musicians agreed with Wilson right away; it took most critics many years to stop arguing about whether Billie's last recordings had depth and appeal and to understand what Wilson apprehended so effortlessly.

Unlike almost all those who are classified as jazz singers, Billie Holiday is basically neither a blues singer nor that type of singer of popular ballads who is identified as a "pop" singer. She draws from both sources but depends on neither. She is, purely and simply, a jazz singer. Three recently released disks trace the musical path she has followed over the last twenty years.

Two are made up of reissued material—*Billie Holiday* (Commodore) and *The Blue Are Brewin'* (Decca). The Commodore collection, recorded in 1939 and 1944, is subtitled, with more than the customary justification, "Twelve of Her Greatest Interpretations." In 1939 Miss Holiday had achieved a happy conjunction of originality of conception, matured discipline in performance and a rich and flexible voice that gave the pieces recorded that year—"I Gotta Right to Sing the Blues," "Yesterdays," "Fine and Mellow" and "Strange Fruit"—a depth and emotional intensity that are paralleled in jazz only in the very best of Bessie Smith's work. She continues to be a vibrant, commanding singer, fully justifying her high reputation, in the 1944 selections, but she seems less deeply involved in these songs and is beginning to drift toward the agonizingly slow tempos that have plagued much of her later work.

In the years since the war, Miss Holiday's singing career has been shadowed by a constant burden of personal problems, although there is little suggestion of this in the Decca recordings, made between 1946 and 1949. Her singing on these is still lithe and assured, but it is of little avail, since the songs are largely second-rate and her accompaniment is quite uninspired. "Big Stuff," the blues recording heard on the juke box in Leonard Bernstein's ballet, "Fancy Free," glistens like a diamond in this lackadaisical collection.

Additional Resources

Today Miss Holiday's voice is a rough-surfaced ghost of what had once been a pliant, precise instrument, but its very limitations have brought out additional resources of craft and skill in her use of it. One hears occasional suggestions of this reorientation in her latest disk, *Lady in Satin* (Columbia), but much of her present potential is stifled in the steady succession of slow, slow ballads and flaccid accompaniment of Ray Ellis' orchestra.

LADY DAY HAS HER SAY
LEONARD FEATHER

Leonard Feather made a fascinating contribution to jazz literature by conducting blindfold tests with prominent jazz musicians. He tested Lady Day for the February 1950 issue of *Metronome* magazine. Billie revealed her self-assurance and taste in music. These are the words of the singer who had the courage of her convictions and refused to alter her style to please club owners.

Some people might be surprised by her antipathy toward Sarah Vaughan's singing style. Billie could hardly have missed knowing about Sarah's gorgeous voice. On the other hand, particularly in the 1940s and early 1950s, Sarah occasionally met up with critics who didn't like her embellishments, which they found excessive. It's possible that Billie didn't like the extent to which Sarah took her progressive jazz style. Leonard Feather must have thought Billie was giving a heartfelt opinion of Sarah's singing; otherwise he might not have included it. But it's far more likely that Billie, who altered songs tremendously, too, didn't like Sarah personally. Billie may have used the blindfold test as chance to get revenge.

In her autobiography, *Lady Sings the Blues*, Billie recounted her experiences in the few weeks following her release from jail after serving a term on narcotics charges.

". . . Bobby [Tucker, her accompanist] insisted on going to see Sarah Vaughan. She was giving a concert and Bobby took me backstage. The people hanging around there were wonderful, the air was full of "Hi, baby" and "oo-pa-pa-da" and everybody telling me how great I looked.

"We waited for Sarah to come off between sets. I was glad to see her. And I expected she'd be glad to see me. All I expected was a little hello—after all, she was working. When she came off she turned up her nose and walked straight by me to her dressing room without a sign. To get this from someone I had worried over and tried to help really hurt.

"I broke down and cried. Sarah made me wish I'd never left jail or, worse, like I was still in or carried the bars around with me.

"She tried to explain later by telling me her husband, George Treadwell, had told her I was hot, just out of jail."

Billie's blindfold test appeared in print about a year later. Although Leonard Feather knew Billie well, he might not have known about her difficulties with Sarah's coldness. If he had known, he might not have asked Billie for an opinion of Sarah's singing.

Billie's other comments remind us of the allure of the now virtually forgotten Little Miss Cornshucks. She had been a very popular singer in the jazz world. Billie praises Duke Ellington, Woody

Herman, Peggy Lee, Jackie Cain, and Roy Kral. Jimmy Rushing may be immortal, but Billie didn't hear much to excite her.

One wonders if she would have softened her attitude, had she lived longer, about Sarah Vaughan. And there's a possibility—and this is entirely speculation—that Billie had developed a grievance against Jimmy Rushing during her months on the road with him in the Count Basie band. Rushing never gambled with Billie and the men on the Basie bus. He held onto his money tightly. He didn't do very much in the way of wailing and raising hell with comrades. He sang the blues, and he loved to eat. These were not the standards which Billie used to measure the worth of friends. Jimmy Rushing was not her type of fellow. Or she may really not have liked his singing—his tone, perhaps—although she, too, had a plaintive, whining quality at times, which she used to enormous advantage, as he did. Billie didn't especially admire Ruth Brown or June Christy, either.

Bebop was essentially new to the world—officially only about five years old on commercial recordings, and ten years old altogether from the start of its development—at the time Billie took this blindfold test. Eventually bebop became *the* mainstream music and the basis of all future developments in jazz. Dixieland, though it has diehard fans to this day, was becoming antiquated. However, to Billie and most people in 1950, Dixieland sounded far less old fashioned and quaint than it does today.

Overall, in her test, Billie tended to depict herself as a child of her own time, on the cutting edge of her time, and a singer "for all time," as Mel Torme would eventually say about her—and an artist with little patience for commercialism or experimentation that could sound exaggerated or unnatural. Even early in her career, she tended more toward parlando—talk-singing—than to blues shouting or operatic ornateness. And she was a fighter. These are elements that seem to have influenced her comments about other singers.

The main problem in conducting a blindfold test with Billie Holiday, or with anyone of her musical stature, is that of limiting the records to a small but comprehensive selection. Personally, I was so interested in investigating Billie's views that a marathon test involving several hundred records seemed mandatory. Considerations of time and space, however, reduced the project to a round dozen discs, on which Billie commented as follows.

1. It's "I Got Rhythm," isn't it? Sounds like Jacquet . . . and now it *doesn't* sound like him. Is that some concert or something? Well, it jumps, it's very exciting at times, but I don't care too much for the rhythm section. Under the circumstances, not a bad record, but this kind of thing is according to the atmosphere you're in. If I had my choice of records I wouldn't pick this. Two stars.

2. Duke! . . . I always loved this—it gets four right now! I've always wanted a band to play under me like that when I sing; they don't mess around or noodle, they just help you. I've wanted it all my life! I almost got that with Gordon Jenkins, on "You're My Thrill," but that was pretty music. This has bounce, too. You know, the only ones who can take a solo while I'm singing and still not interfere with me are Lester Young and Teddy. I always like Hibbler, but he has some tricks I don't care for. And Hodges is always my man. This is an all around great record. Four.

3. Peggy, isn't it? . . . I always loved Peggy—loved her when she first started, and she's been very fortunate; she's always had the kind of background every singer needs . . . That clarinet sounds very familiar. I like it. Sounds a lot like Goodman. Don't tell me it is, I'll die! Three stars.

4. Who's that guitar? . . . The piano is the kind of bop I like; it makes sense. I don't know the alto; he's trying to play like Charlie, whoever he is. I like the tenor; he's nice and even and smooth. And I like that music in the last chorus. I call this bop, and I like it *very* much. Three stars.

5. This is Ruth Brown, and you don't have to play it. I know all about this. I can't stand copycats, and this girl copies Miss Cornshucks note for note. I just do not like her. I'd like to get 'em both together with a good piano player and have 'em both sing; if Cornshucks' "So Long" isn't twice as good, I'll eat my hat. When Cornshucks sings this style, she *means* it. Sure I copied Bessie Smith and Louis Armstrong, but not note for note; they *inspired* me . . . I don't care if she hates me for saying this, it's my opinion!

6. That's Teddy Wilson . . . no, wait . . . yes, I still say it's Teddy. I won't take that back! Bud Freeman on tenor, maybe Joe Marsala on clarinet. I'm not much on this Dixieland, I mean I don't recognize them too well, but they're all swinging and it's a good record. Do I like good Dixieland? Damn right I do—three stars!

7. That's Sarah . . .this is the best record I've heard of hers in a long time. She sticks to the melody; maybe she has to, because of the vocal

background. You know, on "The Man I Love," she goes so far out, it stinks; she got so that even musicians couldn't understand what she was doing. That sort of stuff is for an instrument, not for a voice. Maybe I'm old fashioned, but I just don't like or understand it. But this one is worth three stars.

8. That's whatshisname, "Mr. Blues," Wynonie. He has the best backgrounds on his records of any blues singer of his type. That's Tab Smith on alto. The tenor sounds like Lester . . . It is Lester! . . . No, it isn't . . . yes, it is! Nobody in the world does that but Lester! . . . I like this kind of blues singing. I love T-Bone Walker, too. Four stars!

9. That could be anybody, they all sound alike to me . . . the girl that used to be with Krupa, Anita, or any of them. I guess the band is Stan Kenton . . . June Christy? I like "Willow Weep For Me," but I haven't heard many of their things. This is just fair; the tune, the band and the singing, all fair. Didn't move me. Two stars.

10. That's Jimmy Rushing . . . he never killed me . . . it's Basie's band, and the tenor sounds a little like Lucky Thompson. This is just fair, very fair . . . tell the truth, I'm ashamed of them. That band, I could just cry for what's happened to it, when I think how great it used to be. Two stars.

11. I don't know who the hell this is but it sure is great. The piano player's wonderful! This sounds awfully familiar. Is it Woody's band? Now this is what I call bop, the real thing! It doesn't heckle your ears, you get right up to a pitch with it, come right down; it moves you. The soloists? *Everybody's* great! Four stars.

12. I believe this has my girl on it. Jackie Cain. She's the greatest for this kind of thing; she's made a business, made life out of perfecting it. I think she and her husband are great . . . that's that girl on cello and the girl on drums. The group has a marvelous sound; all they need is a break. At Bop City they didn't have a chance, because their music is soft and not exciting, no clowning, no funny bow ties. They should be able to work in any good hotel, any theatre, anywhere; they're the best. Bop like this is here to stay!

. . .

Records Reviewed by Billie Holiday

Following were the records discussed in Billie Holiday's blindfold test. She was given no advance information about them either before or during the test.

1. Jazz at the Philharmonic, "Endido," Part I, (Mercury,) Illinois Jacquet, tenor. Hank Jones, Jo Jones, Ray Brown, rhythm.
2. Duke Ellington, "Don't Get Around Much Any More," (Columbia).
3. Benny Goodman Orch. & Peggy Lee, "For Every Man There's a Woman," (Capitol).
4. Lennie Tristano, "Sax of a Kind," (Capitol,) Tristano, piano, Billie Bauer, guitar, Lee Konitz, alto, Warne Marsh, tenor.
5. Ruth Brown, "So Long," (Atlantic).
6. Mel Powell, "Muskrat Ramble," (Capitol), Powell, piano, Don Lodice, tenor, Gus Bivona, clarinet.
7. Sarah Vaughan, "Make Believe," (Columbia).
8. Wynonie Harris, "Come Back, Baby," (Aladdin), Tab Smith, alto, Allen Eager, tenor.
9. Stan Kenton, "He Was a Good Man as Good Men Go," (Capitol), June Christy, vocal.
10. Count Basie, "Walking Slow Behind You," (Victor), Rushing, vocal Paul Gonsalves, tenor.
11. Woody Herman, "That's Right," (Capitol), Lou Levy, piano.
12. Roy Kral–Jackie Cain, "Ever-Lovin' Blues," (Atlantic).

THE WILLIS CONOVER INTERVIEW

This is an ideal piece to follow Leonard Feather's blindfold test. Here Willis Conover says right away that Anita O'Day, June Christy, and Chris Connor, whom audiences have loved, followed Billie Holiday's lead. Billie wasn't particularly fond of those Kenton band singers, she said in her blindfold test. But since they were virtually her disciples, one might ask if some hidden passion colored Billie's opinions of them.

She reminds us, in the Conover interview, that she first fell in love with Louis Armstrong and Bessie Smith as her greatest influences. It could be that, to Lady Day, originality and overall sound were of paramount importance. Anyway, it's clear that even at this late date in her life, Billie enjoyed her memories, and she could still laugh.

She was not fourteen in 1933, as she claimed to Conover, but eighteen when she made her first recordings. She could bend the truth as well as the notes.

But it is enlightening to hear her do a critique of her own singing and learn what a perfectionist she was. She was, it appears, intensely concerned about sounding relaxed and natural.

The broadcast transcription has Billie saying that songwriter Andy Razaf helped her write the words and music to her song, "Don't Explain." John Chilton's biography, *Billie's Blues*, claims the same. But in Billie's autobiography, *Lady Sings the Blues*, she says she wrote the tune with the help of Arthur Herzog. Nowhere in Andy Razaf's biography, *Black and Blue*, is the song even mentioned. So it's safe to assume that there was a mix-up in the transcription of the Conover interview. Billie and Herzog have always received the credit for holding the copyright. Also, she said that she wrote "Your Mother's Son-in-Law" after asking her mother for some money, and her mother flatly refused her. Actually the song she wrote at that time was "God Bless the Child."

On the whole, the interview constitutes an intimate, charming, serious visit with Lady Day.

In communist countries, Willis Conover's broadcasts served as a lifeline for jazz lovers and musicians. *Down Beat* gave him a Lifetime Achievement Award. Many stories have been published about him, including one in the *New York Times Sunday Magazine* by John S. Wilson.

Conover: Billie Holiday, about whom at least one critic has said, "If you want to know what jazz is about, listen to Billie Holiday." She's been named by more jazz fans and by more musicians, more consistently and for the longest time, as the greatest jazz singer. Stylistically, from Billie Holiday came Anita O'Day and then June Christy and Chris Connor.

I'd like to ask Billie. From whom did Billie Holiday's voice come?

Holiday: I think I copied my style from Louis Armstrong. Because—I always liked the big volume and the big sound that Bessie Smith got when she sang. But—uh—when I was quite young, I heard a record Louis Armstrong made called "The West End Blues," and he doesn't say any words, you know?—and I thought, "This is wonderful," you know? And I liked the feeling he got from it. So I wanted Louis Armstrong's feeling and I wanted the big volume that Bessie Smith got. But I found it didn't work with me, because I didn't have a big voice, you know? So anyway, between the two of 'em, I sort of (smiling) got Billie Holiday.

Conover: That's very interesting—that the source of so much instrumental music was also the source of such great vocal music as yours: Louis Armstrong. What other musicians have had some sort of influence upon the development of your singing style?

Holiday: Well, I like Lester Young. I always liked—uh—well, Lester came much later in my life, but I liked Lester's feeling. You know, everyone, when he first started, thought: This man, his tone, is too thin, you know? A tenor sax y'know. Everybody thinks it has to be real big; and Lester used to go out of his mind getting reeds, you know, to sound big like Chu Berry, and he was very popular in those days, and I told him, "It doesn't matter, because," I said, "you have a beautiful tone," I says, "and you watch. After a while, everybody's going to be copying you." And it came to be, you know?

And then, uh—well, I made my first record with Benny. And . . . Benny came to a little club, in Harlem, to hear me—the Log Cabin. At that time, he was not "Benny Goodman," he was just another musician. (Laughs) He worked in a studio band, and—down at NBC—and he thought I was wonderful. So he had a recording date under his own name, and John Hammond—you must have heard of him, he's a music critic. And they thought I was it, for the vocalist. And the funniest thing— (Laughs) I got there and I was afraid to sing in the mike. Because I never saw a microphone before. And I says, "Why do I have to sing in that thing? Why can't I just sing like I do at the club?" I was scared to death of it. And, uh, Buck and Bubbles—Buck played the piano on that date. Can you imagine—all those studio men and Buck, he can't read a note, (laughing) he played the piano! Well, that's the way Benny is, he likes music. You don't have to read, or write, or anything, you just play it, you know. So Buck says, "You're not going to let these people think you're a square, are you?" He says, "Come on, sing it!" And I sang, "Your Mother's Son-in-Law," and on the other side was "Riffin' the Scotch."

Conover: Let's see, you were fifteen years old then, weren't you?

Holiday: No, I was fourteen. (Laughs)

Conover: I beg your pardon. Well, which of your records, Billie, give you more pleasure today—or perhaps I should rephrase that. What different kinds of pleasure do you get from the earlier recordings and from the more recent records that you made?

Holiday: Well, I get a big bang out of "Your Mother's Son-in-Law." It sounds like I'm doing comedy. (Laughing.) My voice sounded so funny and high—on there, and I sounded like I'm about three years old. To me, anyhow. But uh I don't like any of my records, to be truthful with you. Because it's always something you should have done; or should have waited here; or should have held that note longer; or you should have phrased—well, you know how it is. So you're never really satisfied with your records. But the things that I like the most—I think the things I've done with strings. Or the ones—the real blues ones, you know, like "Summertime." Y'know, the ones with no music, at all, you know, where we just relaxed? Like the things we did with Teddy Wilson and then Benny and Roy Eldridge. We had . . . I was with Count Basie's band at the time, and we had been on the road—about three months, doing one nighters, you know, and that's pretty rough. And we had no time to rehearse or anything, and we walked right in the studio—no music, and we made six great sides, you know. Those are the kind I like.

Conover: Billie, you've recorded so many songs . . . Which of the songs that you have recorded did you compose yourself?

Holiday: Oh, I did "Billie's Blues" and "Fine and Mellow" and uh . . .

Oh, let me tell you how I did "Fine and Mellow." I was working in the Cafe Society downtown in the Village, and we get up there to make these records, all of a sudden we needed one more side. So I says, "I know. Let's do a blues, and let's make the introduction like an organ grinder, you know (sings) dah-dah, dah-dah, dah." You know. And, uh—right there I made it all up, right in the studio.

And I did "Don't Explain" and, oh, what else? A few more, I can't think of 'em (laughs).

But "Don't Explain" had, uh, I did that with a fellow named Razaf, and he helped with the lyrics. But gee, I was—I'm very proud of that because I think it's a pretty tune, and as a rule I can only write blues, you know. So I thought "Don't Explain" was the end for me (laughs modestly).

Oh—and I did "Your Mother's Son-in-Law" . . . don't let me forget that one, because I wrote that one for my mother. And how it came about, I asked Mother for some money. And she flatly refused me. So I said, "That's all right. God bless the child that's got his own!" I walked out, y'know, and, uh—it sort of stuck in my mind. And my piano player and I were foolin' around the next day. I says, "You know, that's a good title for a song." I says, "Maybe we'll have to make it kind of religious."

So he says, "No-o-o!" So we—I write out the words and we get the melody and we wrote the song. (Laughs.) So I carried it to Marks— the publishing?—he thought it was wonderful, and right away he published it.

So that's how we got "God Bless the Child."

Conover: Are these your favorite records, of those you've made, Billie?

Holiday: No-o-o . . . ! (Laughs) No. Uh, the things—uh, like I told you—the things that I made that I like never got popular. Like "Deep-Song"? You probably never heard of it. (Laughing) It's a Decca. It never got popular . . . "You're My Thrill"—I think it's got a beautiful back-ground, the strings, and the oboe, and—it never got popular.

Like Benny Goodman always says, uh—like this "Some Other Spring" I did. This song, nothing ever happened to it, and it's the most beautiful thing I ever heard in my life. Teddy Wilson—Irene Wilson, his wife, wrote it. And uh—she got inspired when, the night we were all playing up there, Benny Webster and Benny Carter and myself and John Kirby the bass player? We were at her apartment having a jam session there, and she had made some red beans and rice that night (Laughs). And we were just sittin' around playing, and she got inspired and wrote the tune—but like Benny says, "That's not gonna—nothing's gonna happen with the tune; it's too beautiful!" And he just didn't make sense to us, y'know; but he was right. He says, "Maybe in years to come."

Now, for instance, like "Yesterdays," that's a tune that I recorded, and I loved it. But Benny was right, because, uh, well, what was the show? "Roberta?" It came from "Roberta," I think. But anyway, "I Only Have Eyes For You," that was popular, all the other tunes. "Yesterdays," the most beautiful song in the show, is just starting to get popular now! So maybe Benny was right.

Conover: What other songs that you *haven't* recorded would you like to record some day, Billie?

Holiday: Well, I don't know. I, uh, I tell you a song I'd like to sing, and it doesn't have any lyrics to it. I don't think, and that's "Our Waltz," David Rose. You know, things like that. Something nobody else does.

Conover: Well, let's get away from the musical end of Billie Holiday for just a second and ask how the name Lady Day came about?

Holiday: Well, now, that came about when Lester and I were in Count Basie's band, and Lester named me Lady Day, and he named my mother, the Duchess. And there was Count Basie, so we were the Royal Family. (Laughs.)

Conover: I see. Well, how did the gardenia in the Billie Holiday hairdo become Billie's trademark?

Holiday: Well, I've always loved gardenias. And one night I got very, very—how would you say it? . . . well, I guess . . . uh, uh . . . well, I don't know, there's a word for it. Anyway, I just wouldn't go on. I couldn't go on. I couldn't sing without my gardenia. (Laughs) So it became a trademark, and I just thought I couldn't sing if I didn't have a gardenia in my hair.
 And they had to be fresh. (Laughs)

Conover: You're no longer wearing the gardenia, these days, though.

Holiday: Well, no, I, uh, got over that. It was just a childish thing.

Conover: Lady Day. Billie Holiday, our in-person guest today on the Voice of America Jazz Hour. Thank you very much, Billie.

Holiday: Thank you, Willis, for having me here.

PART THREE

Me, Myself, and I:

Billie Holiday
on Record and
in Print

EARLY RECORDINGS
JOHN HAMMOND AND DAN MORGENSTERN

This conversation between record producer John Hammond and then–*Down Beat* editor Dan Morgenstern was made at the time of the release of the film *Lady Sings the Blues* to promote a Columbia album reissuing Holiday's original performances of the songs featured in the film. In it, Hammond reveals the circumstances of these early recording sessions and how he met the singer.

John Hammond championed jazz as a journalist and record producer from the mid-'30s through the '80s. He became one of the most famous of all producers, working throughout his career for Columbia Records, and credited for "discovering" numerous acts, from Billie Holiday and Benny Goodman through Aretha Franklin, Bob Dylan, and Bruce Springsteen. Morgenstern, a noted writer/critic on jazz since the 1950s, is now head of the Institute of Jazz Studies at Rutgers University.

John Hammond: This is John Hammond, the guy who used to record Billie Holiday from the years 1933 off and on through 1940. With me is Dan Morgenstern. We're about to talk of the new Billie Holiday album being put out of the songs that Diana Ross sings in the movie Lady Sings the Blues. *I thought we might talk a little bit, Dan, about some of the sessions that are included here—the titles—and maybe you could ask me some questions about some of the sessions, and maybe I could remember some of the things that happened.*

Dan Morgenstern: I guess the earliest one on the record is the famous session that produced "What a Little Moonlight Can Do" and "Miss Brown to You." That was actually one of the first Billie Holiday records that I ever acquired, and it's been one of my favorites ever since.

John Hammond: Actually that was only the second record she ever made in her life. She made two records with Benny Goodman in 1933; this was the first one she made in that little band I got together around Teddy Wilson in June of 1935. This was a session that I can remember practically every second of, because we got together six guys who had literally never played with each other before. There was Teddy Wilson on piano, John Kirby on bass, Cozy Cole just down from Buffalo, with Jonah Jones and Stuff Smith, Cozy on drums, John Trueheart, Chick Webb's guitar player. Then there were the three horns of Benny Goodman on clarinet, a very unwilling Benny Goodman I might add, Roy Eldridge on trumpet, and Ben Webster on his first recording session in the east. It was absolute dynamite, because here were the seven guys with tunes that were not the best. On that session, probably the best known tune, the only plug* tune, was "I Wished on the Moon," which was from The Big Broadcast of 1936, which was a pleasant ballad. "What a Little Moonlight Can Do" was considered a dog by everybody, including its publisher. "Miss Brown to You" was something that was absolutely unknown but I guess Teddy and Harry Gray, who was the musical director of Brunswick at the time, picked that one out. I tell you Billie Holiday's singing and the instrumentalists improvising made three of these tunes absolute classics.

Dan Morgenstern: In a sense I guess it sort of set the pattern for future recordings by Billie under your direction.

John Hammond: Well, it did, because I tell you I did something I'm really rather sorry about. I proved to Brunswick how cheaply good records could be made, because there were no arrangements, no orchestrations, no paper to worry about. There were seven musicians who got union scale, and that was it, plus a vocalist who got paid a flat fee per side.
    However there was practically no jazz being recorded in 1935. I mean, the record business was really broke, and the only possible thing

*The term for songs being plugged by publishers.

that could help the record business was the jukebox business which was just starting. Capehart had just come out with its first jukebox the year before, and in many locations, particularly in bars catering to black people, there were these jukeboxes that played 12 selections. And they were looking for material that would make their customers drop nickels into the jukeboxes. And the Teddy Wilson–Billie Holiday records were the best thing that Brunswick had at that time.

Dan Morgenstern: When did you first hear Billie?

John Hammond: I first heard Billie in early 1933 when she was working at Monette Moore's gin mill on 133rd street. She was 17. She had been scarred by life already. She was up from Baltimore maybe a year or so before. She was the daughter of a guitar player whom I had known, Clarence Holiday, who was the guitar player with Fletcher Henderson's band. Her singing almost changed my musical tastes and my musical life, because she was the first girl singer I'd ever come across who actually sang like an improvising jazz genius. She was an extension almost of a Louis Armstrong; the way she sang around the melody, her uncanny harmonic sense, and her sense of lyric content was just unbelievable for a 17 year old girl.

Dan Morgenstern: And her time must have been something . . .

John Hammond: It was something else. She was always pretty lucky about the musicians she had around her. The first piano player she had was perhaps the greatest—outside of Teddy Wilson—a guy named Bobby Henderson, who died a couple of years ago up in Albany but who was absolutely one of the fine, fine people in Billie's life. He was her first real boyfriend and a gentleman every which way, and a wonderful musician. And they worked together on and off uptown for about three years until actually Billie finally joined Basie's band in the spring of 1937.

Dan Morgenstern: And that sort of made her famous in a sense because she was exposed to a larger audience.

John Hammond: She was exposed to a much larger audience, but already some of her records had made it with more than just a jazz following, because I guess it was in 1936 we recorded "I Cried for You"— and Billie only sang one chorus on these records or maybe she would come back for a final eight bars—it started with the most beautiful Johnny Hodges chorus possible. And this record sold something like 15,000, which was a giant hit for Brunswick in those days. I mean a giant hit. Most records that made money sold around three or four thousand. It was just terrible to think of what record sales were like in those terrible days when radio had wiped out the record business.

Dan Morgenstern: I guess at a session just around that time she did "Mean to Me," which was one of the first with Lester Young. That was quite a famous relationship.

John Hammond: Well, this was one of the things. We had so much luck in these sessions with Teddy and Billie, because who the sidemen were depended very much on what good bands were in town. If Ellington was in town, you'd find a Johnny Hodges or Harry Carney or Cootie Williams or some of the other great sidemen with Duke backing Billie and Teddy. But when Basie came to New York in October 1936, this is when everything changed. Because when Billie got together with three people, Lester Young, Buck Clayton, Freddie Green, and I have to say two others who were terribly important, Walter Page and Jo Jones, this set Billie as probably the most unique jazz singer of her generation. There was an interplay between Lester, Buck, and Billie that was unique in music. I don't believe we've ever gotten this kind of interplay in the years since Billie's prime, you know, in the '30s and '40s.

Dan Morgenstern: There was a remarkable unity of conception. One thing that strikes me when I listen to the records that Billie made during those days is that in later years her life became very tragic and her songs often became sad, but these songs that she recorded in the '30s are basically happy tunes.

John Hammond: There are only a couple of exceptions on this album—one is the first title, "God Bless the Child." This is a very interesting song, of course. "God Bless the Child (Who's Got His Own)" is a phrase that Billie got from her grandmother. But the whole structure of the song, both lyrics and musically, were by Arthur Herzog, a marvelous guy who's still living in Detroit and who has never gotten proper credit for it. Arthur was a good songwriter and a good poet. He loved Billie's singing and was of enormous help on this date, because he had a little flat on Seventh Avenue between 13th and 14th Streets in New York, and I was down there the night that Billie and Arthur worked this thing out. I don't really mind Billie getting sort of sole credit for it because Billie deserved everything she could get, but actually Arthur Herzog should have a lion's share of the credit for this wonderful song.

The other two, there are actually two more gloomy songs, one is "Gloomy Sunday," which was supposed according to the press agents of the period to have caused waves of suicides throughout Europe.

Dan Morgenstern: Hungarian suicides . . .

John Hammond: And the other was Fanny Brice's classic "My Man." But everything that Billie sang, "All of Me," "You've Changed," "Them There Eyes," "Miss Brown to You," which we mentioned before, "The Man I Love," and "I Cried for You," she made masterpieces of them all. These are among the greatest sides that she ever made.

THE GOLDEN YEARS
RALPH J. GLEASON

The essay was originally written to accompany a 1962 reissue of Billie's Brunswick/Columbia recordings made between 1937 and 1942. It includes a brief overview of her career as well as the importance of these seminal disks.

Jazz musicians liked Ralph J. Gleason personally very much. He wrote pithy, intimate portraits and accurate critiques of their work, and he had the uncanny knack for writing both in the vernacular and with an elevated tone. Here he calls Billie a "social message" and "in her prime . . . the most magnetic and beautiful woman I have ever seen." Then, with one little scene, he renders a vision of her as a lonesome pariah during the last year of her life. Gleason was a witness, an integral part of the jazz world, and he loved the music and the people.

Ralph Gleason was born on March 1, 1917, in New York City. After studying at Columbia University from 1934 to 1938, he began writing about jazz; after World War II, he became associated with *Down Beat* magazine for about 13 years, until 1961. He wrote for the *San Francisco Chronicle* from 1950 until his death, and he contributed to many prominent music periodicals. A founder of *Rolling Stone* magazine, he also produced radio and television jazz shows, and he won ASCAP–Deems Taylor Awards for his articles on jazz and Louis Armstrong.

He died in a car accident in Berkeley, California, on June 3, 1975. Some of his pieces for the *San Francisco Chronicle*, magazines, and album liner notes have been collected in a Da Capo paperback, *Celebrating The Duke and Louis, Bessie, Billie, Bird, Carmen, Miles, Dizzy and Other Heroes*, published in 1995.

"I got my manner from Bessie Smith and Louis Armstrong, honey. Wanted her feeling and Louis' style."

That was the way Billie Holiday once described her singing and she kept saying it over and over in one way or another whenever they asked her, and they asked her a lot. For Billie Holiday's singing style is one of the most unique and personal in all of jazz music.

That's what history will remember of her, solidly supported by the undebatable evidence of the records. She was a singer of jazz, the greatest female jazz voice of all time, a great interpreter, a great actress and the creator of a style that, in its own way, is as unique and important to jazz as the styles of Louis Armstrong, Charlie Parker and Lester Young. The fact remains that after all the lurid stories of her star-crossed, self-destructive life, she did something no other woman has ever done in jazz. Today, if you sing jazz and you are a woman, you sing some of Billie Holiday. There's no other way to do it. No vocalist is without her influence. All girl singers sing some of Billie, like all trumpet players play some of Louis. She wrote the text.

The first time anyone was asked to describe her style, it was disc jockey Ralph Cooper, then emcee at the Apollo Theatre in New York, and he said, "It ain't the blues. I don't know what it is, but you got to hear her."

The description hasn't been topped yet. It ain't the blues, but the blues is in it. In some strange, arcane, witch-like way, Billie made blues out of everything she sang. But Billie's forte was the ballad, the pop tune. That she could take these frequently banal and generally trivial numbers and make them into something lasting, something artistic (most singers at best are *artful*) is a tribute to the way she was, for her time, the voice of Woman.

"I've been told that nobody sings the word 'hunger' like I do. Or the word 'love,'" Billie remarked in her autobiography, *Lady Sings the Blues* (a story made all the more tragic and poignant by the little-girl-turned-hip-kitty style in which it was told), and this may be true. But it is the way Billie pronounced another word that always symbolized, for me, the role in which she was, for better or for worse, cast in her life: the idealized sex symbol for an American generation just starting to recognize what jazz was all about, four letters and all.

You can hear her do it numerous times but nowhere does she achieve quite the promise, the assumption and the wild longing that she does in "Them There Eyes" when she lets out that deep-throated, magnificently sexual cry, "Ahhh, baby." For in Billie's world, which represents the introduction to the twentieth century's social upheaval if we look at it sociologically, "baby" had become the word for "lover" in the most intimate, perhaps even Freudian, sense. And Billie, born in the city and raised in town, was the symbol of a sexual reality that transcended all the celluloid make-believe of the glamor queens of Hollywood. She was real and she was alive and you could *hear* her and she spoke to you in the sulphur-and-molasses voice—the epitome of sex.

The story of her life, in all the grisly, tawdry Sunday supplement detail from illegitimate birth, through prostitution, jailhouse, junk, jailhouse again and the final deathbed scene—under arrest in a hospital room for narcotics, gasping out her final breaths, $750 in $50 bills strapped to her shrunken leg—has been told over and over and over. Please God, let her rest in peace at last; she was tortured enough in life in her own all-too-public hell.

Let us deal here with what will live on as long as there is anything left alive in this culture—her music—and forget for now the rest of it, which even carried over into graveyard quarrels as to who paid for her tombstone. Billie needs no tombstone, ever. These records—and her others—are a monument to her that no stone can ever equal. She is in this album, just as surely as in life, all of her, the good and the bad and the beautiful. It's here in her voice, in the songs and in the titles and the lyrics. You can't miss it.

I heard her say "baby" once, offstage and not in song. It was twelve years ago as these notes are being written, but I hear it yet. She had opened at a San Francisco nightclub and she was with her then manager, John Levy. She was wearing a brown turban, a full-length blue mink coat, green wool suit, brown crepe shirt with a Barrymore collar, pearl earrings and Tiffany diamond and platinum watch. She had waited for Levy to come out of the club and had finally gotten into a car with a group of us. Then he arrived, slipped into the front seat, and she leaned forward and said, "Baaaaaaby, why did you leave me?" In that line was all the pathos of "My Man," "Billie's Blues" and the rest. Nobody could say a word for minutes and she didn't even know what she had done.

It's very possible Billie never knew what she did to people with her voice when she sang. Carmen McRae, in *Hear Me Talkin' to Ya*, spoke vividly of Billie the singer. "I'll say this about her—she sings the way she is. That's really Lady when you listen to her on a record . . . singing is the only place she can express herself the way she'd like to be all the time. Only way she's happy is through a song . . . the only time she's at ease and at rest with herself is when she sings."

And Bobby Tucker, her long-time accompanist, gave us a terrifying hint of Billie the woman: "There's one thing about Lady you won't believe. She had the most terrible inferiority complex. She actually doesn't believe she can sing . . ."

Musically, Billie herself had the most illuminating things to say of her own style. First its origin in Bessie Smith and Louis Armstrong and then, "I don't think I'm singing. I feel like I'm playing a horn. I try to improvise like Lester Young, like Louis Armstrong, or someone else I admire. What comes out is what I feel. I hate straight singing. I have to change a tune to my own way of doing it. That's all I know."

Listening to the performances, which is like living over again the best years of our lives for those of us who were lucky enough to have heard her then, the memories are so strong, one is struck by several things. First, how little, in terms of departure from the melody, Billie actually changes the tune. What she does, as Miles Davis was later to work out for himself, is to take a limited canvas and paint exquisitely upon it. She had no tricks, no vocal gymnastics. She may have hated straight singing, but her way was to sing it almost straight but with a special accent on articulation, phrasing and rhythm. Phrased as she phrased, the words mean something. Many lines in drama are banal on their own, but in context and in performance take on meaning. She did this with pop songs because they held meaning for her of a world she never made and never knew, except when she sang.

The samples here are overwhelming. The way she says "this year's crop just misses" on her very first record with Lester Young ("This Year's Kisses"), for instance. They became not lyrics, but Billie's own expression.

The other thing is how, in retrospect, she really did sing as Lester

Young played. Just listen to the way she comes in on "Them There Eyes." You hear it again and again as she starts a number, as she comes back in for the second chorus or the bridge and in the way she phrases multi-syllable words. It's no wonder that from the time she made her first record date with Pres, in January of 1937 ("This Year's Kisses" is from it), there is an entirely new feeling. Billie was home, musically, at last.

For me, at any rate, aside from all the intense and very personal memories evoked by all of these numbers, it was a delight of the highest order to hear the three tracks, previously unreleased, which are included here. They are airchecks of Billie Holiday singing with the Count Basie orchestra. For my money they rate not only as three of the very best Billie Holiday performances but as three of the great jazz vocals of all time. I am particularly attracted, for numerous reasons, to "I Can't Get Started." Not only does Billie here, as in her other two sides with the Basie band, have a sound of pure, unadulterated joy in her voice, but she and Pres in the second chorus indulge in what can only be described as an unsurpassed duet. With Billie singing and Pres talking to her on his horn, this must be ranked as one of the most exquisite jazz moments preserved for us on recording, and we may thank John Hammond for it.

The sides with Basie and the ones from the studio dates around that time are the end of a period of Billie's sound, if not development. Afterwards, she had many things, but never again, or hardly ever, that joyous thrust to her voice.

So in a strange, twisted way, symbolic perhaps of her strange, twisted life, it was an anticlimax when Billie died.

She had been dying by inches for years. You could hear it in her voice—the ugly sound of death—all the way back to her early days at Cafe Society. It was, perversely, part of her charm, like that of Pres and Bird.

Drink, dope and dissipation were really only the superficial aspects of what was wrong with her. She suffered from an incurable disease—being born black in a white society wherein she could never be but partially accepted.

"You've got to have something to eat and a little love in your life before you can hold still for anybody's damn sermon," she wrote in her autobiography.

There was plenty to eat in the later years, though in her childhood as a classic juvenile delinquent she was hungry for more than food. But money never helped Billie, nor did men. She had plenty of both and she died alone and thin, her great body wasted by disease and deliberate starvation, with a police guard on the door.

She was ridden by devils all her life. In the beginning she was in control most of the time. Those were the days when she made the great records, the classic jazz vocals that comprise this collection.

But Billie was more than a singer. She was a social message, a jazz instrumentalist, a creator whose performances could never be duplicated. It's been tried by a whole generation of singers whose inspiration she was. None of them came any closer to it than sounding like Billie on a bad night.

There were plenty of bad nights, too. In the later years her voice and her sense of time would desert her. At nightclub performances, listeners who remembered her when she was not only the greatest singer jazz had produced but also one of the most beautiful and impressive women of her generation, choked up and cried to see and hear her so helplessly bad.

Billie Holiday, when she was in her prime, in the years covered by these performances, was simply the most magnetic and beautiful woman I have ever seen, as well as the most emotionally moving singer I have ever heard.

I remember when she opened at Cafe Society in December, 1938, for her first big nightclub break. She was simply shocking in her impact. Standing there with a spotlight on her great, sad, beautiful face, a white gardenia in her hair, she sang her songs and the singers were never the same thereafter.

She really was happy only when she sang, it seemed. The rest of the time she was a sort of living lyric to the song "Strange Fruit," hanging, not on a poplar tree, but on the limbs of life itself.

Just as Chaplin never won an Oscar, Billie Holiday never won a "*Down Beat*" poll while she was living, but for jazz and its fans her music is unequalled and as indispensable as Louis' and Duke's.

The fall before she died, I saw her sitting stiffly in the lobby of the San Carlos Hotel in Monterey, the morning after the festival finale. The jazz musicians tried to ignore her. Finally, in that hoarse whisper that could still (after 30 years of terrifying abuse) send shivers down your spine, she asked, "Where you boys goin'?" And when no one answered, she answered herself. "They got me openin' in Vegas tonight."

"They" always had Billie opening somewhere she didn't want to be. That's over now and all that's left are memories and the records and the poor, misguided singers trying to sound like her, God save them.

There's really too much and too little to say of someone like her. We have the memories and we have the records. As for myself, I feel like the young man in Colin MacInnes' novel, "Absolute Beginners," who says, "Lady Day has suffered so much in her life she carries it all for you." It was a long, long road from "Your Mother's Son-in-Law" to "Gloomy Sunday," but Billie traveled it for all of us. We owe her a great deal.

It is sad beyond words that she never knew how many people loved her.

A LADY NAMED BILLIE AND I
MILT GABLER

Gabler wrote this article as president of Commodore Record Corp., Inc., the first to dare to record Billie's "Strange Fruit," when Columbia Records, to which she was under contract, refused to take the chance. Many radio stations prohibited their disk jockeys from airing this controversial recording of an anti-lynching protest song. It's hard to imagine that kind of censorship now. Gabler later acceded to Billie's entreaties again, when no one else would, and recorded her singing "Lover Man" with strings. She knew that strings would enhance the record. And with it, she had her biggest commercial hit.

Gabler's personal friendship and professional relationship with Billie render this memoir especially interesting. He had a long, influential career in the recording industry. He founded Commodore Records out of his jazz-specialty record shop in New York. He then worked for Decca through the '50s, producing both jazz and pop recordings; Billie followed him to that label from the mid-'40s through the early '50s. One of the most famous singers, whose records he produced for years, was Ella Fitzgerald.

"Yesterdays". Like she sang it in the song, it seems that I met Billie only yesterday. The year was 1936 and the music was getting better, real good, and Teddy Wilson walked in to my Commodore Music Shop with two girls, one I believe was Irene Wilson who later wrote that marvelous song "Some Other Spring" for Billie, and the other girl was the Lady herself "Miss Billie Holiday To You", to paraphrase another song which was one of Billie's favorites. Billie had been doing some wonderful singing on the Teddy Wilson Brunswick recordings we had been selling in the shop. In fact she was so good people were asking for her. The record company was launching her as an artist in her own right on their Vocalion label. She had already waxed "Summertime", and "Billie's Blues" and it was moving very well, at the Commodore anyway.

It was a thrill meeting her although at the time neither of us realized that our association would span ten years of recording together making some of the finest sounds this world has ever heard. In 1936 I never dreamed that two years later, on becoming disillusioned with the jazz product the major companies were issuing, or the lack of it, I would start my own record company. At Commodore I had already founded the Hot Club of New York, a chapter of The United Hot Clubs of America. For them I re-issued the original masters of the historical jazz sides the major record companies had discontinued. Hot Club members could buy them through mail order, or over the counter at the record shop at 144 East 42nd Street, in New York City. We were the first to print all of the important data on the record labels, an innovation soon copied by every record company all over the world. In those days there were no album jackets to print liner notes. We also sponsored public jazz concerts and called them "Jam Sessions" in order to publicize the new "Swing" music which was really the same old jazz in a new dress. Bessie Smith (courtesy of John Hammond) appeared at one session, and later Billie Holiday sang at others.

All of the famous musicians had heard or were learning of the Commodore so they would drop into the shop to listen to their discs and those of others and to find out what was happening around town. John Hammond had introduced Teddy to Commodore, and Teddy brought in Billie, and so it went on, and Gabler and the Commodore grew and became a legend. We didn't sell the most records in town, but we sold the best ones, and we knew who played on them and where they were playing if they were working at all.

I first heard of Billie from the musicians who went uptown to Harlem to hear her sing. This was before she came to my record shop. I believe the spot she worked was called the "Brittwood". It was a bar connected with a hotel of that same name, frequented by musicians, and near the Savoy ballroom. John Hammond, Benny Goodman, and Bernie Hanighen who wrote "When A Woman Loves A Man", were the first people I know who raved about Billie and got her started on records. Of course Teddy Wilson was right in there with them. I never got uptown to hear Billie in those days for I kept my shop open from 9 A:M: to 10 P:M: and after that I would generally head for some jazz joint on fifty-second street or Greenwich Village before dragging myself home to the Bronx in the New York subway to get some rest. For years I did most of my sleeping on the New York City subway trains. Today you have to think about it twice, or sleep with one eye open if you sleep at all.

In 1938 I opened a branch of the Commodore Music Shop right in the heart of swing street at 46 West 52. That is the title of a famous jazz recording on Commodore by Chu Berry and Roy Eldridge. I kept the place open until one or two A:M: if there was any action at all. If there was no business I would close up shop and go to hear Billie at Kelly's Stables, or The Famous Door, or The Onyx Club, or I went downtown to the Cafe Society on Sheridan Square in the Village where she was sure to be. There was no sense to going home without hearing the Lady. When she was out of town it was no town.

I made the rounds every night for each Sunday afternoon I ran jazz concerts at Jimmy Ryan's on 52nd Street and I had to book jazz musicians for each Sunday's bash. I slept about four hours a night but it was all I needed at the time. I was rugged. I had a strong constitution with a cast iron stomach, and the whiskey helped. It helped me to forget what time it was. I didn't really drink until after I closed up the record shop and it always seemed that the whiskey and the music went together. I tried grass but it never made it for me. I stayed with the juice and the jazz; besides the weed was illegal and I didn't want to mess with it. I had too many people depending on me for me to tangle with the wrong side of the law.

Billie was my constant love. I don't mean the physical thing although we had a great thing for each other and she respected me. I would never spoil that and Billie had many friends she could run with. She didn't need me. With Billie and I it was the music. But when she was on stage in the spotlight she was queenly and absolutely regal. It was something, the way she held her head up, the way she phrased each word and got to the heart of the story in a song, and to top it all she knew where the beat was. She could swing with the best of them but Billie never did many up-tempo tunes. Torch songs were her bag. I had many of them written to order for her. Some songs she wrote herself and on some like "God Bless The Child" and "Don't Explain" she collaborated with Arthur Herzog, Jr., but to my knowledge the ideas were basically the way Billie felt and spoke.

Billie knew how to appeal to losers, the love sick ones who had loved and lost, or like Billie herself those who were searching for and couldn't find a meaningful love. So Billie packed the clubs she appeared in. I well remember the Cafe Society Downtown where she achieved her greatest triumph. I loved the place. It was a glorified cellar with great murals now long gone. It had a miserable little unventillated stars dressing room right next to the His and Hers wash rooms. If you were not the star you changed clothes in the kitchen which was directly behind the wash rooms. Billie's room was ten feet from the bandstand which could accommodate five or six musicians, with a small grand piano on the dance floor in front of it. The dance floor became the stage when Billie or any other attraction performed. The room was step tiered forum style and it was fairly large for a New York night club. Not bad for a cellar.

The Cafe Society Downtown was a fabulous place, run by Barney Josephson, and every top act played there. A typical bill at the time might showcase Billie Holiday plus either the Frankie Newton Orchestra with Tab Smith, Henry "Red" Allen's band with J.C. Higginbotham and Buster Bailey, or Eddie Heywood's Orchestra with Doc Cheatham, Lem Davis and Vic Dickenson, wizard of the glissando trombone. You also might find Josh White, blues and folk singer, "The Revuers" the first great satirical comedy group with Betty Comden, Adolph Green, Judy Holiday, and a fourth little man who was great but whom I do not know the name of, for the group disbanded when the first three went on to fame in Hollywood and on Broadway. They could do two shows a night without ever repeating their material. Another fantastic comic who started there was Jack Gilford now a top actor on television and film and finally coming into his own and rightly so. In addition there could be the three Kansas City Boogie Woogie giants of the piano Albert Ammons, Pete Johnson, and Meade Lux Lewis along with Pete's sidekick blues shouter Big Joe Turner himself. That was the scene. None of the performers including Billie Holiday made a lot of money by today's standards. How could they? But I never heard of Barney Josephson retiring with a bundle either. In fact he is back in the business now running the "Cookery" in Greenwich Village trying to make it all happen again with piano music, this time by Teddy Wilson, Eddie Heywood, Mary Lou Williams and Dick Hyman. Barney always had good taste.

That was the setting and the time and place for "Strange Fruit." In 1939 the Cafe Society Downtown was the only place that attracted mixed black and white audiences in any sizeable numbers. When black couples went out for an evening they would feel uncomfortable at most other clubs downtown. For the most part they stayed uptown on Lenox and Seventh Avenues in Harlem. However the Downtown Cafe Society was a "liberal" club patronized by "New Dealers", free thinking people, writers, actors, musicians and educators. It was a "swingin'" place in the days when "to swing" meant music with a capital "M". It also attracted a poet named Lewis Allen who had written what was to become the first "protest" poem set to music, an anti-lynching song that catapaulted our lady named Billie Holiday to international fame. The story of how it came to be written and recorded by Commodore and Gabler after a major company was afraid to do it appears in the liner notes for the Billie Holiday album* that Leonard Feather poured his heart into for Commodore. Billie and I were both grateful to Columbia for allowing her to record this important song for my label. If they were against its message they could have refused permission. Eventually I produced sixteen selections with Billie for Commodore but "Strange Fruit" was always the main one for me.

On April 20, 1939 Billie cut her first Commodore sides and the four selections were "Strange Fruit", "Yesterdays", "I Gotta Right To Sing The Blues", and the blues "Fine and Mellow". I wanted to do a twelve bar blues with her because her 1936 "Billie's Blues" always was and still is a favorite of mine. Billie did not sing the blues like a Bessie Smith or "Ma" Rainey, who were more traditional in sound and style than she was. Billie was more like today and had an "original" quality and I put an original sound behind her, a band with a riffing sax figure that Tab Smith set up, and roaming piano by Sonny White with muted trumpet by Frankie Newton. It was the first modern blues record.

The night before the recording session I went down to the Cafe Society to get things set with the band and Billie. I told her I wanted a blues so we sat down at a little "deuce" table just outside of her dressing room door and we started to write down blues verses for the still untitled song. Billie had written and collected various blues lines, which she already had on paper. We didn't need a tune for everyone who was going to be there knew the blues. (If you don't then you should not be reading this story.) However, we did need a "kicker", that is one verse that would make this blues different from any blues ever written before. I am proud to say that I came up with the lines†

> "He wears high draped pants,
> Stripes are really yellow,
> But when he kisses me
> He's so fine and mellow".

That was the "kicker" and that also gave us the title for the song "Fine and Mellow". Billie and I wrote it together.

After the record came out and the song was becoming a hit I received a phone call from Decca Records for a copy of the disc. They reached me

---

*Billie Holiday—*Strange Fruit* lp Atlantic SD 1614
†Words printed courtesy of © E. B. Marks Music Corp.

in my fifty-second street store and although I had about one thousand of the records in my back room I told them I was out of stock on the number. As soon as I would get more of the records in from the Columbia factory I promised to send them a copy. They said okay, and I said goodbye. I was in a panic.

I knew that if Decca wanted a record they soon would be cutting a competitive disc by one of their top blues artists and then they would rush the record out on the market. I had no distributors. With Decca's big distribution and low price they could hurt Billie and myself. So I got busy. I collared the next musician that walked into my shop who could transcribe the music from the record. For a fee of nine dollars and a half dozen good jazz records my man copied "Fine and Mellow" from the disc, right inside one of my record listening booths. I put down Billie Holiday's name as composer of words and music, and the Commodore Music Shop as publisher, then rushed to the Post Office and filled out a copyright card to the Register of Copyrights, Library of Congress, Washington, D.C., purchased the necessary money order to pay for the registry and posted the envelope to the Library of Congress. Billie did not know that I was doing this. I protected her rights for once a song is recorded it is impossible to prevent any other person from making a new version of the same song if they are willing to pay the statutory mechanical license fee. After this was done and I received verification from Washington, D.C. I personally delivered the Billie record of "Fine and Mellow" to Decca Records. At that moment of 1939 I never realized that in November, 1941 I would go to work for Decca, become an A & R man, and later a vice-president of their company. I stayed there for thirty years and recorded everyone from Louis Armstrong and Bing Crosby through Bill Haley and His Comets and Bert Kaempfert and his Orchestra to mention only a few, but that is another story. This story is about Billie and I.

Sometime after the Decca Record "Fine and Mellow" incident (Alberta Hunter made the song for Decca but it was not as good as Billie Holiday's), E.B. Marks Music Corporation wanted to publish "Fine and Mellow" for Billie the same as they were doing with "Strange Fruit" for Lewis Allen. I assigned the publishing rights to them so that Billie could get an advance payment for signing the rights to them. They also published her "God Bless The Child" and "Billie's Blues". I am sure she made money on the deal and received performance money on her songs.

Lady Day's Commodore recordings were her first "pop" hits and her career zoomed upward from that point on. Her earnings in clubs sky rocketed and she played every important jazz location and theatres where the big dance bands were packing them in. Unfortunately for me she was a Columbia artist and I had to be content with rooting from the sidelines. I could not record her again until after her contract expired. When she informed me that she was free and wanted me to try some new sessions with her I was overjoyed and went to Mr. Joe Glaser, her agent and president of the Associated Booking Corporation, long the mentor of Louis Armstrong. It was now the year 1944 and I paid him a very good price for Billie to make three record sessions for Commodore so that I could add them to my first date and have enough material for two ten-inch long play records. I had my favorite girl singer back again and we waxed eleven great standards and one more blues, (Billie's Blues) "I Love My Man".

I had Eddie Heywood who was working at the same club as Billie at the time do the arrangements and we used his band to back her up adding Teddy Walters on guitar for two of the sessions. Eddie, a fabulous pianist, was having great success as he had just recorded "Begin The Beguine" for Commodore and it was a monster record. In addition Heywood was a sensitive musician who loved Billie's singing as much as I loved Billie. He would write his head off, and he was perfectionist, but so was I.

The recording dates were a joy. Billie was in great shape, and artistically at the peak of her career. At that time I was working at Decca until five thirty each afternoon. Then I would rush to my Commodore Music Shop for a few hours before it closed, afterward head for swing street (52nd St.) to hear some live music and Billie if she was working in New York City. Between sets Billie and I would go across the street to Tony's where her good friend Mabel Mercer was rendering her particular magic. Billie would have a Brandy Alexander and I stayed with the scotch. Mabel was and still is the classiest singer of songs in the business. Her choice of material was always something special and her presentation the Rolls Royce of show business. All of the great ones wrote for her, and all of the great performers went to hear, listen, and learn.

Decca never did like my working for two companies, theirs and my own, but my agreement with them allowed this. I never crossed them on artistic decisions that would affect both record labels. I remember one night when I stepped into the club next door to Ryan's to hear Billie and she had the audience spellbound, more spellbound than usual. She was doing a new number called "Lover Man". Jimmy Davis, Roger "Ram" Ramirez, and Jimmy Sherman wrote this song for her. To my trained ears it was a "natural" hit and definitely a future standard. As far as Billie was concerned I had reached "the point of no return" to Commodore. If I made this record for myself I would surely be fired from my job. Now I know better, but in those days I was working with and recording many important artists for Decca and I knew that if I stayed with it I could go to the top.

I broke the news to Billie first and told her that I would sign her to a Decca contract for her next session and do "Lover Man". We had our first difference of opinion on how to do the song. Billie won. She wanted a string section on her next date and I gave them to her. She was the first black artist in her field to record with strings, and it was on the "Lover Man" session that she got them. I had the song writers sign the song over to the Decca publishing firm and it is still there in the MCA Music catalogue. I had many great songs written to order for Billie like "Good Morning Heartache", "Old Devil Called Love", and I remember two young writers, whom I encouraged, who adored her and followed her everywhere. They wrote "Deep Song" for the Lady and it was almost auto-biographical, the story of Billie's life. Their names were George Cory and Douglass Cross and I am very proud of them for later they wrote a song called "I Left My Heart In San Francisco". Those were exciting days for me, and the hours meant nothing.

I could have become a wealthy man with Billie and the songs but somehow I would never have been able to sleep at night, and I wanted to do what was best for Billie. She was becoming a little more difficult to work with. She would arrive late for the record sessions and I would have the band all rehearsed on every number before she started. After a few run-downs her voice would open up, and sometimes with the help of some old brandy we were ready to record. Billie was generally a one take artist. Her renditions would never vary much from one take to another. Within a working forty-five minutes or an hour I would complete Billie's part of the session and we would have our sides. If not, her throat would close up again, and we would call off the recordings. Billie never dogged it, and she always tried to make a good record, at least for me anyway. But the later Deccas were agony for me and not as easy as the Commodores. Billie was her own worst enemy and mixed up with some pretty rough men. Once I had to send her money to get her out of Washington, D.C., and another time she sent her maid down with a note to get the balance of the money she needed to pay off a bail bondsman. My father and brothers gave her cash from the old Commodore till any time she needed it. Billie was in trouble and getting in deeper all the time. The worst thing of all was the legal restriction that kept her from working in clubs in New York for the last twelve years of her life. This kept her away from me as I was chained to my desk at Decca and she did not get in to the big town that often. The company did not want to renew her deal when the contract expired and I was switched to the Coral record label, and not able to record her at all.

I stayed at Decca for many reasons but most importantly the excitement and thrill of working with the talented writers and arrangers, and stars. In addition to Billie I recorded Louis Armstrong, Lionel Hampton, Jimmie Lunceford, Andy Kirk, Lucky Millinder, Buddy Johnson, Louis Jordan, The Mills Brothers, Jimmy Dorsey, Woody Herman, Bob Crosby; and the singers Bing Crosby, Dick Haymes, Ella Fitzgerald, Peggy Lee, Carmen McRae, The Ink Spots, The Four Aces, Bill Haley and His Comets, Burl Ives, Josh White, The Weavers, Red Foley, Brenda Lee, Roberta Sherwood; and the sweet bands like Guy Lombardo, Russ Morgan, Johnny Long, Sammy Kaye, Carmen Cavallaro, the list was endless and I wound up after thirty years with the great Bert Kaempfert with whom I collaborated on many songs, two of them being "Danke Schoen" and "Love". The world of recording artists was and still is my life, and at Decca I was able to express myself.

I have made thousands of recordings of all types starting with jazz (Eddie Condon to Louis Armstrong to Duke Ellington). I eventually did Popular music, Country & Western, Blues, Rock, Soul, Gospel, Latin, Folk, Children and Educational, Film Sound tracks, Broadway Shows, Sacred and Inspirational, Classical and Spoken Word. Listening to jazz taught me to listen better to all of the other types of music and I loved it all. Each artist runs his own race and none has to compete with the other for each category stands on its own merits. Looking back I do not regret one moment of it, I have met many marvelous and talented people from all walks of life, and I have worked with more musicians than I have hair on my head. At the top of the list, for the female contingent, the Lady named Billie Holiday stands right up front. Maybe it is because she got herself into trouble, more likely it is because I can't get her out of my ears or my mind.

LADY GETS HER DUE/THE COMPLETE LADY
GARY GIDDINS

For many years Gary Giddins has reigned as the primary, intellectual, proud and perspicacious jazz critic at the *Village Voice*. Many times he has had the courage to stand up and say that the emperor has no clothes, and he was the first and certainly the most articulate, to my knowledge, to mention that the famed and valuable jazz festival in New York, when it was still called the Kool Jazz Festival, had some shortcomings. His articles marked him as an invaluable analyst of the art of jazz.

Gary Giddins was born on March 21, 1948, in New York. Soon after graduating from Grinnell College in 1972, he became a contributing editor at *Down Beat* magazine. For most of his career, since 1973, he has been jazz critic and jazz editor at the *Village Voice*. He has also taught, founded the American Jazz Orchestra, and written enlivening and enriching books on major jazz figures, among them Louis Armstrong and Charlie "Bird" Parker.

Apropos Billie Holiday, he wrote a fascinating appraisal of the Verve collection in the mid-1980s, then followed it up with an article about an updated version of that collection. His update in 1992 is particularly notable for his opening sentence: "Can we agree that the Billie Holiday controversy, in which her early recordings were used to thrash the later ones, has been put to rest? You don't hear much guff about it anymore, so I'm assuming it's finished." That's the verdict, and it should be the final one.

• • •

Editor's notes: Phil Schaap won a Grammy Award for his liner notes as part of the later Verve package. With his encyclopedic, detailed knowledge of jazz history and recordings, and his love and enthusiasm for the art, and his stamina to share his wealth of memories on countless jazz radio programs, he serves as one of the most important teachers about jazz.

André Hodeir was a prominent, historically important French jazz critic.

Lady Gets Her Due

Lady Day is unquestionably the most important influence on American popular singing in the last 20 years.
—Frank Sinatra, 1958

And yet the matter of influence seems almost academic today. Sinatra was speaking a year before Billie Holiday died, at 44, when countless singers considered themselves directly in her debt, and when her gutted voice, drawled phrasing, and wayworn features were widely construed as evidence of self-immolating decline. Now the verdict is less dependent on what we know of her story and more on what we perceive in her music. Now it's obvious that, like Lester Young, whose career closely paralleled hers, Holiday managed to achieve two discrete musical styles in a short, calamitous life. That their later styles were forced in reaction to outrageous fortunes is a fact that continues to offend naive listeners who look to art for limitless innocence and youth. Holiday's later recordings are all the proof we need of her ability to transfigure hurt and confusion into theme and variation. Had she been able to sing "What a Little Moonlight Can Do" at the end of her life as she did at 20, she wouldn't have been much of an artist—she'd have been what Young contemptuously called a "repeater pencil."

Holiday's influence can be calibrated in the language of musical technique: in her use of legato phrasing, ornamentation, melodic variation, chromaticism. But musicology doesn't suggest the primary impact of her singing, which is emotional. Even in her apprentice years as the golden girl in a man's world, taking no more than the single chorus allotted each instrumentalist and transcending the material no less completely, her technique was limited by any conventional standard, blues or bel canto. As Paul Bowles wrote in 1946, "One of the chief charms in Miss Holiday's art is that she makes absolutely no attempt to approach any of the elements of art singing, at the same time cannily making the most of all the differences that exist between that and her own quite personal style." Despite a thin voice and a range of about 15 notes, she overpowered musicians and listeners with multilayered nuances: She embellished melodies, tailoring them to her own needs and limitations; lagged behind the beat, imparting suspense; harmonized well beyond the ground chords of the composition, projecting a bright authority; and inflected words in a way that made even banal lyrics bracing. Bessie Smith and Louis Armstrong adapted blues and improvisational devices to pop songs, but it was Holiday who pushed their achievement into the realm of unmitigated intimacy. Hers was the art of reflection.

Holiday's craftsmanship rarely failed her, but her subjects—the world and her appetites—often did, and latter-day Holiday was formed in part by those failings. Some of her last records, recorded when her instrument was worn to the nerve endings, are disastrous, yet the overwhelming body of work from her last 15 years is as rewarding as jazz singing gets. The early records expel a golden-age sheen of sunny rhythms and instrumental bravura; later records are built entirely around the singer. The tempo is slower, the ambience more conversational. But her alterations remain provocative and full of surprise; her enunciation is, if anything, more compelling, the emotions urgent. The differences between early and late Holiday are illuminated by a comparison of the Columbias (1933–42), many of them contracted and originally released under pianist Teddy Wilson's name, and the Verves (1952–59); each series evokes a dramatically different mood. The Verves are by no means a qualitative reduction of the Columbias, and a listener could no more confuse their respective values than those of Beethoven's early G-major and late A-minor string quartets. The artist has *changed*, no matter whether the cause was heroin addiction or deafness.

The change in Holiday's case took place during the decade between those two major label affiliations, beginning in 1942. That was the year she apparently began using hard drugs to alleviate difficulties with her first husband, an addict she had married the previous year. It was also in 1942 that she worked two months at Billy Berg's Trouville Club in West Hollywood with the brothers Lee and Lester Young, during which gig she first met Jimmy Rowles, the group's pianist and sole white member (Lester had to assure her "this cat can blow"), and the young producer of the club's jam sessions, Norman Granz. After recording "Travelin' Light" with Paul Whiteman, a major hit from which she received no royalties, she spent a few months in Chicago and had her first encounter with the police. Those events set the pattern for the rest of her life—triumph alternating with catastrophe.

She recorded for Milt Gabler, first at Commodore with written band arrangements, then at Decca, where she became the first jazz singer to use strings, a gamble that paid off handsomely in such milestone performances as "Lover Man," "Good Morning, Heartache," "Don't Explain," "No More," "Ain't Nobody's Business if I Do," and "God Bless the Child." Underappreciated (she never won a *Down Beat* poll) and underpaid, Holiday may have felt that the complement of strings flattered her desire to climb a few rungs in the status of mainstream show biz. In any case, the Deccas can be seen today as transitional recordings. Her voice, still in full bloom, met the challenge of the imposing repertoire, but the staid settings diluted the expressive content of singing.

The addiction began to take over. Her marriage broke up, and she canceled engagements, yet she remained unbowed. Although she seemed to be retreating from life, she asserted herself in ever bolder directions, embarking in 1946 on first solo concerts (the second of which was recorded as part of Granz's Jazz at the Philharmonic package); undertaking an acting role in the disgraceful 1947 movie *New Orleans* as a maid (she walked out in the middle of filming); and hooking up with the superb accompanist Bobby Tucker. In 1947, she took a voluntary cure for addiction, but a few weeks after her release she resumed her habit and was arrested in Philadelphia and sentenced to a year and a day at the Alderson Reformatory in West Virginia. She served nine and a half months.

Upon release, she returned to New York for a glorious concert at Carnegie Hall. Newspapers that previously ignored her singing now sensationalized her troubles, a few radio stations blacklisted her, and New York City refused her a cabaret card (Mayor La Guardia's odious cabaret law remained in effect until 1967), which meant she could never again sing in a New York room that served liquor. The only work she could get was on the road or in theaters. More arrests followed, though none of them stuck. The bad publicity tripled, then quadrupled, her salary; yet in 1950, a *Down Beat* hack referred to her as "Lady Yesterday." She continued to cast dangerous playmates in the role of Lover Man, resulting in betrayals and beatings; her second husband, the unmourned John Levy (not to be confused with the respected bassist-turned-manager of the same name), framed her on a drug rap, which she beat—though the cost was permanent insolvency. After Decca dropped her in 1951, she made one session for Aladdin, which yielded the sublime torment of "Detour Ahead," and drifted until Norman Granz signed her to his Mercury label (the parent of Clef and Verve) a year later. Except for one Columbia album, Granz supervised her records for the remaining seven years of her life.

Since 1970 a producer named Akira Yamoto has worked with the Japanese affiliates of American labels to release every record Billie Holiday ever made. None of these issues has been imported to the United States; the Commodores and Deccas are available anyway, many Columbias aren't. Yamoto recently completed his project with *Billie Holiday on Verve 1946–1959*, a box of 10 records that PolyGram is importing at a retail price of about $100. I have some quibbles about presentation, but his is one of the most satisfying compilations ever produced. Its 135 performances, which constitute an anthology of Holiday's favorite songs, are extremely uneven, including much of her best work, along with painful sessions recorded when she could barely summon the energy to enunciate or stay in tune. Despite all the lapses, mannerisms, and clichés—at least 25 songs end with her most overworked tic, the interval of a ninth or major second down to the tonic—there isn't a side I'm not pleased to have. Nor do I feel morbid or sentimental in saying that. The musical elation she affords is often inseparable from the tension of hearing a great artist wrestle with and frequently surmount technical and personal cumbrances. The great thing about Billie Holiday is that she never stopped wrestling.

Consider two performances: the 1952 "These Foolish Things" (which André Hodeir singled out for praise) and the 1956 "All or Nothing at All" (which John Chilton singled out as "the nadir"). In the earlier recording, her voice is strong and the inspiration of the opening paraphrase is sustained throughout the chorus; in the later one, she's hoarse and her variations are occasionally tremulous. Yet in both instances the overriding impression is of a singer intent on making the songs her own, of an artist refusing to accede to what Holiday called "close-order drill." She feels her way through both songs, refurbishing melodies and lifting rhythms, and if her artistic control is indisputable in "These Foolish Things," as it surely is, "All or Nothing at All" is compelling as well—she consistently takes risks, as in the extremely legato swing of the release.

For all but one of the Verve albums, Holiday returned to a setting that superficially resembled her Columbia recordings. Once again she was surrounded by an intimate coterie of brilliant improvisers. The resemblance stops there. The tempos have stalled to a medium nod-time, fit for ruminating, often sensuous. The singing is economical, and so are the arrangements, which were mostly improvised. Instead of a couple of wind instruments escorting her through the harmonies, as on many of the Teddy Wilson classics, she is most frequently heard in dialogue with one soloist. (Harry Edison's obbligati throughout are beyond praise.) Holiday draws you into these songs: They are translucent baubles held to the light and languidly examined. And whereas once she transcended silly lyrics with the intensity of her rhythmic and melodic skills, now she makes them work for her. Every stanza seems autobiographical. When she was 20, in 1935, she made "What a Little Moonlight Can Do" a rowdy jaunt, precocious and exhilarating; 22 years later, worn down by numberless ills, she makes a valiant and winning effort to sing it for the crowd at Newport, and for the first time you hear the words and suddenly what is banal on paper—"You only stutter 'cause your poor tongue/Just will not utter the words/I love you"—is jarring in performance.

The earliest session, her 1946 appearance at a JATP concert in Los Angeles, represents Holiday at her best. Her conceits on "The Man I Love" are as ingenious as those on the Columbia version, although this time Lester Young's contribution is confined to an obbligato in the second chorus. Listen to the way she glides over "seems absurd," or rushes "someday, one day," or bends "my" over two notes. The 1952 and 1954 studio sessions are ornamented with masterly work by Charlie Shavers and Flip Phillips, though the heavy-handed Oscar Peterson is inattentive to her needs. It hardly matters; nothing could bring Holiday down when she was singing this well. In 1955, she was chaperoned by a more orderly Tony Scott ensemble (with Shavers at his peak) and consistently worthy material. She freely reharmonizes key phrases in "Always" and "Ain't Misbehavin'," italicizes the witty lyric of "Everything Happens to Me" (note the inflection on "measles" and the percussive push on "thought you could break this jinx for me"), adds the verse to her classic "I Wished on the Moon," and debuts the first of two sublimely personal versions of "Do Nothin' till You Hear from Me," on which Budd Johnson perfectly echoes her disposition.

Perhaps the best sessions are those with Jimmy Rowles, Harry Edison, and either Benny Carter (his "What's New" improvisation is a song in its own right) or Ben Webster (wailing on the second and superior "Do Nothin'"). In the '70s, a small label released a taped rehearsal conversation between Holiday and Rowles; she exclaims, "It's a pleasure working with you again. Jesus Christ! I've been with some pretty big shots, and they don't dig me no kinda way." On the Verves, Rowles trails her like a bloodhound, his footing as savvy and sure as hers—for example, "Day In, Day Out" and "I Didn't Know What Time It Was" (with verse). Edison (who was Sinatra's preferred trumpet player during the same period) is startling, booting her final chorus on "I Get a Kick out of You," feeding her shots on "One for My Baby," answering her every phrase on "Do Nothin'." Holiday occasionally sounds exhausted, but she regularly comes up with fresh twists, such as the curtailed rest at the opening of a shyly romantic "Isn't This a Lovely Day?" A 1956 session with Tony Scott and Wynton Kelly is sluggish, and the big band album with Ray Ellis, recorded four months before her death on July 17, 1959, can be a trying experience. The voice is haggard, though its soulful cry still penetrates. I find several of these performances deeply moving.

Billie Holiday on Verve comes with a 39-page booklet that includes the most comprehensive discography to date, plus a list of album compilations and four cardboard facsimiles of 10-inch album jackets designed by David Stone Martin. This is the kind of loving production that gives a remarkable artist her due even as it shames the relative negligence and unimaginativeness of American labels. Still, I mentioned quibbles, and they include the singular unattractiveness of the box (the drawing of Holiday has a nose that more closely resembles her Chihuahua's); countless typographical errors; the senseless segregation of her live performances on two final discs (the other sessions are presented chronologically); the deletion of Gilbert Millstein's fine readings from her autobiography at the 1956 concert (you have to buy *The Essential Billie Holiday* to hear them); the absence of a song list with dates and personnel (you have to annotate the booklet to keep from constantly flipping its pages); and poor liner notes rendered poorer by a pidgin English translation—surely PolyGram could have justified the expenditure of a few hundred dollars for an English-speaking proofreader.

When it comes to jazz, domestic indifference has rendered the United States a colony of Japan—and of England. Last year, the BBC broadcast a 98-minute documentary called *The Long Night of Lady Day* that is far and away the best film ever made about her. A wave of interest in Holiday crested in 1972 with the release of Hollywood's unspeakable and slanderous *Lady Sings the Blues*. Diana Ross won't be around to confuse the issue, should that tide return in the wake of the BBC film and the Verve project. Perhaps the recent homages to Edith Piaf on TV and in the theater will now spill over to our own diva of vernacular heartaches. I've often suspected that Piaf was an easy object of mawkish veneration because her problems reflect on another country. Holiday's tragedy reflects the racist Philistinism of our own time and place. Her mature recordings remain controversial not least because they vividly incarnate her indictment of the world, as well as the spirit and dignity she sustained through all its blows.*

*Recently Columbia issued all the Holiday records from the years 1933 to 1942 on nine compact discs. The sound of the early ones is icily inexpressive but improves as the series continues. A three-CD Holiday compilation was subsequently released by the label as *The Legacy*. The selections, originally masterminded by John Hammond for the juke-box trade, are largely indispensable and include most but not all the high points ("When You're Smiling," "Sugar," and "It's a Sin to Tell a Lie" have been passed over for inferior performances). A few oddities are included—an excerpt from Ellington's film short "Symphony in Black," containing Holiday's first recorded vocal—as well as two 1958 songs and the 1957 "Fine and Mellow," taken from a recording session and not the superior telecast, *The Sound of Jazz*, as claimed on the box. The compiler's notes are tastelessly autobiographical, but he is not the first and will not be the last adult reduced to a howl of reflective longing by this incomparably seductive music. The complete Verve recordings, discussed in my essay, were scheduled for release on CD in 1992.

Can we agree that the Billie Holiday controversy, in which her early recordings were used to thrash the later ones, has been put to rest? You don't hear much guff about it anymore, so I'm assuming it's finished. In any case the rear guard never much existed except among reactionary journalists. Musicians and the public surely did not see it that way. Several of the Verve albums were constantly in print: the musical equivalent of postwar noir, they spoke to audiences directly, without need for explanations or apologies. The best of earlier Columbias are beyond praise: sublime explosions of youthful genius, the work not merely of an inspirational singer but of a generation of princely musicians who burnished her vigilant joy with a glowing, compassionate optimism. Holiday is the linchpin, but the results outshine any one participant, even her. The collective spirit of the many individual voices—chiefly Teddy Wilson, Buck Clayton, and, imperially, Lester Young—playing with and for her, irreverently turning Tin Pan Alley dross into gleaming metal, invariably carries the day.

With the Verves, Holiday is at the musical and emotional center of nearly every performance; when she is radiant, the musicians are correspondingly radiant. When she falters, the entire session is as a rainy day, a rehearsal (come back tomorrow, fellas, we'll get it right then). And yet, conceptually, the recordings are similar, as are many of the selections— what a gorgeous irony that the dog tunes she got stuck with in the '30s became so immutably associated with her that 20 years later people requested them as though they were greatest hits. Once again she was bolstered by individual voices—chiefly Jimmy Rowles, Harry Edison, and, imperially, Ben Webster—but now they took their cues from her. The spectacle of Young and Holiday jogging shoulder to shoulder could never be duplicated. She was no longer a girl singer, which is to say, one of the boys. She was now a diva, and they were gentlemen in waiting. The rehearsal banter, much of which has been preserved, may suggest otherwise, but the music is definitive: the obbligato is respectful, which is to say unequal.

If a backlash is in the making, with people saying they *prefer* the Verves to the Columbias (I don't mean to disparage the Commodores, Deccas, and Aladdins, but they represent transitional recordings between her two longest and most prominent label affiliations), a partial cause will be the manner in which the two companies have reissued her work. The Columbias were poorly remastered for CD, though the late volumes improve and the strangely sour liner notes belittle many performances, pinching whatever joy the consumer might have derived from them. The Verves are expertly engineered, and the often embarrassingly hyperbolic notes shout *Event!* in your ear, until you may be persuaded to find enjoyment where none exists. Columbia is Bush; Verve is Clinton. For some Truman-esque plain speaking we'll have to wait at least another generation. But I doubt we'll ever get a more comprehensive edition of the Verve era than the just issued 10-CD cube, *The Complete Billie Holiday on Verve 1945–1959*.

In 1985, Polygram imported the 10-LP Japanese-produced *Billie Holiday on Verve 1946–1959* (the earlier start-up year on the new set merely reflects a change of date for two selections, "Body and Soul" and "Strange Fruit," from her first Jazz at the Philharmonic concert), the most sumptuous presentation of her later work released up to that time. I discussed then the music at length (cf. *Faces in the Crowd* at your favorite bookstore), and noted only a few quibbles: the ugly cover drawing, the segregation of her live performances, and the omission of the Gilbert Millstein narration at her 1956 Carnegie Hall concert. None of those complaints apply to the new edition, which is chronologically arranged and mightily handsome: a black cloth box contains a black cloth binder (not unlike an old 78s album) and a matching booklet filled with musician interviews, photos, recording data (though not the complete discography that graced the Japanese edition), and assorted notes, plus reproductions of four David Stone Martin LP jackets. It's a snug fit—a bit too snug. You've got to shake it all out.

The recordings, too, are packed tight, though not all of them are musical. This time the production was overseen by that most obsessive of anal obsessives, Phil Schaap, who never heard a scrap of studio dialogue, a warm-up, or a false take he didn't find revelatory. Fortunately most of the chatter is confined to two discs, and one of them is an expanded (by 30 minutes) and reedited version of the rehearsal with Jimmy Rowles that was released in 1973 as a Paramount LP and in 1987 as a Mobile Fidelity CD. Less rewarding is a rehearsal at the home of William and Maely Dufty that only the most tenacious of voyeurs will listen to in its entirety, and no one will listen to twice. (Unlike the Rowles tape, it offers little genuine conversation; it would have made an intriguing bonus, but with the box going for a suggested $160 you pay full price for it. Bill Dufty, incidentally, was then a *New York Post* reporter who wrote Holiday's memoir, *Lady Sings the Blues*, as well as a superb series of page-long pieces at the time of her death that has never been reprinted.) Also included are sometimes irritating false starts and a 1954 German concert, with a forthright Holiday skimming the surf of Carl Drinkard's hyperventilating piano. Still, if the surprises are less than riveting, the major concerts and studio sessions have never sounded better. The audio restoration is first-rate—occasionally startling in its brightness and intimacy. As a fan's homage, *The Complete Billie Holiday on Verve* is slightly overbaked, but infinitely treasurable.

MISS HOLIDAY
WHITNEY BALLIETT

This review of Holiday's later recordings gives both an outstanding analysis of her vocal technique and unique insights into part of her catalogue that is sometimes slighted.

Toward the end of her life, Billie Holiday, who died at the age of forty-four, had become inextricably caught in a tangle of notoriety and fame. It was compounded of an endless series of skirmishes with the police and the courts (she was shamelessly arrested on her deathbed for the alleged possession of narcotics); the bitter, vindictive, self-pitying image of herself established in her autobiography, published in 1956—a to-hell-with-you image that tended to repel rather than attract compassion; and the fervent adulation still granted her by a diminishing but ferocious band of admirers. Her new listeners must have been puzzled by all this turmoil, for she sang during much of the fifties with a heavy, unsteady voice that sometimes gave the impression of being pushed painfully in front of her, like a medicine ball. She seemed, in fact, to be embattled with every song she tackled. Nonetheless, her admirers were not mad. Between 1935, when she popped out of nowhere, and 1940, Miss Holiday had knocked a good portion of the jazz world on its ear with a hundred or so recordings, several dozen of which rank with the greatest of non-classical vocal efforts. Part of the success of these recordings, which have an uncanny balance of ease, control, unself-consciousness, emotion, and humor, is due to the accompaniment provided by small bands made up of men like Lester Young, Buck Clayton, Roy Eldridge, Benny Goodman, and Teddy Wilson. Though their work—in obbligatos that underline the grace of her voice, in exemplary solos, and in tumbling, laughing ensembles—often takes up as much space as the vocals, it is Miss Holiday who continues to astonish.

Until she appeared, genuine jazz singing had been practiced largely by a myriad of often obscure blues singers led by Bessie Smith, and by a hand-ful of instrumentalists led by Louis Armstrong. Bessie Smith leveled a massive lyricism at limited materials, while Armstrong's coalyard rumblings, though irresistible in themselves, occasionally seemed to have little to do with singing. Distilling and mixing the best of her predecessors with her own high talents, Billie Holiday became the first full-fledged jazz singer (and, with the defection in recent years of Ella Fitzgerald and Sarah Vaughan, possibly the last). She could sing anything, and her style was completely her own. She appeared to *play* her voice rather than sing with it. In addition to a hornlike control of melody and rhythm, she had an affecting contralto that took on innumerable timbres: a dark-brown sound, sometimes fretted by growls or hoarseness, in the lower register; and a clear, pushing, little-girl alto in between. Her style came in three subtly different parts. There was one for ephemeral popular songs, one for the more durable efforts of George Gershwin and his peers, and one for the blues. Since she was primarily an improviser, not an interpreter, she was often most striking when handling pop songs, like "Yankee Doodle Never Went to Town," "It's Too Hot for Words," and "What a Little Moonlight Can Do," which she spattered with a mocking, let's-have-some-fun-with-this air. Thus, at a fast tempo, she might loll back in half time, and not only elongate each word, so that it seemed nothing but vowels, but flatten the melody into a near-monotone of four or five notes. Then, in the last eight bars or so, she would suddenly pounce on the beat, pick up the melody, and close in a here-I-am rush. (If the evil was in her she might stomp such a number all the way through, rocking it relentlessly back and forth and coating it with dead-serious growls.) At slow tempos, she would use the full range of her voice, adding exaggerated smears to her phrases or dotting them with series of laughlike staccato notes. At the same time, she was busy fashioning a deceptively simple and thorough melodic variation on the tune, smoothing its wrinkles, toughening up its soft spots, and lending it far more lyricism than it usually deserved. This was accomplished not by superimposing melodic candelabra on her material, in the manner of Sarah Vaughan and her baroque students, but by unobtrusively altering its melodic and rhythmic structure with a flow of marvelously placed phrases that might wander around behind the beat, and then suddenly push ahead of it (each syllable urgently pinned to a staccato note) or slide through legato curves full of blue notes and generous vibratos. Miss Holiday's rhythmic sense had much in common with Lester Young's, who would sooner have gone into another line of work than place a note conventionally. Moreover, her enunciation of pop songs was a mixture of clarity and caricature, bringing into action that rule of ridicule that the victim be reproduced perfectly before being destroyed. Her "moon"s and "June"s rang like bells, and one didn't hear their cracks until the sound began to die away. The composers of the pop songs she sang should be grateful; her renditions ("Ooo-ooo-ooo/What a lil moonlaight can do-oo-oo"), and not the songs, are what we remember.

Her approach to Gershwin and such was almost reverent in comparison. In a number like "Summertime," she allowed the emotion that she had spent on lesser materials in sarcasm or near-flippancy to come through undisguised. Ceaselessly inventive, she would still shape the melody to fit her voice and mood, but in such a way that its beauties—and not hers—were pointed up. (The number of popular singers, to say nothing of jazz singers, who have been able to slip inside their material, instead of plodding along beside it, is remarkably small.) "Summertime" became a pure lullaby, "But Not for Me" a self-joshing lament, and "Porgy" a prayer. When there were superior lyrics on hand, she underlined them with diction and an understanding that shunted the meaning of each word forward. More than that, she would, at the best, lend a first-rate song a new and peculiarly heightened emotion that, one suddenly realized, its composer had only been reaching for. And the effort never showed.

Miss Holiday simply let go when she sang the blues. She was never, however, a loud singer, nor did she depend on the big whisper of most of her microphone-reared successors; instead, she projected her voice firmly, keeping in steady balance her enunciation, timbre, and phrasing. She was, in fact, a model elocutionist. Free of the more complex structures of the standard popular song, she moved through the innumerable emotional pastures of the form, ranging from the down-and-out to the joyous to the nasty and biting to quiet, almost loving blues.

Then, in 1944, when Miss Holiday started recording again (after the recording bans), the magic had begun to vanish. Perhaps it was the increasing strain of her private life, or the mysterious rigor mortis that so often freezes highly talented but untrained and basically intuitive performers. At any rate, she had become self-conscious. Although her voice had improved in resonance and control, her style had grown mannered. She ended her phrases with disconcerting, lachrymose dips. She struggled with her words instead of batting them about or savoring them. The melodic twists and turns lost their spontaneity. One could accurately predict her rhythmic patterns. Even her beauty—the huge gardenia clamped to the side of her head; the high, flashing cheekbones; the almost motionless body, the snapping fingers, and the thrown-back head; the mobile mouth, which seemed to measure the emotional shape and texture of each word—implied careful calculation. From time to time, some of this stylization lifted—she never, of course, lost her *presence*, which became more and more melancholy—and there were glimpses of her old naturalness. After 1950, her voice grew deeper and coarser, and her sense of pitch and phrasing eluded her, and finally she became that most rending of spectacles—a once great performer doing a parody of herself that could have been bettered by her inferiors. Her still devoted partisans clamored on; they would have done her greater service by doffing their hats and remaining silent.

Miss Holiday's most recent records chronicle her work from 1944 until a year or two before her death. Among them are "An Evening with Eddie Heywood and Billie Holiday" (Commodore), "The Billie Holiday Story"(Decca), and "The Unforgettable Lady Day" (Verve). By and large, they proceed steadily and sadly downward. The first record includes four Holiday numbers—three standards and a blues—that were done in 1944. (The rest are instrumentals by Eddie Heywood's small band, which also provides her accompaniment.) The best of them is a slow blues, "I Love My Man," in which, dropping her mannerisms, she nearly equals her classic rendition of another blues, "Fine and Mellow," recorded five years before. The Decca collection brings together twenty-four numbers—most of them standards—recorded between 1944 and 1950, and it varies sharply in quality. The accompaniment runs from the indifferent to the stifling. Nevertheless, in numbers like "Lover Man," "I'll Look Around," "Deep Song," "My Man," "Good Morning, Heartache," and "Solitude," she sings in her best forties style.

The Verve album, which consists of twenty-three standards recorded between 1949 and 1957 with a variety of small groups made up of such men as Ben Webster, Harry Edison, Charlie Shavers, Oscar Peterson, and Benny Carter, begins—give or take a little overlapping—where the Decca set stops. There are some valuable things. Six of the numbers were set down at a concert in 1949 on the West Coast, and Miss Holiday sings throughout with an ease and confidence that result in two first-rate efforts—a medium-slow "Man I Love," which ranks with any of her work in the forties, and a fresh, peaceful "All of Me." The eleven numbers from 1952 are not far behind; the notable ones are slow versions of "I Can't Face the Music" and "These Foolish Things." The cracks begin to show in the two 1954 numbers, and then, amazingly, there is a medium-tempo "Please Don't Talk About Me When I'm Gone," done a year later, in which Miss Holiday magically reverts to the late thirties, delivering the first chorus in a light, bantering, husky voice that is memorable. ("When Your Lover Has Gone," apparently made at the same session, is, nevertheless, curiously heavy and uncertain.) With the exception of the last chorus of a 1957 "Gee Baby, Ain't I Good to You," in which Miss Holiday virtually rocks herself into effective shape, the rest of the album is rewarding only for the accompaniment of Webster and Edison. But one is cheered by the recent news that Columbia is considering reissuing the best of the 1935–40 Holiday sides hidden away in its vaults. It would be inhuman not to.

LADY IN SATIN AND HOLIDAY'S LAST RECORDINGS
GLENN COULTER

Coulter's piece is fascinating for its ardent, though primarily negative opinion about the value of Lady Day's last recording, *Lady in Satin*, written at the time of its release. She herself loved the album done with strings; she thought she sounded exactly the way she had always wanted to. Charlie "Bird" Parker endured a similar sort of criticism when he recorded with strings. The results, as Lady Day's effort was, were romantic. Although the passage of time has rallied many critics to the side of these albums, not everyone agrees yet with their champions. Coulter wrote his witty precis of *Lady in Satin* and several other albums by Billie very well, and his analysis opens a window to let in a breeze from another direction.

LADY IN SATIN, Columbia CL 1157. Ray Ellis and his Orchestra: *I'm a Fool to Want You; For Heaven's Sake; You Don't Know What Love Is; I Get Along Without You Very Well; For All We Know; Violets for Your Furs; You've Changed; It's Easy to Remember; But Beautiful; Glad to Be Unhappy; I'll Be Around; The End of a Love Affair.*

BODY AND SOUL, Verve MGV 8719. Jimmy Rowles, *piano*; Barney Kessel, *guitar*; Ben Webster, *tenor sax*; Harry "Sweets" Edison, *trumpet*; Alvin Stoller, *drums*.

Body and Soul; Darn That Dream; Comes Love; Moonlight in Vermont.
Same personnel except Larry Bunker, *drums*:
They Can't Take That Away from Me; Let's Call the Whole Thing Off; Gee, Baby, Ain't I Good to You; Embraceable You.

THE BLUES ARE BREWIN', Decca DL 8701. Sid Cooper, Johnny Mince, *altos*; A. Drelinger, Pat Nizza, *tenors*; Bernie Privin, *trumpet*; Billy Kyle, *piano*; Jimmy Crawford, *drums*; Joe Benjamin, *bass*; Everett Barksdale, *guitar*; Louis Armstrong, *vocal*; on first two tunes.

You Can't Lose a Broken Heart; My Sweet Hunk of Trash; Now or Never.
G. Dorsey, Pete Clark, *altos*; Fred Williams, Budd Johnson, *tenors*; Dave McRae, *baritone*; Shad Collins, Buck Clayton, R. Williams, *trumpets*; G. Stevenson, Henderson Chambers, *trombones*; Horace Henderson, *piano*; Wallace Bishop, *drums*; J. Benjamin, *bass*; E. Barksdale, *guitar*:
Do Your Duty; Gimme a Pigfoot and a Bottle of Beer.
G. Dorsey, J. Mince, *altos*; Fred Williams, Budd Johnson, *tenors*; Ed Barefield, *baritone*; B. Privin, Tony Faso, Dick Vance, *trumpets*; H. Chambers, M. Bullman, *trombones*; H. Henderson, *piano*; G. Duvivier, *bass*; E. Barksdale, *guitar*; drummer unidentified:
Keeps on Rainin'.
G. Dorsey, Rudy Powell, *altos*; Joe Thomas, Lester Young, *tenors*; Sol Moore, *baritone*; Jimmy Nottingham, E. Berry, Buck Clayton, *trumpets*; G. Matthews, Dickie Wells, *trombones*; H. Henderson, *piano*; Shadow Wilson, *drums*; G. Duvivier, *bass*; M. Lowe, *guitar*:
Baby Get Lost.
Lem Davis, *alto*; Bob Dorsey, *tenor*; Bobby Tucker, *piano*; D. Best, *drums*; John Simmons, *bass*; R. Reese, *trumpet*:
The Blues Are Brewin'; Guilty.
Joe Guy, *trumpet*; Billy Kyle, *piano*; Kenny Clarke, *drums*; T. Barney, *bass*; Jim Shirley, *guitar*:
Baby, I Don't Cry over You.
Joe Springer, *piano*; Kelly Martin, *drums*; Billy Taylor, *bass*; Tiny Grimes, *guitar*; Joe Guy, *trumpet*:
Big Stuff.
Milt Yaner, *clarinet and alto*; John Fulton, *flute, clarinet and tenor*; Bernie Leighton, *piano*; Bunny Shawker, *drums*; J. Lesberg, *bass*; T. Mottola, *guitar*; Bobby Hackett, *trumpet;* and five strings:
Somebody's on My Mind.

THE LADY SINGS, Decca DL 8215.

Deep Song; You Better Go Now; Don't Explain; Ain't Nobody's Business If I Do; God Bless the Child; Them There Eyes; Good Morning Heartache; No More; No Good Man; I'll Look Around; Easy Living; What Is This Thing Called Love.

On 1, 2, & 11, orchestra directed by Bob Haggart; on 6, orchestra directed by Sy Oliver; on 8, orchestra directed by Camarata; 10, Billy Kyle and his Trio; orchestra unidentified on others.

HOLIDAY CLASSICS, Commodore FL 30008. Frankie Newton, *trumpet*; Tab Smith, *alto sax*; Kenneth Hollon, Stanley Payne, *tenor saxes*; Sonny White, *piano*; James McLin, *guitar*; John Williams, *bass*; Eddie Dougherty, *drums*.

Yesterdays; I Gotta Right to Sing the Blues; Strange Fruit; Fine and Mellow.
Eddie Heywood, *piano*; Doc Cheatham, *trumpet*; Lem Davis, *alto sax*; Vic Dickenson, *trombone*; Teddy Walters, *guitar*; John Simmons, *bass*; Big Sid Catlett, *drums*:
I'll Be Seeing You; I'll Get By; I Cover the Waterfront; How Am I to Know; My Old Flame.
Eddie Heywood, *piano*; John Simmons, *bass*; Big Sid Catlett, *drums*: *Lover, Come Back to Me; She's Funny That Way; On the Sunny Side of the Street.*

LADY IN SATIN is the name of a new Columbia record of twelve more or less insipid songs done by Billie Holiday against the neon arrangements of Ray Ellis. It is very nearly total disaster. The fault is not wholly that of the arranger, though one is tempted to say so. Still, the ideal accompaniment for a jazz vocal is a many-noted commentary which does not interfere with what the singer is doing, but rather provides a texture of the utmost contrast and a springboard of rhythm. Ellis provides the hit-record approach, slow, sleek insufficiently subordinated counterpoint, as rugged as Reddi-wip and so continuous that Billie's timing is thrown off, for want of anything to brace itself against. The instrumental richness (to say nothing of the heavenly-choir effect furnished from time to time: it is at any rate simply, *aah*, not *doo-aah*) also cancels out her own unique sonority, that rasp or snarl which in itself preserves her from expressing mere self-pity.

It is a burden to hear the Ellis arrangement systematically frustrating Billie's intentions through every measure of *Easy to Remember*, which might have been, in any but this chenille setting, a real accomplishment. But whoever selected the material for this date is as much to blame as Ellis. True, Billie (like Armstrong, Toscanini, and most established performers) usually prefers to handle the same few numbers over and over. Doubtless someone designed this record to introduce her, as the phrase has it, to a wider audience, and also to a broader repertoire. The results are not happy. At best, Billie must contend with songs for the most part of indifferent quality, on which her grasp is too uncertain to allow any exercise of power or insight—anything that might make them worth attention. At worst, she has not even taken the trouble to find out how they go: *Glad to be Unhappy* (and it is the most substantial tune in the set) is a discreditable travesty which should never have been released.

With these stimuli to unease, it is no wonder that Billie's voice fails her. Nowadays, whenever she has to fight undesirable circumstances—inappropriate accompaniment as here, or uncongenial surroundings as at Newport II—she mistakenly responds by forcing, with a result that must make every listener's throat ache sympathetically. (On the other hand, when there is no untoward pressure, as at Lenox in the summer of 1957, her voice is intact. Critics lately have praised her for showing "flashes of the old brilliance" so frequently that one might well mistake hers for the eternal fire of the Arc de Triomphe.) It is no pleasure to describe most of these performances, the gritty tone, the wavering pitch, the inability to control an instrument that is nothing without control; many times one can't name with any certainty the notes she is striving for. Billie's superiority (I am sure it remains, and will remain after this record has been deleted) has always rested in transcending her materials: hacking off melodic excess, and attacking the words with, alternately, deeper conviction and greater contempt. The ambiguity is, in her best performances, elusive and unpredictable, gives even rather foolish songs a startling resemblance to real existence, and since the process is just as musical as it is verbal and operates like opposing mirrors, results in fascination rather than monotony. Naturally, when sheer articulation becomes difficult, none of this can come into play. It does in this set only once: *You've Changed* is remarkably free of flaws, and one is likely to play it over several times in delight without realizing how absurd the text is.

In a better world than this, Columbia, on its side, would have reissued more of the Wilson-Holiday masterpieces, now more than twenty years old. On her side, Billie might better have stayed with Granz. For the last of her Verve records to be released BODY AND SOUL, is a better product in every way. Here are eight tunes suited to Billie, and in place of the heavenly choir Webster and Edison supply obbligatos and solos. Webster is particularly good; his sonority alone is music to read F. Scott Fitzgerald by. Billie's voice is as clear as it can be these days, though there is a straining after high-lying passages, as in the title song, and the amplification of her voice, though necessary, is excessive, yielding a sound darker and coarser than the reality. *They Can't Take That Away from Me* demonstrates the advisability of having the instruments get out of her way early: she begins like the guillotine blade in slow motion, and Webster, when his turn comes, has a solo that is all jaunty nostalgia. Billie teases *Comes Love* along: just imagine how arch another singer would be, or how self-consciously sultry. (Next to Billie, others singing of love sound like little girls playing house.) It was not to be expected that Lady should surpass her 1944 *Embraceable You*, but she has. Her second chorus is more than an embellishment of the melody; it is a new melody, a sort of inversion of the original or shadowy melody that offsets its descent by overleaping the climactic note. It is a striking line indeed, and her commanding manipulation of it exceeds the ability of every other active singer of jazz.

Billie Holiday's desire to phrase like a horn, not just to sing, enhances words as well as music. It is a strategy that involved attacking each note separately, a vocal approximation of the instrumentalist's bowing or plucking or whatever it is, and stifling the voice's natural vibrato in favor of one that is rare and eccentrically placed. These characteristics of her style mean that each syllable seems unnaturally distinct, as if each were a stone plopped into a pool of still water, and, because she delights in staying well behind the beat, critics have been fooled into dismissing her as a kind of precious *diseuse*, momentarily interesting but not to be compared with a real jazz artist, like, say, Sarah or Anita.

This misunderstanding might be most readily cleared up if such critics would try listening to Lady's voice as they would to a horn, to the way it burns through *Fine and Mellow* (when Blesh ridiculed this he must have been too busy beating time to notice how the angry wail blazes throughout—or does he think the tone of a buzz-saw enervated?)—but then, it would be too bad to overlook what happens to the text.

Fine and Mellow is one of twelve songs done for Commodore now newly reissued on LP. Even God gets tired of too much alleluia, and it would be fruitless to invent fresh ways of commending performances which Commodore rightly calls classic. Among other which are better known, I would single out two: *My Old Flame* is done with a jauntiness not often associated with Billie and beautifully in keeping with the spirit of the text. It would be difficult to imagine an emptier song than *How Am I to Know*; yet Billie seems to charge it, from the release on, with some fleeting but true significance.

A jazz collection without these performances would be a poor thing indeed.

Billie Holiday's work for Decca (1946-49) has been transferred to LP, and two of the records which make up this praiseworthy venture afford an amusing and instructive contrast. As might be expected, the last issue, THE BLUES ARE BREWIN', is the least in merit, the bottom of the bin. Two tunes linked to the name of Bessie Smith—*Gimme a Pigfoot* and *Do Your Duty*—remind us of what Billie's work lacks: informality, joy, spontaneity. A pair of duets with Louis are well sung but disfigured by stale ad libs. None of these should be taken seriously anyhow; they are music-hall material, only incidentally jazz. The rest of the set contains mediocre pop tunes performed with due (but unintentional) insipidity—except for a Leonard Bernstein tune which it would be better to deal with further on.

Most of the backing for both sets is supplied by sizable bands. Brasses make the kind of din that is, science tells us, fatal to mice, yet the arrangements are not bad as support and they are idiomatic.

THE LADY SINGS is the other Decca, and indeed she does. It seems wasteful to attempt any description of these performances: anybody of a certain age must have taken cognizance of them when they were first issued. (The sound, incidentally, has paled in the transfer.) What was not so apparent when they were released two by two was their expressive variety: the cold dismissal of *No More*, the contorted pathos of *You Better Go Now*, the perhaps excessive virtuosity of *Ain't Nobody's Business*. *I'll Look Around* is a lesson for all who would be jazz singers, the line sustained from first to last, the approach to it just suspenseful enough to make it live, the words forced to generate real meaning. But there is no pat explanation of how Billie can make a quite common interval, say a major third, seem an unusual and difficult leap, nor of how she can isolate and break down for analysis the counterwords in her lyrics.

This unique method—of course the word is misleading: I do not suggest any gnawing consciousness that the words are trash—of battling the weakness of the material is only intermittently successful.

INDIGENOUS MUSIC
NAT HENTOFF

This review of Holiday's later sessions, including studio chat, gives insight into another side of Holiday's artistry. Nat Hentoff gives readers the feeling that they are eavesdropping on the jazz scene, as he himself acknowledges in the opening of his review that doubles as "a slice of life."

Nat Hentoff was born in Boston on June 10, 1925, where he graduated from Northeastern University and attended Harvard University. By the 1950s he was writing and editing for *Down Beat* magazine, and he also became renowned as a jazz writer for his books *The Jazz Life* and *Hear Me Talkin' to Ya*, the latter co-authored with Nat Shapiro. He was a coeditor with Martin Williams of the *Jazz Review*. Since the early 1960s, he has built a reputation as a writer on civil liberties, publishing regularly in the *Village Voice*. In 1995, he published a new collection of his recent music criticism, and the jazz world still regards him as one of its best chroniclers.

Like many eavesdroppers, I am fascinated by shop talk—lawyers chortling about how they play upon the foibles of judges or Sy Hersh telling how he so boxes in a source that the leads start pouring out. And so it is in jazz— at rehearsals, between sets, after hours, the shop talk can be remarkably illuminating, more so than critical treatises by the most diligent outsiders. But unless you hang out with musicians, there's no way to audit these jazz seminars—except for one utterly unprecedented recording: *Billie Holiday/Songs & Conversations* (Paramount Records/Famous Music Corp.). Released a couple of years ago, it has been largely and inexplicably ignored, but no jazz library should be without it.

The set was taped at a rehearsal toward the end of Lady Day's life, although she doesn't sound at all ready for the last chorus. Billie sounds as I remember her at a mutual friend's home one evening years before— pungently funny about the dreadful squares who run the music business and ceaselessly curious about better ways to make a song move. The supporting cast at the rehearsal consisted of bassist Artie Shapiro and pianist Jimmy Rowles, the Gerald Moore of jazz accompanists.

Rowles was trying mightily to reach a consensus with Billie about key signatures (she expected him to fill in whatever he liked so long as it fit); and he was also working with her on some songs that were new to her repertory. From time to time, you do hear her singing. Her approach to *Please Don't Talk About Me When I'm Gone*, for instance, is the very definition of swinging jazz time. And elsewhere (as in *I'm Restless*), the process by which she starts to learn and then comes to entirely possess a tune new to her is a fundamental lesson in the rare art of instrumentalized jazz lieder. (That is, Billie sang like a most supple horn.) For other songs, by talk and then by example, Billie focuses specifically on problems of phrasing, rhythm placement and texture. "I do not got a legitimate voice," she says, laughing, at one point. And not having a "legitimate" voice, she extracted from it—even toward the end when the voice was cracked and gravelly—such subtly variegated, emotionally exact colors that she could transform the most banal lyrics into swiftly piercing epiphanies.

For much of this rehearsal time, however, Billie felt like reminiscing. About the year, for instance, when "They ran me out of Chicago. The owner of the Grand Terrace," she mimics that worthy's heavy, indignant incomprehension, "tells me I got to get out because I sound like I'm tired, like I'm sleeping. Man, it took me ten years for people to pick up on what I was doing." And another time, confronted by the explosive Joe Glaser, her booker and manager and a man well connected in the nether world, Billie refuses his command to sing commercially. "Look, you son-of-a-bitch," she laughs again at the mellow memory of standing up to Glaser, "you want it sung that way, *you* sing it! I'm gonna sing *my* way."

It is a singular document, this album, telling much about Lady Day and about jazz itself, psychologically as well as musically. Of course, it won't mean much to those millions of people who know Billie only through the grotesquely ignorant film version of her "life," *Lady Sings the Blues*, with Diana Ross who is to Billie Holiday as Rod McKuen is to W. H. Auden. They finally did commercialize Billie, posthumously. Still, this recording of her true grit remains, as do a number of entirely musical reissues, the best of which to begin with is *Billie Holiday/ Golden Years* (Columbia).

As is quite timelessly evident on these recordings, including the passages of singing on the rehearsal date, Billie Holiday was the most deeply and durably evocative of all jazz singers—from floating, mocking, good-time highs to unsparing poignancy. Or, for that matter, tragedy, jazz indeed being "serious" music.

LADY SINGS THE BLUES
ORRIN KEEPNEWS

Keepnews, who lived much of his life in the jazz milieu, wrote an insider's view of Billie's semi-faux autobiography. He knew its strengths and weaknesses—she darted around and over the facts with the skill of a racing car driver—and his insights should guide anyone approaching the book now.

Keepnews was born on March 2, 1923, in New York City, where he graduated from Columbia University in 1943. He started writing for the *Record Changer* in 1948, and, with his friend and former classmate Bill Grauer began reissuing albums of important early jazz artists in 1952 for RCA Victor. That enterprise led to their founding the recording company, Riverside, in 1953. Keepnews produced albums by Thelonious Monk, Bill Evans, Sonny Rollins, Wes Montgomery, and Cannonball Adderley, then moved to the Milestone label from 1966 to 1972, and then to Fantasy, which acquired the Prestige, Riverside, and Milestone catalogues. Keepnews reissued albums from those labels. A vice president of Fantasy in 1980, he resigned from the company with the goal of producing more albums for that label and others. He founded the Landmark label in 1985, for which he produced many important younger artists ranging from vibist Bobby Hutcherson to pianist Mulgrew Miller to singer Weslia Whitfield. The label was eventually sold to Muse Records.

Keepnews has always written extremely engrossing, historical articles and liner notes about the jazz world, including annotations for Thelonious Monk albums.

The "celebrity autobiography" is a type of book that undoubtedly will always be with us. Promising, and sometimes even delivering, glamor and backstage secrets and lots of casual name-dropping, such books have a very understandable appeal. But for those readers who consider the person whose life story is involved to be an "artist" rather than a "celebrity" (and the difference is of course a vast one), such an autobiography can be a source of squirming annoyance that is strictly in the fingernail-across-the-blackboard category.

Applying the above generalization to the book at hand—which is Billie Holiday's *Lady Sings the Blues*—let me very quickly add that I'd recommend it to most readers of this magazine. Not that you're apt to be satisfied with it. But, coming to the book with the background knowledge and special interest that most *Record Changer* readers have, you're in a position to find it more valuable and more comprehensible than the non-jazz public will.

The basic trouble with *any* "celebrity autobiography" is that it is not honestly conceived. (There may be exceptions to this sweeping statement, but none come to mind as I write this.) When a living, still-active professional entertainer writes, or causes to be written, an account of his life and career, it seems inevitable that it turns out to be motivated by press-agentry, ego, or a desire for self-justification. These are simply not good reasons for writing books, even though interesting books may sometimes inadvertently result. (I'm sure the same objections apply to the life stories of politicians and authors, but that's beside the point at the moment.)

Now if the celebrity involved is outside of my field of special interest, I don't care very much. But when it is a jazz personality, I can't keep from feeling . . . well, *embarrassed* is probably the best word to describe it. For in almost every case, and no matter what the writer's motives were, it strikes me as one more case of the exploitation of the jazz artist. I get this feeling whether the person involved is someone I deeply respect as a creative artist (Louis Armstrong, Miss Holiday) or someone I don't (Mezz Mezzrow, Eddie Condon). So I suspect that it is not the specific individual I sympathize with—after all, nobody forced them to do or to permit this. It is, rather, that I feel a sense of betrayal: a betrayal of the whole cause of jazz, and of that constant negative battle that so many of us automatically keep fighting—the battle to keep jazz from being so completely publicly misunderstood. Now I realize that there is probably a good deal of impracticality in what I have just written, but it is something I feel too deeply to keep quiet about. And I suspect that I am not alone in feeling this way.

It is, let me emphasize, somewhat unfair to use *Lady Sings the Blues* as the jumping-off place for this dissertation. It is by no means the worst of its kind. I'm reasonably sure that Doubleday published this book largely because of its sensational aspects—dope, prison, and the rest of Billie's well-headlined troubles, and its view of some of rough behind-the-scenes aspects of the Negro musician's world. But there may also have been some feeling of presenting a social document. And in any event, this book avoids that musical self-righteousness and little-boy preening about being "bad" that was so constantly evident in Mezzrow's book. It also avoids the tasteless egotism and contrived brashness of Eddie Condon's autobiography. *Lady Sings the Blues* is, like most of its kind, a ghost-written book ("by Billie Holiday with William Dufty" is the credit line), and it does have its share of that artfully ungrammatical and doggedly colloquial writing that is supposed to seem "natural" and always sets my teeth on edge. But in this respect it is far less offensive than Ethel Waters's masterpiece of hokum and even less irritating than the recent Louis Armstrong book (which wasn't ghost-written, but merely neatened up a bit). Mr. Dufty, who is an assistant to the editor of the liberal New York newspaper, *The Post,* cannot be accused of over-indulging in dialect jokes. His main defect, actually (apart from the extent to which he can be blamed for the things I complain about in the paragraph that follows), is that he tends to indulge in little moral sermons on occasions. While they are not marked off as his, they are quite plainly not Billie's creations, and at least one (on narcotics and what to do about the problem) struck me as in highly dubious taste.

What is wrong with *Lady Sings the Blues* more than anything else is that people to whom Billie Holiday is only a name, a few records, and some concert and night-club appearances are either going to be woefully misled by it or terribly annoyed by it. For it is not a particularly honest book. It would appear to be frank and accurate up to a point—and it is quite probably a true (and often a very moving) picture of some prisons, of Southern *and* Northern Jim Crow in the music business, of real poverty in Harlem. But there is a pervasive air of self-pity that gets me down, and there is a distressing (and rather transparent) vagueness at key points. We gather, for example, that Billie's first arrest on a narcotics charge came after she had gone through a successful cure; but, thereafter, I defy any reader to tell from the text whether she is saying she is "on" or "off" the stuff at any given point. Similarly, the whole previous matter of how she first acquired a habit is glossed over rather bewilderingly. All this seems part of the unfortunate overall "almost everybody done me wrong" spirit that led one jazz magazine to headline its review of the book: "Billie Wails."

In a sense, however, this lack of full candor cannot be called surprising. Not, all least, to those of you who can—as I noted at the start of this piece—bring something more with you to the book than the "average" reader can. You can appreciate, certainly, that an up-from-poverty, kicked-around, jailed Negro singer has to hold something back, and has to push her side of the story to the fullest. To do otherwise would, under all the circumstances, be superhuman. And you can set her words against a context that includes the actual musical product created by Billie and by others whom she deals with here. Keeping these things in mind tends to increase tremendously the meaning of what you read. It's not really fair to a reader, of course, to ask for this sort of extra work. But the point is, if you approach this book forewarned and forearmed and interested in learning from it (and not necessarily in learning precisely what the author herself chooses to emphasize), you'll surely find it worth having read.

In all such books, the general accuracy of the facts presented is of importance, if only as an indication of how careful and reliable a job has been done. I found very few mistakes: Don Redman's name is given as "Redmond," which perhaps bothered me more than it should, but this is nothing at all in comparison to my favorite boner, found in Mezzrow's book, where the Chicago-born patron of Negro jazz let his ghost writer refer to pianist Lovie Austin as a "blues singer." (Editor's note: She was a pianist.) Miss Holiday's writer is guilty of one important failure to clarify that did make me quite angry, and I'd like to clear it up right here. In the late '40s, Billie was involved unpleasantly with a promoter-agent type named John Levy, who, she says, tricked her into taking the rap for him on a dope charge, etc. Mr. Levy's present whereabouts are unknown to me. However, on the current scene is a John Levy who is the personal manager for George Shearing and others, and who was Shearing's bass player until about 1951. He is not the same man; as far as I can discover, there is no connection whatsoever between the two men. I wish Billie or Bill Dufty had seen fit to make this distinction in the book.

PART FOUR

Don't Explain:

Billie Holiday and Her Contemporaries

THE FEMALE SINGERS
JOACHIM E. BERENDT

Translated from the German, the short but sweet analysis of Billie Holiday contains a brilliant explanation of her charisma during the last years of her career: "It is extraordinary to discover just how much a great artist has left when voice and technique and flexibility have failed and nothing remains except the spiritual power of creativity and expression. To hear this on recordings made by Billie Holiday in the fifties is an almost eerie experience: a vocalist devoid of all the material and technical attributes of her profession who still remains a great artist."

More questionable is Berendt's opinion that: "It can be said that because of Billie Holiday, modern jazz had its beginning in the realm of singing earlier than in the field of any instrument." The voice was the first instrument, but in the jazz world, one cannot lose sight, sound, and influence of Louis Armstrong's trumpet playing and vocalizing, which preceded Billie's emergence.

As fascinating as anything Berendt says is his position as an erudite, serious jazz critic in Germany in the mid-twentieth century. Musicians and their retinues and satellites in the jazz world recognized early in the game that jazz received more serious attention in Europe than in the United States. Berendt gives not only jazz its rightfully deserved respect as an art music but Billie her due as "the most important figure" among improvising singers. She is at least one of the most important. His remarks exemplify the bright, refreshing criticism written abroad.

The history of female blues singing starts later than male blues singing. No female singers from "archaic" times are known to us. Folk-blues singers like Blind Lemon Jefferson, Leadbelly, or Robert Johnson did not have female counterparts; nor do their contemporary successors. The simple, rural world of folk blues is dominated by man; woman is an object.

This changed as soon as the blues moved into the big cities of the North. At that time—in the early twenties—the great era of classic blues, whose "mother" was Ma Rainey and whose "empress" was Bessie Smith, began. In the section on Bessie, we discussed the classic blues period in detail. Singers like Bertha "Chippie" Hill, Victoria Spivey, Sippie Wallace, and Alberta Hunter carried on the message of classical blues, while Big Mama Thornton incorporated it into rhythm and blues. But it is important to note that in the late twenties the musical climate was already changing, shifting the accent away from the blues and toward the song.

The first female singers important in this field (who are worth listening to even today) are Ethel Waters, Ivie Anderson, and Mildred Bailey. Ethel Waters was the first to demonstrate, as early as the twenties, the many possibilities for jazz singing in good commercial tunes. Ivie Anderson became Duke Ellington's vocalist in 1932 and remained for almost twelve years; Duke called her the best singer he ever had. Mildred Bailey, of part-Indian origin, was a successful singer of the Swing era with great sensitivity and mastery of phrasing. She was married to Red Norvo; and with him, Teddy Wilson, and Mary Lou Williams she made her finest recordings. Her "Rockin' Chair" became a hit of considerable proportions; it was a blues, but an "alienated," ironic blues.

The songs of the female singers in this "song line" were—and are—the ballads and pop tunes of "commercial music," the melodies of the great American popular composers—Cole Porter, Jerome Kern, Irving Berlin, George Gershwin—sometimes even tunes from the "hit parade," all sung with the inflection and phrasing typical of jazz.

In this area, improvisation has retreated to a final, irreducible position. The songs must remain recognizable, and of course the singers are dependent upon the lyrics. But in a very special sense there can be improvisation here, too. It lies in the art of paraphrasing, juxtaposing, transposing—in the alteration of harmonies, and in a certain way of phrasing. There is a whole arsenal of possibilities, of which Billie Holiday, the most important figure in this branch, had supreme command. Billie was the embodiment of a truth first expressed by Fats Waller (and after him by so many others): In jazz it does not matter so much what you do, but how you do it. To pick one example among many: In 1935, Billie Holiday recorded (with Teddy

Wilson) a banal little song, "What a Little Moonlight Can Do," and what resulted was a completely valid work of art.

Billie Holiday sang blues only incidentally. But through her phrasing and conception, much that she sang seemed to become blues.

Billie Holiday made more than 350 records—among them about seventy with Teddy Wilson. She made her most beautiful recordings in the thirties with Wilson and Lester Young. And in the intertwining of lines sung by Billie Holiday and the lines played by Lester Young, the question which is lead and which is accompaniment, which line is vocal and which instrumental, becomes secondary.

Billie Holiday is the great songstress of understatement. Her voice has none of the volume and majesty of Bessie Smith. It is a small, supple, sensitive voice; yet Billie sang a song that, more than anything sung by Bessie Smith or the other female blues singers, became a musical protest against racial discrimination. This song was "Strange Fruit" (1939). The "strange fruit" hanging from the tree was the body of a lynched Negro. Billie sang this song as if she were stating a fact: That's the way it is. Any blues by Bessie Smith, even a simple, everyday love song, was sung with more emphasis and pathos than this: the most emphatic and most impassioned musical testimony against racism to become known before Abbey Lincoln's interpretation of Max Roach's "Freedom Now Suite" of 1960.

Charm and urbane elegance, suppleness and sophistication are the chief elements in the understatement of Billie Holiday. These elements can be found everywhere—for example, in "Mandy Is Two" (1942), the song about little Mandy, who is only two years old but already a big girl. And this is expressed so straightforwardly and warmly! How simple and unpretentious it is! Nothing rings false, as is the rule with commercial ditties attempting childlike naiveté. It is almost inconceivable that something seemingly destined by every known law to become kitsch could be transformed into art.

Billie's singing had the elasticity of Lester Young's tenor playing, and she had this elasticity prior to her first encounter with Lester. Billie was the first artist in all of jazz—not just the first woman or the first jazz singer—in whose music the influence of the saxophone as the style and sound-setting instrument became clear. And this took place, only seemingly in paradoxical fashion, before the beginning of the saxophone era, which actually only began with the success of Lester Young in the early forties. The "cool" tenor saxophone sound is apparent already in Billie Holiday's first recording—"Your Mother's Son-in-Law," made in 1939 with Benny Goodman. It can be said that because of Billie Holiday, modern jazz had its beginning in the realm of singing earlier than in the field of any instrument.

It had its beginning with Holiday also because she was the first to realize—certainly subconsciously—that not only was her voice the instrument but also the microphone. Holiday was the first vocalist to understand that a singer using a microphone has to sing in a totally different way from one not using a mike. She humanized her voice by "microphonizing" it, thus making subtleties significant that had been unknown in all singing up to that point—in fact, that had been unnecessary, because they could not have been made audible.

The life story of Billie Holiday has been told often and even more often has been effectively falsified: from servant girl in Baltimore through rape and prostitution to successful song star, and through narcotics all the way downhill again. In 1938 she worked with Artie Shaw's band, a white group. For months she had to use service entrances, while her white colleagues went in through the front. She had to stay in dingy hotels and sometimes couldn't even share meals with her associates. And she had to suffer all this not only as a black but also as the sole woman in the band. Billie felt she had to go through all this to set an example. If it could work for one black artist, others could make it too. She took it . . . until she collapsed.

Before that, she had appeared with another great band, that of Count Basie, and had suffered the reverse kind of humiliation, possibly even more stinging than what she had to endure in Shaw's band: Though Billie was as much a black as any of Basie's musicians, her skin color might have seemed too light to some customers and it was unthinkable at that time to present a white female singer with a black band. At a theater appearance in Detroit, Billie had to put on dark makeup.

In the last years of her life—she died at the age of forty-four in 1959—Billie Holiday's voice was often a mere shadow of her great days. She sang without the suppleness and glow of the earlier recordings; her voice sounded worn, rough, and old. Still, even then her singing had magnetic powers. It is extraordinary to discover just how much a great artist has left when voice and technique and flexibility have failed and nothing remains except the spiritual power of creativity and expression. To hear this on recordings made by Billie Holiday in the fifties is an almost eerie experience: a vocalist devoid of all the material and technical attributes of her profession who still remains a great artist.

Billie Holiday stands at the center of great jazz singing. After Holiday comes a host of female singers whose common denominator was, and still is, their application of Billie's accomplishments to the particular stylistic field to which they belong.

LADY DAY . . . BILLIE HOLIDAY
WILL FRIEDWALD

"One word from Holiday is worth a thousand pictures," writes the intensely analytical jazz critic and musicologist Will Friedwald about Billie in performance. The rarefied atmosphere of his writing and his musings about Billie Holiday serve, in effect, as a fine companion to this "companion" book. He concentrates very little on her drug addiction and related suffering. It's intriguing in the extreme that Friedwald can separate this singer's experience from her artistry. His emphasis makes his work unique.

This excerpt is drawn from his classic work, *Jazz Singing*, one of the rare histories of the art form. Friedwald has written a book, *Sinatra: The Song Is You*, focusing intensely on Frank Sinatra's musical achievements, published in 1995, and a few years before that, annotated a celebrated Nat King Cole collection issued by Mosaic Records. His articles have appeared in the *New York Times*, the *Village Voice*, the *New York Observer*, *Down Beat*, the *Wire* in London, and many other magazines and newspapers.

> "I cannot hide what I am: I must be sad when I have cause, and smile at no man's jest; eat when I have stomach, and wait for no man's leisure; sleep when I am drowsy, and tend to no man's business; laugh when I am merry and claw no man in his humour."
> —*Shakespeare, Much Ado About Nothing*

> "The whole basis of my singing is feeling. Unless I feel something, I can't sing."
> —*Billie Holiday, Lady Sings the Blues*

Billie Holiday's art is the kind that takes you deeper inside yourself and ultimately out again. . . .

Holiday creates a five-senses reality out of the lyric to a song, yet her abilities as a musician equal or surpass any "pure" instrumental improviser to work in jazz. To some, the actual tonal quality of her voice sounds off-center and requires effort to fathom its miraculous beauty; Fitzgerald makes melodies, whether a songwriter's or her own, soar through skies of aural heaven, and creates a no less effective, no less emotional kind of drama through purely musical means. While her voice, even on first hearing, is quite the loveliest in all music, it takes time to appreciate its depth.

Both are capable of slapstick comedy and epic tragedy* and all the gradations of feeling that fall between. Being true daughters of jazz, both can sing the blues, and both can swing—interpreting these foundation elements of the music no less personally than they do an individual song.

The swing era serves as a convenient nexus for both careers (who wouldn't trade in their CD players to have been there on that night in 1939 when Chick Webb "battled" Count Basie at the Savoy Ballroom in Harlem, with Fitzgerald and Holiday as competing canaries?). Fitzgerald, born in Virginia, in 1918, the first important victor of an Apollo Theatre amateur show, enjoyed a longtime collaboration with one of the most crucial of black bandleaders, Chick Webb. With Webb she landed a career-establishing hit ("A-Tisket, A-Tasket") very early on, and she even led the band for two years after Webb's death in 1939.

Holiday, born in Baltimore in 1915 (or earlier), worked on the fringes of the big-band epoch, although she toured with both Count Basie and Artie Shaw for just under a year apiece. The bread-and-butter recording work of early career—when she worked with bands that were not big, did not tour, and did not necessarily exist outside the studio—came through her original rabbi, John Hammond. He had first heard Holiday singing at a small Harlem club in 1933 and arranged for her debut session (vocal refrains with Benny Goodman's pretouring studio band); her long-running series of small-group dates under Teddy Wilson's leadership began two years later.

Apart from being the year in which Goodman discovered that large numbers of people would pay to dance to big-band swing, 1935 is also significant as the year, according to Frank Driggs, that saw the invention of the modern jukebox, a contraption that was to have great ramifications for jazz, the recording industry as a whole, and Billie Holiday in particular. Studio-only bands had produced acres of jazz and more conventional dance music in the twenties, though with the depression only a few

---

*I disagree with Martin Williams's assessment that Fitzgerald is incapable of tragedy.

sweeter in-house bandleaders carried on. The jukebox provided a shot in the arm for small bands just as Goodman launched the boom for big ones, and the "combo" records made largely for juke consumption differed from most jazz small-group recordings of other times (and other considerations, such as Artie Shaw and Goodman's band-within-a-band records) in their heavy emphasis on current pop tunes and vocals. They featured either a singing instrumentalist (Red Allen, Lionel Hampton, Wingy Manone, Louis Prima, Fats Waller, or, in England, Nat Gonella); an occasional band warbler (Fitzgerald, Helen Ward) on a small-group holiday along, perhaps, with some of her fellow sidemen; or in-house studio vocalists including three holdovers from the early electric years, Dick Robertson, Chick Bullock, and Red McKenzie, and relative newcomer Billie Holiday, either just on the date or getting top billing on the label.

For the rest of her career, Holiday raved about producer Bernie Hanighen for making possible for her the transition from "with vocal refrain by Billie Holiday" to "Billie Holiday and Her Orchestra," which made more of a career difference than a musical one. Except that her vocal usually comes first, Holiday was apparently only minimally more in charge than on the Wilson dates. As she explained in a 1955 interview with disc jockey Gordon Spencer, "I didn't lead, honey, we just sort of went in the studio. And here's Cozy Cole, here's Roy Eldridge, here's Billie Holiday, here's Teddy Wilson, here's Ben Webster, or here's Lester Young, and we got four sides to do. Now, the man that's running the studio says, 'I want a blues, I want a sweet tune, I want something that moves.' So I think, let's do 'Man I Love,' let's do 'All of Me,' let's do some blues in E flat. And that's the way it went, and we did it. No music, nobody's worried from nothin'. We'd get the beat and I'd say, 'Ben you make this introduction,' or Lester, you make the introduction,' or 'Teddy, you make the introduction,' and we get the tempo and we're gone!"

That the song publishers largely controlled the repertoire of these sessions has led many an ignorant commentator (most being far greater hacks than the songwriters they put down) to complain that the songs Holiday sings are unworthy of her. The jazz press has always tended to view the pop mainstream as an enemy, and while I can see doing this within one's own generation, to extend this pejorative judgment back fifty years is ludicrous—there are almost as many derivative critics who claim that Holiday, or Pops or Fats, turned "dross into gold" (a favorite phrase of Brit crits who can't quite comprehend American pop) as there are witless reviewers who think it droll to quote the opening line of Holiday's autobiography. In many ways, this is the same dog-brain logic that led as otherwise sensible a body as the Chicago AACM to ban all but original music from their performances—from Cole Porter to Sonny Rollins.

But listen, folks, those one-shot songs that Billie Holiday does are wonderful. Even party-line purists who don't care for pop, big bands, Broadway, or Busby Berkeley have to admit that Tin Pan Alley, at least before its standards were corrupted by the likes of Mitch Miller and Allen Freed, was one of the greatest friends jazz ever had, no less than the blues. Sure, Holiday improves on them, but no more than she does "They Can't Take That Away from Me" (1937, Vocalion) or "The Man I Love" (1939, Vocalion) or the way she turns standard blues material into performances as special as "Billie's Blues." What's more, these songs are precisely what this young singer needs to polish her chops. A few of the rhythm novelties, like "Swing, Brother, Swing" (1939, Vocalion) and "One, Two, Button Your Shoe" (1936, Vocalion) suggest Fitzgerald-style concentration on the riffish melodies while giving little attention to the somewhat minimal lyrics. But on a few very early quasi-ballads ("A Sunbonnet Blue" [1935, Vocalion]) she acts equally unconcerned with the narrative. Holiday grows out of this quickly, and the transition is something to hear. By 1936 she can make the most out of a parallel between a descending melody line and story line on "You Let Me Down" (literally!, Brunswick); by 1937 she's mastered conversational directness, making tune and libretto sound like a natural extension of speech on "It's Too Hot for Words" (again, an idea suggested by the song title, Brunswick). By 1938 she effortlessly communicates screwball comedy chutzpah in "Here It Is Tomorrow Again" (Brunswick).

Hammond, Hanighen, and Morty Palitz, who produced most of Holiday's jukebox-period records (for the ARC Corp.: Vocalion, Brunswick, and Okeh) from 1935 to the early forties, were already known as A&R men, meaning artists and repertoire men. While it's common critical currency to knock the "R," the "A" involved in these dates has long been accepted as one of their chief attributes. I've mentioned how her voice, sandwiched between instrumental solos, challenges the vocal refrain concept—in which everything else stops while the canary indulges herself—by desegregating players and singers. You might call her voice hornlike, but I think it's more a matter of sharing common concepts of rhythm and phrasing (how melodies are divided up into breath-sized chunks) with her fellow musicians. Trumpeter Buck Clayton, trombonist Benny Morton, and tenor man Ben Webster all share Holiday's warm and very human vibrato, and their improvisations on the chord changes are just as valid dramatically as Holiday's melodic and dramatic embellishments make sense musically (her extension of the interval between "of" and "you" in "The Way You Look Tonight," for instance [1936, Brunswick]). "In the good old days of Billie," Joe Williams explained to Leonard Feather, "the soloists would wait until there was a space and play something that would corroborate the vocal statement." As Holiday asserts in "Getting Some Fun Out of Life" (1937, Vocalion), when she wants to sing, she sings.

The musicians on these sides function as collaborators more than sidemen, none more so than Lester Young. "Lady Day . . . is the last word," Jimmy Rushing once told Burt Korall. She admired Lester Young so [much] that she used to play his records over and over to get the phrasing." The ninety minutes or so of recorded sound they produced together stands as a milestone in Western music, from Bach to Mozart to Ornette. Holiday's round, chubby voice (which matches the zaftig young Billie captured in contemporary snapshots) and her off-center way of attacking the beat so perfectly matches Young's feathery alto-tenor (his own term) tone, strikingly original melodic concept, alternately languorous legato, and ferociously up-tempo use of time. You can sense they had an understanding of each other far beyond what musical terminology or metaphoric imagery can describe. It's beyond mere obbligato, even on the level of Armstrong and Bessie Smith, beyond matched vibrato, a level of understanding of which I can find no counterpart, which happened only this once. Almost everyone who knew them has taken pains to assure us that they were not lovers, including Holiday herself. "Lester likes to eat good home cooking, so I took him home to Mom one night," she told Gordon Spencer. "So, Lester moved in and he was like her son." (But, like John O'Hara on the death of Gershwin, I don't have to believe that if I don't want to.) Like "The Chink and the Child" in D. W. Griffith's *Broken Blossoms*, Holiday and Young were two miraculously kindred souls who found in each other shelter from a world of violence and brutality.

After taking the art of collaboration to its zenith, it's no wonder Holiday's next series of recordings, made for Milt Gabler's Commodore label from 1939 to 1944 (which began because of ARC's refusal to record the controversial "Strange Fruit" and dovetailed with her last few years under contract to that corporation), reinstate her voice at the center of attention, demoting the musicians back to humble accompanists. Beginning with the overdramatic but startlingly effective "Strange Fruit" (1939, Commodore), Holiday experiments with slightly suppressing her melodic embellishment as a means to turn lyrics into personal videos of the mind. If you're in the right frame of mind, any reasonably competent singer can make you sad with a tender ballad or spiteful with a vindictive blues, but only Holiday can take Jerome Kern's rather stately "Yesterdays" (1939) and make it swing gently while at the same time retaining its drama, and only Holiday can take Oscar Hammerstein's deliberately archaic (full of backward constructions) and somewhat pompous lyric (forsooth!) and make it breathe; only she can make you visualize the waterfront she covers in search of the one she loves, only she can implant in your mind the horrifically powerful image of lynch mob victims hanging from the trees like so much strange fruit. One word from Holiday is worth a thousand pictures.

In the early forties Holiday put the finishing touch on her art of the minuscule. Even the tiniest of nuances assumes epic grandeur; the lightest of inflections takes on tremendous significance (and films and TV appearances reveal that she moved not more physically). Her mastery of time grew stronger, as she had perfected the dramatic effect of dropping behind the beat for disconcerted off-balance feeling and then shifting back on top of it, and maintaining control at superslow tempi. As early as parts of 1936's "Pennies from Heaven" and "The Way You Look Tonight" (both Brunswick), and by the Commodore recordings, she worked some ballads in half time, making the audience hang on to every syllable. "How Am I to Know?" becomes simultaneously a heavy and a light dirge, Dorothy Parker's poignant question going unanswered by the horns in the background, who sidestep conventional harmonic support to sort of comment softly on the action like a Greek chorus.

Though Gabler ran the pure-jazz Commodore label out of his own pocket, by this time he had a "day job" at Decca Records where he was trusted to bring potential hits to their attention. Already having a good track record with Holiday's big seller for Commodore, "Fine and Mellow" backed with "Strange Fruit," Gabler smelled money in the song "Lover Man" and brought both it and Holiday to the big label, which was better able to afford Holiday's then-surprising request for a string section. Gabler's instincts proved correct, and both he and Holiday remained at Decca for six years.

As the informality of the jukebox years deferred to the high drama of the Commodores, the stark, open spaces of the Commodores would soon be filled by strings and occasional choirs; you'd think they'd curtail Holiday's creativity, but she finds sweet uses of adversity in any situation. To my ears, she gets friskier when the strings behind her ensure a serious tone, whereas on the earlier "I'll Be Seeing You" (1944, Commodore) she seems compelled to take the tempo as slow as she can possibly stretch it without stopping altogether and to restrict her melodic playfulness for fear of breaking the spell (she didn't have to worry, but Gabler was the good witch who let her find out for herself).

In spite of a few middle-brow misfires, largely bought on by the presence of arranger Gordon Jenkins, who simultaneously put the anal in banal but also the taste in tasteful, Holiday's forties sessions mark the most entertaining and polished in her whole career. Surprises abound in this underappreciated period, appearing along with the Holiday trademarks she's taught us to expect, just as her playful, melodious lines are both interrupted and accentuated by her emphasizing dramatically appropriate words in offbeat ways: Never has the word "cute" sounded legitimately cuter or "flirting" more flirtatious than on "Them There Eyes" (the soft vowel squeezed like a mustachioed nightclubber getting fresh with a cigarette girl), and the brisk, somewhat wacky tempo she and arranger Sy Oliver ascribe to it typifies the period. Even most of the ballads ("What Is This Thing Called Love?," "Crazy He Calls Me," "Good Morning Heartache") come rolling out faster than anyone else could do them and still touch you, "Solitude" surprisingly taking the original Ellington medium-retard tempo (and Ducal muted brass) as a model. She reserves the more traditional real slow speeds for the two least traditional numbers, her definitive "Porgy" and "My Man," from her sole rhythm-section-only session for Decca (1948). Both songs depict a woman looking for love (no amount of pronoun substitution would render them suitable for a man to sing), and neither uses the standard AABA structure, following their twisting trails into unexpected new patches of melody; both keep going where a conventional pop song just stops. She travels (to quote another song by Gershwin) the music's bumpy road to love way down into the dark depths on the flipside of romance's dizzy heights, beyond the blatant masochism—at once archaic and modern—of the lyrics, to unearth truths even bleaker and more unsettling.

In the second chorus of the above "Them There Eyes," Holiday's audacious mood puts on the gloves and goes a few rounds back and forth with Oliver's pugnacious, blustering ensemble (at times its roughness anticipates Lester Bowie's Brass Fantasy). The same brashness and exuberance pervades her blues-oriented numbers of the forties, practically the only ones in her career *not* to use her stock "Fine and Mellow"/"Billie's Blues" pattern. Both "Now or Never" and "Baby, Get Lost" could have been played by Lionel Hampton for the R&B-style rowdiness, invective lyric, and climactic stop-time episodes, and her minicycle of Bessie Smith homages in 1949 touches on this same raucousness. She "covered" (to use a rock 'n' roll term) four Smith classics: one pairing, "T'ain't Nobody's

Business" and "Keeps on A-Rainin'" from 1923, the beginning of Smith's recording career; and another from the end in 1933, "Do Your Duty" and "Gimme a Pigfoot." Slight lyric modernizations update the specifics of these songs; in "Gimme a Pigfoot," what the folks up in Harlem do on a Saturday night is described by the bebop figure "Klook-a-mop" rather than "tut-tut-tut," and they're too busy doing "The Hucklebuck," a popular dance modeled on Charlie Parker's "Now's the Time," to be bothered by the arresting officers when the wagon comes (the old-fashioned reefers are omitted altogether—now they partake in unmentionable substances). However, Holiday shares Smith's jaunty defiance, underscoring her right to do as she pleases, whether that means something we can sympathize with sixty years after Bessie and forty years after Billie (sexual service in "Do Your Duty," hell-raising in "Pigfoot") or not (more masochism and wife-beating in "T'ain't Nobody's Business").

The forties also saw Holiday's greatest flowering as a songwriter, and considering that music has produced only a few individuals who can both sing and write (Mel Torme and Lee Wiley are two others), it's unfortunate that this aspect of her work hasn't received more attention. After her first triumph with the socially conscious "Strange Fruit," she penned one of the most effective of all torch songs, "Don't Explain," and then "God Bless the Child." Not a religious song but a song about religion that's both sacred and profane, it describes, in poetically abstract fashion, how man's knowledge of God has no effect on his treatment of other men. Arranger Gordon Jenkins either thought it was a hymn or, knowing of his formidable (if not always well-applied) smarts, wanted you to think he thought it was hymn, for in addition to backing her with a bleached-out Protestant choir, he put the ersatz-sacral "This Is Heaven to Me" on the disc's B side.

Along with the standout "Crazy He Calls Me" and her two scrumptious duets with Louis Armstrong, these signify her last days at Decca. After the death of Jack Kapp, the corporation demoted two of his producers, Gabler and Kapp's brother Dave, and dropped many of their black artists, including R&B stars Buddy Johnson, Louis Jordan, and Billie Holiday. She made no studio dates at all (excepting a one-shot session for Aladdin Records memorable for the only "official" version of "Detour Ahead") until going to work for Norman Granz in 1952.

The operative word for her last seven years is erratic. Too unpredictable an artist to provide those who would cop out critically with a simple cutoff date, Holiday does work that varies wildly from session to session (the same holds true for Tony Bennett and Frank Sinatra today, but, my God, they're twenty and thirty years older than Holiday!). The first Granz date in March 1952 sounds as if twenty years have passed, not just two, since the final Decca in March 1950, but the July 1952 session captures a vastly rejuvenated set of chops. On August 14, 1956, she's at her absolute peak, turning in a "Speak Low" that puts all other versions to shame (she's the only one who gets full effect from Ogden Nash's magnificent bridge, making "time" sound genuinely "old" and "love" truly "brief"), but on the next date, four days later she sounds as if she's spent the whole time on a sleepless bender. And then there are her three extant television appearances. Her masterpiece blues "Fine and Mellow" from CBS's "The Sound of Jazz" in December 1957 captures the fullest, most perfect Holiday you can imagine, while the two July 1958 "Art Ford Jazz Party" shows reveal a great artist in decline. The voice is thinner, but we don't notice it as much because we're too absorbed by her emaciated figure, her ribs fairly sticking through a loose summer dress. Bearing this in mind, as well as the knowledge that she dies in July 1959, you'd expect Holiday to resemble a walking skeleton on her February 1959 BBC-TV performance. Instead, we get the full-voiced, full-control, full-figured Holiday of the old days. The skeleton, however, as photographed by bassist-historian Milt Hinton, returns on her last studio date (MGM) one week later: with zero windpower, every breath sounds like it might be her last. Not to say this album, *Billie Holiday*, isn't worth hearing, or worth hearing for reasons more substantial than Sinatra—*Only the Lonely*—like wrist-slashing nihilism, for Holiday interlaces the prevailing mode of despair with the most faintly discernible traces of defiance and even hope, flowers sprouting in a graveyard.

Many of Holiday's most sublimely perfect moments come from her last seven years. A&R-wise, she and Granz appropriately picked and chose from her own past, remaking the best of her previously recorded songs in definitive versions, and drawing upon both ARC-style small groups with heavyweight soloists as collaborator-accompanists on most of the Clef/Verves and strings on her last two albums (for Columbia and MGM), as well as any number of tempo gradations between the crawl speeds of the Commodores and the brisker ballads of the later forties. Instead of sandwiching her vocals between instrumental solos, here her beginning and ending choruses frame their statements, these being full two- or three-chorus LP-era outings as opposed to the terse thirty-two or sixteen-bar one-liners of her thirties 78s. Though these four- and five-minute dramas all use the same script (usually vocal-solos-vocal) and the same cast (trumpet, sax, four rhythm) and the same ending (one note sliding down into another), never once do they get repetitious or fail to command our attention.

Granz deserves praise for assigning Holiday to do virtually all the classic

American songs of the "Golden Years" from 1925 to 1945, though Holiday rarely ventured far afield from her rather small established repertoire on extant live performances (the same ten or so songs over and over!). Granz made a mistake in not including any of the worthwhile new tunes of the postwar era (what she could have done with "Teach Me Tonight" or "Along the Way") and also in not letting her record with Mal Waldron, the last of the great Holiday pianists (after Teddy Wilson, Bobby Tucker, and Jimmy Rowles), whose sensitive, post-Monk shading of mood and time made him the perfect partner for Holiday's twilight years.

Still, there's morbidness in some of her later work, which developed partly out of her successful exploitation of her personal life. After the minor scandal that followed her arrest and internment on a narcotics charge, seekers of cheap thrills began to flock to her appearances (for the same reason that Robert Mitchum's star rose after the bulls caught him with cigarettes that had no printing on them). When writer William Dufty put together a brief biography, *Lady Sings the Blues*, based on interviews with Holiday, illegitimacy, prostitution, and inconceivably nasty abuse from husbands added to the mounting list of Holiday horrors (as a child she's forever trapped with corpses). To read it without knowing Holiday's music is to agree with Robert Reisner's portrait of Holiday as a "professional sufferer."

Yet even on the surface there's more than suffering in her work; laughter abounds as much as tears. As one of many wildly confessional autobiographies in jazz (not as fine a piece of literature as the more Augustinian *Mr. Jelly Roll* or *Straight Life*), it doesn't nearly depict her struggles with racism as vividly as her singing of her own lyrics to "Strange Fruit" or abusive husbands as well as "Don't Explain." Nonetheless, from its supermarket-tabloid shock value opening line to its more revealing closer (a quote from her oft-sung French Apache sop to masochism, "My Man"), it's a compelling read, and perhaps even helped exorcise more traces of "poor me" attitude out of Holiday's system.

Holiday didn't have to suffer on either an amateur or professional level; two in-depth studies, John Chilton's well-documented biography, *Billie's Blues*, and John Jeremy's mesmerizing BBC documentary, *The Long Night of Lady Day*,* leave one with the impression that much of her pain was voluntary, that she had never worked to find a way of life that

---

*Mesmerizing if you get the right version: the one released commercially in Japan being more effective, with more music and less yammer-yammer than the one edited for American TV.

didn't include it (other remarks to the contrary, suffering is no more essential to great singing than heroin). Perhaps her agony was inflicted because of the unwritten laws she violated, a single all-important rule of popular music. Before Holiday, the pop song was a harmless medium. Even when its lyrics had acid in their veins and its melodies stinging wit, the form itself was escapist and unreal; originally, pop songsmiths felt compelled not to make their wares more complicated than amateurs could play or sing. Holiday changed all that. Armstrong had made great music with a pop foundation by transcending the songs, Al Bowlly made them work for him by fine-tuning his own naïveté to match theirs, but Holiday made her songs real by depriving them of their innocence. After Holiday, pop singing could never go home again.

THE GREAT AMERICAN POPULAR SINGERS
HENRY PLEASANTS

Published in 1974, Pleasants's book stands as one of the earliest and most interesting books on the art of jazz and popular singing. In his chapter on Billie, he attempts to analyze her autobiography, her life, and her art. He finds the book's validity lies in the impressions it delivers about her. Her version of the facts is less important than the way she expresses herself. The same idea can be applied to her singing style. And as a great French writer once said about a writer's style, "Le style, c'est l'homme"—the style is the man.

Born in Philadelphia, Henry Pleasants studied at the Curtis Institute there. He then spent the rest of his life writing music criticism for newspapers such as the *International Herald Tribune* with headquarters in Paris, France, and music periodicals such as *Stereo Review* in the United States. Among his other books have been *The Great Singers: From the Dawn of Opera to Our Own Time*, *The Agony of Modern Music*, and *Serious Music—And All That Jazz*. With his wife, Virginia Pleasants, a harpsichordist, Mr. Pleasants settled in London, where he now lives in retirement.

Certain leads or opening sentences to articles or books stick in one's mind. I have always remembered and cherished, for example, the opening sentence of Rafael Sabatini's *Scaramouche*: "He was born with the fit of laughter and a sense that the world was mad." It was my favorite until I opened Billie Holiday's *Lady Sings the Blues* and read: "Ma and Pop were just a couple of kids when they got married. He was eighteen, she was sixteen, and I was three."

This was more than just a flip gambit. It established immediately the setting and background for one of the most troubled careers in the annals of American music. The book traces, with significant candor, not only the professional life of a great singer, but also a sordid history of adolescent prostitution and subsequent drug addiction, the scene switching back and forth between more or less prestigious nightclubs, supper clubs, theaters and auditoriums to police courts, reformatories, sanatoriums and jails.

Billie Holiday made a lot of news, most of it bad. She made and spent a lot of money. Her two-hundred-odd records constitute a legacy of much that was finest in her era of jazz, a precious documentation of her own unique art as a singer and of the art of the splendid musicians, both white and black, who worked with her. But it was her losing struggle with adversity, bad luck, and personal weaknesses and inadequacies, rather than her hoarsely eloquent voice and her way with a phrase or a song, that made her a legend in her own time.

She is to be numbered among the self-destructive waifs of modern musical history, along with Mildred Bailey, Bix Beiderbecke, Judy Garland, Charlie Parker, Edith Piaf, Bessie Smith and Hank Williams. They were all gifted beyond the lot even of those destined to become the most accomplished professionals. But they were denied the compensatory attributes of self-knowledge and self-discipline, prerequisites for survival in the merciless world of show biz. Toward the end of Billie Holiday's career, a magazine asked her for the "real lowdown inside story of her life." She summed it up in a single sentence. "I wish," she wrote, in *Lady Sings the Blues*, "I knew it myself."

She didn't know it. but both her book, written with William Dufty, and her work on records offer clues. From the book, for example:

It's a wonder my mother didn't end up in the workhouse and me as a foundling. But Sadie Fagan loved me from the time I was just a swift kick in the ribs while she scrubbed floors. She went to the hospital and made a deal with the head woman there. She's told them she'd scrub floors and wait on the other bitches laying up there to have their kids so she could pay her way and mine. And she did. Mom was thirteen that Wednesday, April 7, 1915, in Baltimore, when I was born.

It is an eloquent paragraph, not just because it tells a story of desperate nobility so simply and so affectionately, but also because it projects succinctly and ingeniously the juxtaposition of feigned or ingrained toughness and vulgarity on the one hand, and on the other, the real pride and tenderness that characterized and complicated Billie Holiday's public and private performance throughout the forty-four years of her life.

Her vocabulary was as unoriginal and unimaginative as it was coarse. Women were bitches, girls were chicks, lesbians were dikes, musicians were cats, money was loot, whores were whores and policemen were fuzz. To be arrested was to be busted. This from the singer who was known throughout most of her professional life as Lady Day, or Lady, for short.

Her Christian name was Eleanora, but her father, Clarence Holiday, a jazz musician, called her Bill because she was such a tomboy. She changed it to Billie after Billie Dove, her idol on the silent-movie screens of her childhood. "Lady" was conferred upon her early in public career by the other girls at Jerry Preston's Log Cabin in Harlem when she refused to pick up tips from customers' tables without using her hands. Lester Young, then playing tenor in Fletcher Henderson's band, and who later played some of his most beautiful choruses behind her, combined it with the "day" of Holiday to make Lady Day. She returned the compliment by calling him "Prez," thus putting him on a pedestal alongside another of her idols, President Roosevelt.

Max Jones, veteran critic of *Melody Maker*, saw behind the mask when he met her, wrapped from head to toe in blue mink, at a London airport in 1954. "She was outspoken, bright, tough and transparently sincere most of the time," he wrote not long afterwards. "She was obviously an imposing woman, an inch or two taller than I had expected, with a strong, well-boned face and a lot of natural magnetism and dignity."

The operative word is *dignity*. She had it. She could not always sustain it, least of all when it was overlooked, ignored, offended or defied by others. Thanks in part, no doubt, to an Irish (Fagan) great-grandfather on her mother's side, she had a low boiling point. Exposed to real or imagined slights, she could respond in an undignified fashion, sometimes with her fists, sometimes with any hard movable object within reach.

Louis Armstrong characterized her for the benefit of the producer, director and stage crew on the set of *New Orleans* in Hollywood in 1946, when Lady Day, unhappy at being cast as a maid, but unable to escape her contract, broke into tears. "Better look out," said Pops. "I know Lady, and when she starts crying, the next thing she's going to do is start fighting."

Many elements in the Billie Holiday story recall the career of Ethel

Waters. Both were children of the Northern slums. Both were born illegitimately to slum children, and both were grownups before they were even properly adolescent. Ethel was first married, it will be recalled, when she was thirteen. Billie was raped when she was ten. Both did menial work, Ethel as scullery- and chambermaid, Billie scrubbing the famous white steps of Baltimore's brick row houses. Both served a rough, tough apprenticeship as singers in the swinging gin mills of prohibition Harlem.

More significantly, perhaps, both tasted Jim Crow under circumstances more galling, even, than those experienced by their less renowned black contemporaries. They had to endure the outrage of being admired, even loved, by whites as artists while being directed to the tradesmen's entrance and excluded from hotels, dining rooms and restaurants as persons. They earned well. They were accorded many privileges normally denied black Americans at that time. But their apparent good fortune only made the facts of black life seem blacker.

Billie Holiday had an especially grueling time of it as the first black vocalist to be featured with a white band. The year was 1938. The band was Artie Shaw's. As she remembered it nearly twenty years later:

> It wasn't long before the roughest days with the Basie band began to look like a breeze. It got to the point where I hardly ever ate, slept or went to the bathroom without having a major NAACP-type production.
>
> Most of the cats in the band were wonderful to me, but I got so tired of scenes in crummy roadside restaurants over getting served, I used to beg Georgie Auld, Tony Pastor and Chuck Peterson to just let me sit in the bus and rest—and let them bring out something in a sack. Some places they wouldn't even let me eat in the kitchen. Sometimes it was choice between me eating and the whole band starving. I got tired of having a federal case over breakfast, lunch and dinner.

Continual humiliation on this order left both Billie and Ethel, to use their own terminology, salty. Ethel was the stronger character of the two, certainly the more self-reliant. Billie fought, and fought hard, both against society and against the person that society had made of her. But there was something pathetic about the performance. The odds against her were too great.

Lena Horne came to know her well in New York in the early 1940s, when Billie was working at Kelly's Stable and Lena at Café Society Downtown, and as she remembered her in *Lena*:

Her life was so tragic and so corrupted by other people—by white people and her own people. There was no place for her to go, except, finally, into that little private world of dope. She was just too sensitive to survive. And such a gentle person. We never talked much about singing. The thing I remember talking to her about most was her dogs; her animals were really her only trusted friends.

Small wonder that she was, as an admiring white singer once said of her to me, "a hard one to get through to."

Her career and Ethel Waters', after Harlem, differed considerably and significantly. Their respective ages had something to do with it. Ethel, twenty years older than Billie, was early enough on the scene to make a career in both black and white vaudeville, a preparation that revealed the talent and established the professional accomplishments for her subsequent triumphs as an actress in *Mamba's Daughters* and *The Member of the Wedding*.

Ethel was, in any case, far more a woman of the theater than Lady Day, not only in terms of experience, but also in terms of disposition and predilection, and it showed in her singing. In just about every song that Ethel Waters ever sang she projected a character. Hers was, indeed, an art of characterization, whether she was playing a part or singing a song. Billie Holiday never projected anybody but Billie. This was reflected even in her stage deportment. She had no routine. As Martin Williams remembered her in an article for *Jazz Journal*, "Billie Holiday—Actress Without an Act," "she came out, sang, bowed and left—no vaudeville showmanship."

The article is misleading only in the title. It might better have been called "An Act Without an Actress." But it wasn't even an act—discounting the white dress, the white gardenia and, as she ruefully appended to her own description of her stage appearance, the white junk. It was just Lady Day, who was Billie Holiday. Her way with a song was to take it apart and put it together again in her own image.

Even the image would change with the circumstances of the moment and according to her mood and passing fancy. "I hate straight singing," she used to say. "I have to change a tune to my way of doing it. That's all I know." Her way of doing it changed, too: "I can't stand to sing the same song the same way two nights in succession, let alone two years to ten years. If you can, then it ain't music; it's close-order drill, or exercise, or yodeling or something, not music."

There were other reasons why she changed the music. She had to fit a song not only to herself, to her state of mind and body, and to an extraordinarily acute sense of style, but also to a meager voice—small, hoarse at the bottom and thinly shrill at the top, with top and bottom never very far apart. She had hardly more than an octave and a third. She worked, as a rule, as Bessie Smith had worked, within an octave, tailoring the melody to fit the congenial span.

Given these physical limitations, what she achieved in terms of color, shadings, nuances and articulation, and in terms of the variety of sound and inflection she could summon from such slender resources, may be counted among the wonders of vocal history. She did it by moving, with somnambulistic security, along—or back and forth across—the thin, never precisely definable, line separating, or joining speech and song.

This accomplishment, or ambiguity, has always been characteristic of the greatest blues singers. In this respect, Billie Holiday was a child of Bessie Smith, although she rarely sang a traditional blues. Her 1936 recording of "Billie's Blues" gives us a glimpse of what a blues singer she might have been had she chosen to be one.

Playing back to back the records made by Ethel Waters and Billie Holiday at about the same time in the early 1930s, one notes how much closer Ethel Waters was to Broadway. She was more versatile, more professional and, stylistically, whiter. Ethel was of a generation of black vaudeville and recording artists greatly influenced by the white headliners of the time—Nora Bayes, Ruth Etting, Al Jolson and Sophie Tucker. Played today, her records sound a bit dated. They are certainly easy to date.

In those years, Billie Holiday, then in her late teens and early twenties, seemed untouched by Broadway and show biz. She probably was. The only vocal models she ever acknowledged were Bessie Smith and Louis Armstrong. As a child in an East Baltimore slum, she had run errands for a whorehouse madam just to be allowed to sit in the front parlor and listen to Louis and Bessie on the Victrola. "Unless it was the records of Bessie Smith and Louis Armstrong I heard as a kid," she recalled later, "I don't know anybody who actually influenced my singing, then or now. I always wanted Bessie's big sound and Pops' feeling." Lady Day was probably entitled to say, as she did, that "before anybody could compare me with other singers, they were comparing other singers with me."

Bessie's big sound she never had, nor do her records suggest that she tried for it. She may have belted a bit in the very early days, working without a mike in Harlem clubs. But hers was not a voice that would have responded generously or amiably to the kind of treatment that Bessie's voice rewarded with that big sound. On records and on mike in clubs, Billie's breath was wonderfully light on the vocal cords, which is why a voice neither rich in texture nor ample in size could be so eloquently tender. This lightness of the breath on the cords also contributed to immaculate enunciation, as it has with subsequent singers, notably Nat Cole, Ella Fitzgerald, Peggy Lee and Frank Sinatra.

Louis' feeling she had, and then some, although one wonders what precisely she meant by "Pops' feeling." It can hardly have been feeling in an emotional sense, for Louis' involvement with any song was always more a matter of exuberant and affectionate virtuosity than of personal commitment. She may have meant his feeling for words and phrases, and his way of shaping, or reshaping, a song to suit his own musicality. In this she equaled and may even have surpassed the master.

Louis can be heard in just about every phrase Billie ever sang. His example is conspicuous in her way of wrapping a sound around a word or syllable, enveloping it, so to speak, in an *appoggiatura*, a slur, a mordent or a turn, in her habit of widening the vibrato during the life of a sustained tone. But what was musical fun and games to Louis Armstrong, who lived the better part of his seventy years at peace with the world, was life in the raw to Billie Holiday. What you had when she finished with a song was not just invention tempered by superb craftsmanship, although there was plenty of each, but untempered autobiography.

Lady Sings the Blues, when it appeared in 1956, three years before her death, was welcomed as a recital of the facts of her life—or at least some of the facts—but regretted for its failure to reveal much of the woman behind the facts. It did, indeed, fail in this respect. But the failure was inconsequential. Anyone who has heard Billie Holiday sing, in person or on record, "Strange Fruit," "God Bless the Child," "Come Rain or Come Shine," "Don't Explain" or "Prelude to a Kiss" does not need to look for her in a ghostwritten autobiography. "She, of all singers in jazz," wrote Max Jones, "laid herself most bare when she sang; and it was primarily this raw, human quality, communicated through her voice and her technique, which troubled the hearts and minds of her listeners."

What little voice Billie ever had deteriorated toward the end of her life. In her progress along the dividing line between speech and sustained melody she wandered more often, and ever farther, in the direction of speech. She also tended to wander farther and farther from pitch. She favored ever slower tempi. She was always a languorous singer except in out-and-out up-tempo songs, in which she could achieve and sustain astonishing speeds. Listening to the records she made in the mid-1950s, I am always reminded of George Bernard Shaw's description of Lady Hallé, in London, setting a tempo for the first movement of the Beethoven Septet "at about two-thirds of the lowest speed needed to sustain life." Lady Hallé's tempo may have been prompted by either conviction or discretion. Billie's tempi, on some occasions, at least, were probably dictated by vocal insecurity. But generally they would seem to have been determined by her lifelong love affair with words.

She herself preferred her later records to the earlier ones, and not without reason. She had learned a lot, both about life and about her own singing. She was more resourceful. Her ornamentation was richer and more varied. The voice, formerly weak at the bottom, now had lovely dark tones down to the low G and F and even below.

"Anybody who knows anything about singing," she wrote at that time, "says I'm for sure singing better than I ever have in my life. If you don't think so, just listen to some of my old sides like 'Lover Come Back' and 'Yesterdays,' and then listen to the same tunes as I have recorded them in recent years. Listen, and trust your own ears."

She was probably right. But speaking for myself, and probably for others, I find that the earlier records have an imperishable charm, especially those she made with Teddy Wilson and a number of upcoming studio sidemen at the very beginning of her recording career. While she had not then the artistic accomplishment of a later time, the raw material was there, and the genius too, a spontaneous, original, fearless and irresistible way with voice and song.

There was something special about the backings, too, both in those early recordings and in those of a few years later, after she had established her association with the Count Basie band in 1937. Her work with the Basie men remained the happiest memory of her recording career, and her recollection of it offers a delightful and fascinating insight into how records were made in those days:

> Most of my experience with bands before then had been in hanging out with Benny Goodman. I used to listen to him rehearse with high-paid radio studio bands and his own groups. He always had big arrangements. He would spend a fortune on arrangements for a little dog-assed vocalist. But with Basie we had something no expensive arrangements could touch. The cats would come in, somebody would hum a tune. Then someone else would play it over on the piano once or twice. Then someone would set up a riff, a ba-deep, a ba-dop. Then Daddy Basie would two finger it a little. And then things would start to happen.

Half the cats couldn't have read music if they'd had it. They didn't want to be bothered anyway. Maybe sometimes one cat would bring in a written arrangement, and the others would run over it. But by the time Jack Wadlin, Skeet Henderson, Buck Clayton, Freddie Green and Basie were through running over it, taking off, changing it, the arrangement wouldn't be recognizable anyway.

I know that's the way we worked out "Love of My Life" and "Them There Eyes" for me. Everything that happened, happened by ear. For the two years I was with the band we had a book of a hundred songs, and everyone of us carried every last damn note of them in our heads.

Billie herself could not read music. Her art might have survived literacy. But it would have gained nothing from it. What she heard in her mind's ear and translated into vocal utterance had nothing to do with the notes on a printed page. Nor has it come down to us in any printed form. Even her records account for only a part of her musical estate. Hear it from one whose art has been an embodiment of her legacy:

With few exceptions [wrote Frank Sinatra in an article for *Ebony*] every major pop singer in the United States during her generation has been touched in some way by her genius. It is Billie Holiday, whom I first heard in 52nd Street clubs in the early 30s, who was, and still remains, the greatest single musical influence on me.

He had not changed his mind fifteen years later. An album released just after the announcement of his retirement in the spring of 1971, and recorded in October of 1970, includes a song called "Lady Day"—a tribute to Billie Holiday.

She would have been pleased.

THERE WAS NO MIDDLE GROUND WITH BILLIE HOLIDAY
LESLIE GOURSE

At the time this was written in 1982, the most appealing book on Billie, for the reader who was not a stickler for veracity, was her own *Lady Sings the Blues,* and the most ambitious for accuracy was *Billie's Blues* by John Chilton. The Linda Kuehl tapes, which spawned the intriguing study, *Billie Holiday: The Many Faces of Lady Day,* and a graphic emotionally exhilarating and depressing biography, *Wishing on the Moon*, weren't available. The best sources of information were Billie's old friends, among them first and foremost Bobby Tucker, and also Buck Clayton, Mal Waldron, Sylvia Syms, Helen Forrest, Carmen McRae, Barney Josephson, Etta Jones, Patti Bown, and Big Nick Nicholas. Photographer Raymond Ross was a friend of Louis McKay, Billie's last husband.

The chapter exists because of the kindness and perceptiveness of those people and others who knew Billie. Many times as I was writing the book on jazz singing history, including the chapter on Billie, I turned to listening to her recordings for a thrill, for a reminder of the most inspired jazz singing, and, oddly enough, considering the turmoil of her life, for my own peace of mind. I think my closing remarks in the chapter, about the legion of protégées who constantly reanimate her, put her legacy into perspective.

Bobby Tucker has corrected me about the night Billie started wearing a gardenia. The hat check girl at the club provided it for her, not Sylvia Syms. But Sylvia, sitting the hat check booth, probably witnessed the action.

"Originality should be the highest goal . . . without it, art or anything else stagnates and eventually degenerates,"* said Lester Young, who played tenor saxophone as languidly as Billie Holiday sang.

Unlike Young, who could sing the praises of his soft-toned, articulately original music, Billie Holiday reacted instinctively, stunned by artistic criticism and racial persecution. She and Lester Young were musical "soul mates," one of the finest teams in jazz. And they were kindred spirits in despondency. Both drank themselves to death in the late 1950s. But Billie's excesses were not the source of her misery. She emerged from a childhood of crushing abuse, armed only with a potent voice and a slender memory of an affectionate grandmother, and found that a great number of people disliked her singing style. It was not commercial. The world abused her, too, as a black and as a woman. So she tranquilized herself with drugs against the memories and the ongoing brutal experiences. Eventually she switched from heroin to alcohol, which gave her cirrhosis of the liver. Weakened by alcoholism, she died of a kidney infection at age forty-four.

Much of what was written about her is inaccurate, her friends have said. She beclouded her own autobiography to make it commercial.

*From *Billie's Blues*, by John Chilton.

Furthermore, she didn't come under close scrutiny as a cult figure and a musical innovator until after her death. Bobby Tucker, her good friend and accompanist in the late 1940s, before and after she served a jail sentence for drugs, has discounted the veracity of her autobiography with its attention-getting opening paragraph: "Mom and Dad were just a couple of kids when they got married. He was eighteen, she was fifteen, and I was three." Tucker himself intuitively preferred not to ask questions about the truth.

John Chilton wrote *Billie's Blues*, a postmortem biography as accurate as anything published about her personal life. Friends and acquaintances have shed some light on aspects of Miss Holiday, called Lady Day or simply Lady by her friends, a title conferred by Lester "Prez" Young. (She in turn gave him his title, "President of the Tenor Saxophone.")

In her autobiography, not Chilton's work, Billie said that her mother left Baltimore to find work in the North. Billie, a young girl at the time, stayed in the care of an aunt and vicious cousins who abused her. An affectionate grandmother died in Billie's arms. Eventually her mother, Sadie Fagan, returned to Baltimore and took Billie to live with her. The father, Clarence Holiday, a guitarist, had been long gone from the scene, leaving Sadie and Eleonora (Billie's real name) to fend for themselves. Billie took her stage name from Billie Dove, an actress.

She began her métier by cleaning the steps of a local whorehouse, and as payment, she listened to the house's records of Bessie Smith and Louis Armstrong. Other sources say Billie worked in the house as a prostitute. As a child, she had already been raped by a neighbor and sent to jail for his crime, accused of enticing him. Her mother remarried a dockworker briefly. But he was killed in an accident on the job. Probably traumatized and bereft, Sadie never remarried. Then that elusive, or in any case inconsistent, mother left for the North again.

Billie followed but didn't join Sadie right away. Billie tried her luck for a while as a maid and then as a prostitute. When she and her mother met again, Sadie maintained an exploitative attitude toward Billie, perceiving the teenager in part as a meal ticket, according to Billie's autobiography. Billie occasionally importuned Clarence Holiday for money at stage doors—to his chagrin. Billie grew to be a tall, stately teenager, and for a while weighed about two hundred pounds. Finally, desperate for money, with her mother sick in bed, Billie looked for work as a dancer in a Harlem club, she said. She danced pathetically, then started to sing. That was how she got her first paying job as a singer, Billie reported, though Chilton's book said musicians remembered her singing professionally at joints around New York City before the Harlem gig.

Billie began attracting attention right away. John Hammond, with a great eye and ear for talent, discovered her at another club and pushed for record dates. She was booked at the Apollo Theater. John Chilton wrote of her stage presence: "The sight of this tall, buxom, beautiful girl with the exquisite coloring was enough to make any neck swivel. On looks alone, Billie was potential star material, but her voice was her greatest asset, for she sang in a style that was new to the world."

Clarence Holiday did not agree at first. He disliked her style, predicted her failure unless she changed it, and tried to deny his paternity because it interfered with the impression he was trying to make on young women. (He had remarried and also taken on a mistress, with whom he had children.) He did not evince any pride in Billie until she was rebooked at the Apollo. She in turn called herself Billie Halliday, until her father's attitude toward her softened. He died, a relatively young man, of pneumonia in 1937, a virtual stranger to Billie, just as her musical reputation began to spread. He never survived to see his existence as a musician become a mere footnote to his daughter's major influence on jazz.

Billie continued making records and gigging in clubs. In 1939 she sang at the Onyx Club, one of many Fifty-second Street joints in full swing then, possibly the one where Sylvia Syms, then a young, hopeful singer, stood outside on the sidewalk, transfixed by Lady's music.

"I listened to everybody and knew who I wanted to sing like when I heard Lady," said Sylvia. "She was the first one who made sense to me. She had an innate animal sense of what she was singing. Others I listened to so I could learn what not to do. Lady was intelligent, articulate, feelingful. She understood far more than anyone would think she could. She was not an intellectual. She wasn't educated. But Billie had a wit. It was unbelievable."

Bobby Tucker, Billy Eckstine's accompanist since Tucker left Billie in the late 1940s, recalls a night when Billie and Eckstine were bantering. Billie said to him, "You're a real pretty mother-fucker, but you ain't as pretty as Buck Clayton." At the time Buck Clayton, with gray-green eyes, was "the prettiest man anyone ever met," Sylvia Syms said. And many years later, teaching at Hunter College, he was still very attractive. But Billy Eckstine, whom Billie was teasing, was nationally known as a formidably handsome singer.

"Billie loved to laugh," said Sylvia Syms. "She doesn't sound sad to me, not at all. She was really a wild-looking girl in those days, sexy, tall. That was before her arms looked bad. She was very endowed, not heavy and very stylish."

Syms added that she supplied Billie, nine years her senior and her idol, with a gardenia to wear behind her ear. The flower became Billie's insignia.

"I didn't preconceive it," says Sylvia. "I didn't sit hours all night and dream up ways to make her look better. She was stoned one night in the dressing room and burned a hunk out of her hair with a hot comb. We couldn't find anything to hang on her head. A hole so big! The checkroom girls used to sell favors—nuts, stuffed animals, anything to make a couple of bucks. So I got a few gardenias and wired them together. It was easy to pin on her because of the wires in the stems.

"I heard living in her music. I heard the most music in her music of any singer. She had a purity of intention. There are a lot of scat singers. But she never deviated from her sentence. And somehow she brought into view a proper picture of what she was feeling musically, articulately.

"Billie sang the blues. She migrated to guys who treated her like hell and didn't want anything to do with her. So she sang 'Billie's Blues' and 'Traveling Light' about traveling without a man again. These were the things she knew best. Without even trying, she knew everything. She could swing the blues. And I think she improvised so beautifully because she never knew the tune and played within the changes that the guys were playing, too.

"I was a young and floundering kid, but, from listening to her, I realized the goal was (a) to relate things you're telling to people who are listening to you, and (b) not to lose sight of your story and what it means to you."

Billie alternated at the Onyx with Leo Watson, the fastest scat singer in the world, and his Spirits of Rhythm, a bill which must have made extremely engaging entertainment. By 1938 Billie traveled with the Basie band.

"Billie's pitch was in such a key that the trumpet player had to play high or low for her," Buck Clayton remembered about the months when a young, plump Lady worked with Basie. "Normally 'Body and Soul' was played in middle range, but with her you had to play high or low. If it were in the key of B flat, Billie would sing it in F. And it was hard to play for her. She changed the original key; sometimes I would have to play it so high that the trumpet would screech. So then I would have to play it low. There was no middle ground with Billie.

"I would keep watching her mouth to see if she were fixing to close it. Then I'd fill in and play two or three notes until she was ready to sing again. Then I cooled it. That was the best way to play with Billie. I had more fun playing with her than with any of the others in the Basie band. More than with Helen Humes second and Jimmy Rushing third.

"She liked sharp-looking guys who were pimps. They tried to take her money, her royalty checks. I don't think until her last marriage [to Louis McKay] that she found someone not trying to get her money. The others would take it and beat her up. Every time she got paid, she had to give her money to her 'old man,' whoever he was at the time. Not Freddie Green [Basie's guitarist since the thirties, with whom she had a brief affair]. Although he was a nice-looking guy, he wasn't slick. He wasn't married at the time they had an affair. He was the only one in the band that she cared about in that way. With Lester Young [whose small-toned horn playing along with Billie's singing sounded like a musical expression of the same soul] she would go places. People thought they were having an affair, but it was just a friendship based on the music. Billie and I were just friends, too," added Buck, a slender, exceptionally handsome black man with a long, aquiline nose and cheeks sculpted into rivulets. A narrow-brimmed tweed hat can put the finishing touch on his resemblance to Rex Harrison.

Bobby Tucker: "I told Billie that I could line up a platoon of men in front of her and, blindfolded, she could pick out the two lemons." Tucker, who worked with Billie during her relationship with John Levy, thought Levy could have qualified easily as two lemons all by himself. Levy, a clubowner in New York, met Billie soon after her release from prison in the late 1940s on drug charges. Billie wrote in her autobiography, *Lady Sings the Blues*, that Levy bullied and probably fleeced her on the pretext of helping her, giving her presents but not cash from her earnings for several years. And, she wrote, he appeared to have gotten her arrested for possession of opium at a time when she wasn't using drugs.

That happened about ten years after she had endeared herself, drug free except for a taste for marijuana, to other young musicians traveling with Basie.

Clayton: "She would shoot craps on the bus and be one of the boys and do things to help pass the time, so we wouldn't go crazy."

One day in 1938, Clayton went to work and found that Billie had suddenly left the band. He isn't exactly sure what happened: a never-explained disagreement with Basie that had some connection to money, Billie's moodiness and inconsistency. Although Basie and the band loved her improvisation, she did have an odd Sound, without commercial appeal because of the unusual timbre of her voice and the relaxed phrasing—so slow and drawled, with a subtle vibrato. The very thing that she was most famous for—laying back on the beat—caused her the most grief commercially. But she sang melodies with a whole lot of notes that she put in so deftly you would never know how she did it. Her style, despite her laid-back attitude toward professional work habits, may have rescued her from oblivion.

(As a foil and comparison, consider Lena Horne, Billie's opposite number. Lena Horne spent many years learning from her husband, the late Lenny Hayton, and all the marvelous musicians he associated with and introduced her to. She became a wonderful soul singer. In her one-woman show on Broadway in the early 1980s, preceded by her tour with Tony Bennett, Lena Horne sometimes sang ahead of the beat. The trick gave her songs runaway excitement and drive; commercial socko at the box office. The accountants are still trying to catch up.)

After Billie left Basie (who usually called her "William," according to Chilton), Basie said about her: "Billie is a marvelous artist, who remains unappreciated by the world at large."

He suggested that her pride and belief in her music made artistic and racial shocks all the more difficult for her to absorb. Her days with Basie may have been among the most carefree in her complex life. On the Basie bus, the Blue Goose, she had traveled with her special friends: Prez, Buck, trumpeter Hot Lips Page and Freddie Green. If they had been traveling light, they had done it together.

She quickly joined Artie Shaw and faced difficulties as the first black singer on the road with a white band. (June Richmond sang with Jimmy Dorsey in the thirties; Lena Horne briefly with Charlie Barnet; and Ella Fitzgerald recorded a few tunes with Benny Goodman's band for Victor. Ethel Waters worked with white musicians, too, and Fats Waller with Lee Wiley. But not on the road.) With Shaw, Billie had the support of her well-intentioned, complicated bandleader. He helped her face down some ugly incidents with hotels, restaurants, club and ballroom owners. However, in St. Louis, Shaw deferred to a ballroom promoter who insisted that Shaw hire a white singer with a commercial sound. Helen Forrest, whom Shaw had heard sing months earlier in Washington, got the job for the ballads, while Billie kept the blues. She was "too artistic" to have enough of the common touch, as well as too light-skinned to be considered truly black by some businessmen and too dark to be accorded whatever politeness a white singer could command. For Helen Forrest the road offered a blessed improvement over her difficult childhood, with some seaminess reminiscent of Billie's. For Billie the road offered, sadly, more of the same.

Back in New York City, Shaw's band moved into the Lincoln Hotel's ballroom. Management forbade Billie to mingle with the customers as white musicians did. One version said she had to sit alone in a little room, waiting for her turn to sing while the band played or drank at the bar. Helen Forrest remembered that she and Billie stirred up controversy by sharing a ringside table, waiting to sing.

In short, Billie had to deal with the principle of "Every Tub." The lyrics, supplied by bebopper Jon Hendricks in the 1950s to a Basie tune, say that every tub stands on its own feet, a metaphor for every black standing his or her ground, an "every man for himself" philosophy, in the face of racial prejudice—and incidentally a universal metaphor for man's fate to stand alone and up for himself.

After quitting Shaw, Billie went to work for Barney Josephson at Café Society Downtown, the Sheridan Square club in Greenwich Village, where black and white patrons mingled freely in the audience. Billie gained self-confidence as a performer. Josephson attributed her improved attitude to his evenhanded race policy.

"A singer had full view of the door and could see her people ushered to prominent tables. So the singer feels better and sings better. In addition, her boss gives her a song to sing. 'Strange Fruit' by Lewis Allen. That was his songwriting name. Abel Meeropol was his real name. Abel and his wife, Anne, adopted the children of Julius and Ethel Rosenberg, Michael and Robbie Meeropol. But I knew him as Allen. He showed me the music and lyrics. I don't know music, but I like the lyrics. I'm a left guy. 'What do you want to do with it?' I said. 'It would be great if you could get Billie Holiday to sing it.' 'Okay, stick around. When Billie comes in, I'll get her to listen.' Billie said, 'What do you want me to do with that?' I said, 'Be great if you did it. Great song.' 'Okay, if you want me to sing, I'll sing it.' She did—and became internationally famous for that song. It gave her status as a black singer with a brain, a mind, an awareness, something to say. Though Billie was apolitical. Not a fighter."

Josephson also retold the story of Billie's "Moon over Manhattan," when she was part of Café Society's show with three acts. "The first two acts were bands. If their instruments permitted it, the musicians would come down on the floor near the audience. The singer was told to do three songs and go off and take bows. Billie was told to do that and to honor all her encore calls, too; if she had one or five, to do them all.

"We had one little dressing room. Everybody came in there, disrobed and put on their evening gowns. One night, Billie comes in, slips her gown on and goes out to do the show." (She was fairly high on marijuana, Josephson recalled, too; although he didn't permit marijuana in the club, he knew that she sometimes took a taxi for a turn around town and smoked.) "She sings with one little spotlight on her face in this black room. Afterwards, the applause is coming. She turns around and does like this." Mr. Josephson turned around and mimicked a woman throwing up her dress and showing her bare ass to moon the audience. "She did that. She was high and uninhibited. I went backstage and said to her, 'What are you doing?'

"She said, 'Fuck 'em.'

"I said, 'What happened?'

"She said, 'Don't bother me.'

"I couldn't get anything out of her. But I can guess what had happened. She must have overheard somebody say something. Somebody in the audience must have made a remark about black performers and a mixed audience. That kind of thing went on all the time. So many of these musicians and singers don't have the words. They can't express themselves with words. So Billie told them: 'You can kiss my black ass.' That's what she was saying. No, I didn't fire her. Of course I didn't fire her."

Billie often got into wild fights with club owners who disliked her odd sound. (Not Josephson.) They yelled at her to sing faster and louder or get out. She told them to sing their way, and she would sing her way. She got out, never peaceably.

Call Billie's work a monotone with a bounce, or a dreamy reverie, or a lazing conversation. Call her sound the greatest nonclassical vocalizing on records, as John Hammond did. The overwhelming charm of her small Sound has the effect of bombast. She achieved an arresting catch of laughter in her voice with her staccato notes, Whitney Balliett explained. In her last years, these notes became a mechanical and melancholy imitation. Her style hinted at her private confusions; her Sound became a patina. But in the young Lady's song, there was an indefatigability. The nearly tone-deaf can carry her haunting sound in their memories long after the music has stopped.

By 1943 Billie rued never having won a *Down Beat* poll. She watched disconsolately as other singers, who imitated her, won instead. But in 1943 jazz critics voted her the winner in a Critics' Choice poll. Billie trounced Ella Fitzgerald by 23 to 4 and Mildred Bailey by 23 to 15. A 1950 *Down Beat* review called her Lady Yesterday. Then the same magazine relieved the sting by giving her an award in 1954 as "one of the all-time great vocalists in jazz."

She also had enough prestige that she was polled to pick her favorite young singers. In 1946 she picked Perry Como and Jo Stafford. Another time she selected a group including Etta Jones—to Etta's everlasting joy. "You always think your idol doesn't even hear you," she said.

By that time Billie was deeply involved with drugs. She married and lived briefly with Jimmy Monroe, the ne'er-do-well younger brother of New York City club owner Clark Monroe. When Buck Clayton saw her again, in California, years after she left Basie, Billie was using drugs. "She was clean when she left Basie. When I saw her again, she was . . . messed up." Billie said that she started using drugs with Jimmy Monroe to give them something in common and hold their shaky marriage together.

By the late 1940s, she was constantly embattled by the law, primarily because of drugs and then, too, because of her increasing unreliability about dates. In 1947 she spent time at the Federal Reformatory for Women at Alderson, West Virginia. In her autobiography she related her grim experiences in prison with a Dostoyevskian attention to detail that conveyed a sense of her crushing depression. She did not sing a note there. Afterward, when she performed, she wore her trademark gardenia less often.

Divorced from Jimmy Monroe by the 1950s, she married Louis McKay, her second and last husband. Not only Buck Clayton but other musicians who knew the couple say that McKay loved Billie, though Bobby Tucker has mused that Billie may have cared only about Jimmy Monroe and an even earlier love, Bobby Henderson, one of her first piano accompanists, a married man. She wrote about him without using his name in her autobiography: "It was the first time I was ever wooed, courted, chased after. He made me feel like a woman. He was patient, loving; he knew what I was scared about, and he knew how to smooth my fear away." Whomever Billie preferred of all her men, Big Nick Nicholas, a veritable honeydripper of a singer himself, who was playing tenor saxophone at a regular gig in an uptown club, recalled that Billie and McKay would drop by to listen to Big Nick's sweet brand of music. Billie seemed happy, laughing; she was still good-looking. McKay, who was quiet, appeared to care about her. Ray Ross, a veteran photographer on New York's scene, said that McKay tried to get Billie clean of all drugs.

"But she was too far gone by that time," Ross added, for McKay to do much good.

Even so, for many years she was often able to keep up appearances. In the late 1950s, not long before she died, she was filmed for a CBS-TV show, *The Sound of Jazz*, singing "Fine and Mellow" in a group including Mal Waldron, her last accompanist, on piano, Lester Young on tenor saxophone, and the legendary drummer Jo Jones on drums. Billie was a beauty—with a high forehead, hair backswept into a chignon, eyes alight and keenly fixed on Lester Young; she sang his licks exactly as he blew her words. Clearly engulfed in his sound, she paid little attention to the other musicians.

Not long after that, pianist Patti Bown, who met Billie in her last years, recalled seeing the insides of Billie's arms. "They looked like punch boards, with scar tissue all around. Some scars are permanent. It breaks your heart to look at it, especially because you know it's some kind of self-abuse. Your heart goes out." New to New York, young Patti, who had worshiped Billie from afar and written a tune for her, was also taken aback by Billie's profanity in the dressing room. Patti couldn't bring herself to talk about the song. "One time I saw her wearing a leopard coat, taking a walk with her dog in Central Park. She looked so bad, so sad. At Town Hall she gave a concert. It was horrible. She could barely make it to the concert. Those were the hardest years."

Billie's story is not about a singer and her men, nor her women, nor any of the appetites for which she became infamous. If the right man could have fixed all the problems that assailed Billie Holiday from the start, then Louis McKay might have provided the remedy, despite their tumultuous ménage in which Billie got physically bruised sometimes. But no one person could ever provide the reason or antidote for Billie's short, fast life. Eventually she and McKay separated. Essentially alone, she lived out her last, degenerating years singing with a combat-weary, battle-scarred voice. Some fans have said that by the 1950s she sang with more maturity and feeling because of her experiences. Others have perceived her, at best, as dispirited. The odd Sound became even odder—the high voice eerily and artificially pitched instead of buoyant. Still, it mesmerized.

Mal Waldron, her last accompanist from 1957 to 1959, recalled those downhill years. She liked to cook for a lot of people and "set fantastically good meals before them, but wouldn't eat anything herself. She said: 'The cook only samples the food in the kitchen but doesn't eat her own food.'" She always had a drink in her hand, he said, "except on the bandstand." And although only in her early forties, she talked about her death, telling Waldron that she didn't want to be buried underground because she wouldn't be able to breathe. "She wanted to have her ashes spread over the ground from a plane," he recalled. He also remembered her laughing at his jokes with quite a lot of energy left, even in those grim days.

In the New York City hospital where she died, he visited her. So did a Czechoslovakian woman named Alice who helped Billie care for herself in her final years in a West Side apartment. So did clarinetist Tony Scott. Chilton's biography said that Louis McKay visited often. But Mal Waldron never saw him there. Nor did Billie ever mention that McKay visited.

Billie Holiday died on a Sunday. Patti Bown, who was living on Christopher Street in Greenwich Village, recalled: "One faggot [sic] kept playing 'Gloomy Sunday' over and over again."

Billie was buried next to her mother in St. Raymond's Cemetery in the Bronx. Eventually Louis McKay put a marker on the grave.

It had been a terrible fight all the way for a lightly armed woman. She had the stamina to withstand the rigors for a little while. But a legion of protégées has seen her reanimated.

As soon as they heard her records or saw her in live performances, scores of singers singled her out as their ideal: Dinah Washington, Anita O'Day, Etta Jones, Ernestine Anderson, Sylvia Syms, Helen Merrill, Sarah Vaughan and Carmen McRae, to name a few, owe more to Billie than to anyone else—all of them Billie's children as well as Louis Armstrong's.

PART FIVE

Strange Fruit:
Legacies

THE REAL LADY DAY
NAT HENTOFF

Throughout his career as a jazz writer and civil libertarian, Nat Hentoff has been regarded as one of the most astute critics and best writers, with a warm, kinetic style. Hentoff's essays provide a feeling of the scene and the people who lived the jazz life. His viewpoint on the biographical movie about Billie's life is supported by his personal relationships with the singer and the musicians in her real life. Particularly interesting are his intimate observations during the filming of "The Story of Jazz," the CBS program made as part of a series, "The Seven Lively Arts." Billie's incandescence made the jazz film an enduring work of art and an everlasting symbol of the emotionality and intimacy of the art of jazz.

Billie Holiday was on television, part of "The Sound of Jazz," on a Sunday afternoon in December, 1957, less than two years before her death. The program, which was coming "live" from C.B.S. studios on Manhattan's West 57th Street, was going well and about to move into "Fine and Mellow." Billie, perched on a high stool, faced a semicircle of musicians who were all standing—except for one. Lester Young. Prez (as Billie had nicknamed him long before) was sick. He had been so weak that most of his solos during a previous segment with Count Basie's band had been split among other reedmen. Now Prez was slumped in a chair, his eyes averted from Billie, whom he had not spoken to for some time. I didn't know the reason for their discord, but throughout the rehearsals they had ignored each other.

Lady Day began to sing; and in the darkened control room, the producer, the director and the technical staff leaned forward, some of them mumbling expletives of wonder. The song, which she had written, was one of the blues in Billie's repertory, and this time she was using it to speak not so much of trouble but rather of the bittersweet triumph of having survived—with some kicks along the way. Despite the current myth that Lady, toward the end, invariably sounded like a cracked husk of what she had been years before when she wouldn't sing without a gardenia in her hair, that afternoon she was in full control of the tart, penetrating, sinuously swinging instrument which was her voice.

It was time for Prez's solo. Somehow he managed to stand up, and then he blew the sparest, purest blues chorus I have ever heard. Billie, smiling, nodding to the beat, looked into Prez's eyes, and he into hers. She was looking back, with the gentlest of regrets, at their past. Prez was remembering too. Whatever had blighted their relationship was forgotten in the communion of the music. Sitting in the control room, I felt tears, and saw tears on the faces of most of the others there. The rest of the program was all right, but this had been its climax—the empirical soul of jazz.

Later, a woman in White Plains wrote in to say how startling it had been to see on television "*real* people, doing something that *really* matters to them."

Music did indeed really matter to Billie. Carmen McRae, a friend of hers and now the pre-eminent *real* singer of jazz, once said to me about Billie: "Singing is the only place she can express herself the way she'd like to be all the time. The only time she's at ease and at rest with herself is when she sings. I mean when she can sing, not when she's under the influence of liquor or whatever she's on."

Billie was happy with that television program because it had been almost entirely music, with minimal script, and everyone had been encouraged to dress in what was most comfortable and natural for them. Some of the jazzmen wore their hats, as they would at a recording date or an after-hours session. They smoked and talked with each other when they felt like it. Billie, her hair in a ponytail, was in slacks. Initially, that had taken some doing. Along with Whitney Balliett, *The New Yorker*'s jazz critic, I had helped set up the program; and when I first told Billie, a few weeks before, that the ambiance was going to be the direct opposite of that on the Ed Sullivan show (the bare studio was our set) Lady had been furious. "I just spent 500 goddam dollars on a gown," she said. But once we started working in the studio, she fell into easeful spirit of the occasion; and on camera, Lady made her entrance walking gaily through the ranks of the Basie band, kidding several of her long-time colleagues as she ambled along. After the show, she kissed me on the cheek, smiled, and said, "Well, I guess I can use that dress some other place."

Very little of the Billie, the one to whom music mattered so deeply, is in the 1972 film, *Lady Sings the Blues*. Prez isn't in it at all, nor are any of the other jazz musicians who meant so much to Billie. Nor does that Billie seem to figure prominently in the rest of the present, growing mystique which is creating what I suppose can be called her legend. The emphasis now is on Billie as a victim—of herself, of society. The rhythms she moved to were a junkie's beat, according to the legend. The music— well, that's part of the background, and in the movie is so foolishly misunderstood that Michel Legrand (who is to jazz what Rod McKuen is to the world of letters) was commissioned to write the score.

Not that Billie was not a victim and was not hooked on drugs for much of the last 18 years of her life. And she did come up hard, although she was all too vulnerable inside until the day she died. Her mother was 13 when Billie was born; and her musician-father, Clarence Holiday, not only abandoned the family but always considered Billie an accident. ("She was just something I stole when I was 15," he said years later to another musician.)

Eleonora Fagan—she changed her name to Billie when she was young because Eleonora was "too damn long for anyone to say"—started scrubbing white folks's steps in Baltimore when she was 6. She also ran errands for the madam and the other professionals in a whorehouse in return for being allowed to listen to Bessie Smith and Louis Armstrong records on the house Victrola; was almost raped at 10 and put away in a Catholic institution as punishment, presumably for "enticement"; and left school at 13, having gone only as far as fifth grade.

"Up" South, in New York, Billie worked briefly as a maid, a role she despised both then and in her one Hollywood picture, *New Orleans*, with Louis Armstrong. By the age of 15, Billie was turning tricks in a brothel on 141st Street. ("I had someone doing my laundry," she observes in the book, *Lady Sings the Blues*, written with and considerably oversimplified by William Dufty.) She was soon in jail again for having refused to accept a too-rugged customer who happened to be somewhat of a power in Harlem.

Because of that experience, and for reasons of pride, Billie stopped turning tricks and began to sing in Harlem clubs. Her reputation grew rather swiftly, in part because of the proselytizing work of John Hammond, the Magellan of jazz (his finds having ranged over 40 years from Count Basie to Bob Dylan).

"It was around 1933," Hammond told me recently, "and in a club uptown there was this chubby girl going around the tables, singing. I couldn't believe my ears. No chick I'd heard sounded like this—like an instrument, like Louis's trumpet. And the way she improvised. When those girls were working, they had to sing a route which ran to 20 to 30 tables. That required an extraordinary amount of musical resourcefulness, and if you didn't have it, that was clear right away. She had it."

Hammond also recalls that, although the other girls working the tables were expected to collect their tips by lifting their dresses, using their labia to pick up the dollar bills, Billie would not. It was at that point, by the way, that she first started to be called Lady, at first derisively by her less punctilious associates. Lester Young later expanded the sobriquet to Lady Day, taking the addition from her last name.

In 1933, John Hammond persuaded Benny Goodman to use the 18-year-old Harlem singer on a record date, Billie's first. Many more recordings followed, including a notable series of small band sessions under Teddy Wilson's direction. The recordings helped establish Billie, though not financially. "I made over 200 sides between 1933 and 1944," she wrote in *Lady Sings the Blues*, "but I don't get a cent of royalties on any of them. They paid me 25, 50, or a top of 75 bucks a side, and I was glad to get it . . . But royalties were still unheard of."

Although Billie was working New York clubs fairly regularly, the monetary returns were slight from those sources too. Consequently, she went on the road with Count Basie, and then with Artie Shaw. Billie, traveling light, failed to make her fortune, stringing one-nighters together, but she added to her store of experiences concerning the depth and diversity of Jim Crow in the American grain. Billie was angered and disgusted by bigotry, but her response was considerably more resilient and defiant than is apparent in the soap opera movie which purports to be about her life.

There was the time the Basie band arrived in a small Southern town which didn't even have a "colored" hotel. Quartered at the home of a local black minister, the Basie band and Billie had just finished an idiomatic but nearly indigestible dinner. One of the number, a very light-skinned member of the orchestra, had been missing from the table. On the street, they saw him jauntily emerge from the best white restaurant in town. He pretended not to recognize his co-workers; and Billie, placing herself in front of him, shouted for all the town to hear: "All right for you, Peola!" (Peola, elder readers may recall, was the young Negro woman who tried to pass for white in the then popular movie, *Imitation of Life*.)

Back in New York, Billie became a star, as she somewhat wryly put it, after two years of singing at Barney Josephson's Cafe Society. When she left, as she also claimed, she was still making the $75 a week at which she had started. But gradually, Billie's price rose, and she could have become a moderately affluent woman if she had not become involved in a series of ruinous affairs with exploitative men, and if she had not acquired a most expensive drug habit.

I have neither the qualifications or the inclination to try to explain the specific dynamics of Billie's penchant for self-destruction; but it is germane to cite a point made by pianist Bobby Tucker, who for some years was Billie's accompanist. "There's one thing about Lady Day you won't believe," he said. "She had the most terrible inferiority complex." Billie puts it another way. Speaking of her childhood—the attempted rape; the times she had been locked up while she was still in her teens; the lack, to put it mildly, of a secure sense of family—she emphasized that those experiences had left her feeling "like a damn cripple." And she always insisted on telling any man with whom she had a relationship of "the things that had happened to me when I was a kid."

In any case, Billie, until then, had a hard time believing she was a star, even a falling star. She would be genuinely, almost ingenuously, touched when someone told her how much her singing meant to him. I do not mean she ever lost, for any length of time, her stubborn pride. Quite the contrary. Billie would hoot at such myths about her, as in the movie of *Lady Sings the Blues*, that without the support of one good, strong man, she would have had an even untimelier end. Of all the men she knew, she said, "I was as strong, if not stronger, than any other of them. And when it's that way, you can't blame anybody but yourself."

Not always, but often, Billie retained her sardonic wit in the worst of times. And she also kept her sense of rage when she felt she was being victimized by forces for which she could not and would not take the blame. There was the persistent harassment of Billie, for example, by those police, Federal and local, who specialize in enforcing the narcotics laws. When she once went to a private sanitorium to kick her habit, and succeeded for a time, a narcotics agent appeared there on the day she left, keeping track of her. Some of her arrests for drug possession were legitimate; others were not; and always she had the sense of being tailed. There's more than one kind of monkey that can be on your back.

What most galled and depressed Billie was her inability to work in New York clubs for 12 years after she had served a 10-month term for drug possession at the Federal Women's Reformatory at Alderson, W. Va. At that time, anyone with a police record was refused permission to work in any New York room where liquor is sold. Billie was in show business, although she was also an artist to those of us who believe that jazz is America's classical music. And she knew, as Lenny Bruce later knew, that an entertainer exiled from New York suffers extensive career damage. As she did.

The hounds of the narcotics squads, imbued with faith in irredeemable sin, pursued Billie quite literally to her death bed. A friend of Billie's, and of mine, Maely Dufty, who was once Charlie Parker's manager, has described Billie's last days in the notes for an ESP Records album of Billie Holiday radio performances.

In June, 1959, her liver badly damaged, Billie, in a coma, was taken to Metropolitan Hospital where she was placed in an oxygen tent. After 12 days she regained consciousness, but "still remained on the critical list, having to be fed intravenously while receiving blood transfusions. One morning, nine hours after I had left her bedside the night before," Maely Dufty wrote, "I found her in a deep rage . . . 'You watch, baby, they are going to arrest me in this damn bed.' And so they did. The night nurse claimed she had found a deck of heroin in Billie's handbag, which was hanging from a nail on the wall—six feet way from the bottom of her bed. It was virtually impossible for Billie—with hundreds of pounds of equipment strapped to her legs and arms for transfusions—to have moved one inch toward that wall. One hour later the police arrived and arrested Billie Holiday in her hospital bed. Charge: use of narcotics."

Even assuming the police charge to have been accurate, what followed underlines Billie's long-held contention that, to the authorities, being a drug-user is to find oneself on "a one-way street."

"To make the arrest of a woman in a hospital bed seem more real," Maely Dufty continued, "the police confiscated her comic books, radio, magazines, a box of Whitman chocolates, and Italian ice cream, and then stationed two cops at the doorless, tiny gray hospital room. When I screamed at the authorities that they could not arrest a woman on the critical list, I was told that problem had already been solved. Billie Holiday had been removed from the critical list."

That issue was soon academic. Billie died in that hospital bed. She was 44.

If that were all of Billie, or most of Billie—the victim of herself and of the authorities—the substance of the Holiday legend might indeed be legitimately restricted, though without present distortions, to the tale of the Black Lady of the Gardenias. A latter-day Camille of the jazz grottoes who lit her candle at both ends. But that way of fashioning legend leaves out the essence of Lady Day—her music.

This was a woman who was as deeply pervasive an influence on jazz singing as Louis Armstrong and Charlie Parker were on jazz instrumental playing. Though herself influenced by Armstrong and Bessie Smith ("Honey, I wanted her feeling and Louis's style"), Billie, by the time she was in her 20's, had created a way of singing that was unmistakably her own. Or as Ralph Cooper, then the *compere* at Harlem's Apollo Theater, said many years ago about Billie: "It ain't the blues. I don't know what it is, but you got to hear her."

Billie Holiday, for one thing, excelled all jazz singers who had preceded her in her ability to make the lyrics of a song (and some of the songs she was to record were most ordinary) take on nuances of meaning and feeling that lifted whatever she sang to significance, to many levels of significance. And as John Hammond instantly recognized when she was 18, Billie did sing like a horn. ("I try to improvise like Prez, like Louis, or someone else I admire. I hate straight singing. I have to change a tune to my own way of doing it. That's all I know.") No singer in jazz, before or since, has phrased with such supple inventiveness as well as with such graceful, illuminating wit. Although nonpareil as a speleologist of the poignancy of ballads, Billie could also be the blithest of mocking spirits. And there was also her timing—her risk-taking playing with the beat, as only the most assured jazz instrumentalists are able to bend time to their feelings.

All these qualities were fused into a story-teller who could make waitresses stand still, cash registers remain unrung, and bring musicians backing her to applaud—as happened at a Carnegie Hall concert shortly after she was released from the Federal Women's Reformatory.

This bardic quality was hers to the end. There were stumbling off nights, but the later Lady Day could be more compellingly expressive than the younger lady of the gardenias. In his book, *The Reluctant Art*, Benny Green, a British musician turned essayist, noted of Billie's singing in the nineteen-fifties: "The trappings were stripped away, but where the process would normally leave only the husk of a fine reputation it only exposed to view once and for all, the true core of her art, her handling of a lyric. If the last recordings are approached with this fact in mind, they are seen to be, not the insufferable croaking of a woman already half-dead, but recitatives whose dramatic intensity becomes unbearable, statements as frank and tragic as anything throughout the whole range of popular art."

So it was less than two years before her death, Billie sang "Fine and Mellow" on "The Sound of Jazz" with such tender yet acrid power that we cried in the control room and Lester Young was lifted to his feet to, briefly, rejoin Lady Day's life and art. That scene is not in the movie, *Lady*

Sings the Blues. That scene is real, as Billie's music can still be so real an experience to those who go to the only remaining source, Lady Day's recordings, to find out who Billie Holiday was.

Of course, for many reasons I wish Billie—and not only her voice—were still present. I'd give a lot to hear her response to socialite Maureen McCluskey who, as reported in *The Times* by Charlotte Curtis, said at a benefit supper party after the premiere of *Lady Sings the Blues*: "Doesn't everybody look marvelous? Of course, if I could come back again after I die, I'd come back black."

I would expect that Lady's reaction to that costless fantasy probably could not be printed in this newspaper.

BILLIE HOLIDAY: SLEEPLESS NIGHTS
ELIZABETH HARDWICK

This piece is distinctively different from nearly all the other writings about Billie in this book. Hardwick cannot be pigeonholed as a critic, historian, musicologist, or biographer. She's a novelist, whose talent lies in her subjectivity, and so she has expressed first and foremost her own perceptions and poetic imaginings about Billie with, on the whole, exciting success.

Billie is seen by turns close up and at a distance, and as a mysterious, intelligent artiste and a pathetic social misfit, as a glamorous dowager of the night world and the art of jazz singing and an outlandishly disorganized drug addict and alcoholic. Above all, Billie is an inspiration, virtually a muse, for Elizabeth Hardwick, who, to some degree, expresses her own interior weather when she is confronted with the task of interpreting Billie's impact as an artist and a woman on other people.

Completely absent is the sense that Billie loved to laugh. Her friends knew that well. And Hardwick also came up with some controversial ideas—saying, for example, that Billie lived "gregariously and without affection." That was at least debatable, and her friends and close associates refuted it.

Nevertheless, Hardwick made some astoundingly apt observations about Lady—for example, about her relationship with her childish, inept, unattractive, perhaps even competitive mother—

long before the Linda Kuehl tapes became available. And it was true that, in part, Billie's "message . . . was style." It is probably true, too, that Billie's "people, those around her, feared her." Without doubt, she was awesome, as Leonard Feather suggested when he described his first meeting with her, when both of them were young, with nearly all their adult lives before them. The most recent biographies reveal Billie's physical strength in a fight. She once knocked out two sailors who tried to intimidate her. Lady was fearless.

Miss Hardwick's brooding, intelligent, emotion-fraught writing transcends criticism and biographical sketches to portray Lady Day accurately as a personage with a touch, at times, of the grotesque.

"The unspeakable vices of Mecca are a scandal to all Islam and a constant source of wonder to pious pilgrims." As a pilgrim to Mecca, I lived at the Hotel Schuyler on West 45th Street in Manhattan, lived with a red-cheeked, homosexual young man from Kentucky. We had known each other all our lives. Our friendship was a violent one and we were as obsessive, critical, jealous and cruel as any couple. Often I lay awake all night in a rage over some delinquency of his during the day. His coercive neatness inflamed me at times, as if his habits were not his right but instead a dangerous poison to life, like the slow seepage from the hotel stove. His clothes were laid out on the bed for the next day; and worst of all he had an unyielding need to brush his teeth immediately after dinner in the evening. This finally meant that no fortuitous invitation, no lovely possibility arising unannounced would be accepted without a concentrated uneasiness of mind. These holy habits ruined his sex life, even though he was, like the tolling of a time bell, to be seen every Saturday night at certain gay bars, drinking his ration of beer.

My friend had, back in Kentucky, developed a passion for jazz. This study seized him and he brought to it the methodical, intense, dogmatic anxiety of his nature. I learned this passion from him. It is a curious learning that cuts into your flesh, leaving a scar, a longing never satisfied, a wound of feeling hard to live with. It can be distressing to listen to jazz when one is troubled alone, with the "wrong" person. Things can happen to your life that cause you to give it up altogether. Yet under its dominion, it may be said that one is more likely to commit suicide listening to "Them There Eyes" than to Opus 132. What is it? ". . . the sea itself, or is it youth alone?"

We lived there in the center of Manhattan, believing the very placing of the hotel to be an overwhelming beneficence. To live in the obscuring jungle of the midst of things: close to—what? Within walking distance of all those places one never walked to. But it was history, wasn't it? The acrimonious twilight fell in the hollows between the gray and red buildings. Inside the hotel was a sort of underbrush, a swampy footing for the irregular. The brooding inconsequence of the old hotel dwellers, their delusions and disappearances. They lived as if in a house recently burglarized, wires cut, their world vandalized, by themselves, and cheerfully enough, also. Do not imagine they received nothing in return. They got a lot, I tell you. They were lifted by insolence above their car loans, their surly arrears, their misspent matrimonies.

The small, futile shops around us explained how little we know of ourselves and how perplexing are our souvenirs and icons. I remember strangers to the city, in a daze, making decisions, exchanging coins and bills for the incurious curiosities, the unexceptional novelties. Sixth Avenue lies buried in the drawers, bureaus, boxes, attics, and cellars of grandchildren. There, blackening, are the dead watches, the long, oval rings for the little finger, the smooth pieces of polished wood shaped into a long-chinned African head, the key rings of the Empire State building. And for us, there were the blaring shops, open most of the night, where one could buy old, scratched, worn-thin jazz records—Vocalion, Okeh, and Brunswick labels. Our hands sliced through the cases until the skin around our fingers bled.

Yes, there were the records, priceless flotsam they seemed to us then. And the shifty jazz clubs on 52nd Street. The Onyx, the Down Beat, the Three Deuces. At the curb, getting out of a taxi, or at the White Rose Bar drinking, there "they" were, the great performers with their worn, brown faces, enigmatic in the early evening, their coughs, their broken lips and yellow eyes; their clothes, crisp and bright and hard as the bone-fibered feathers of a bird. And there she was—the "bizarre deity," Billie Holiday.

At night in the cold winter moonlight, around 1943, the city pageantry was of a benign sort. Young adolescents were then asleep and the threat was only in the landscape, aesthetic. Dirty slush in the gutters, a lost black overshoe, a pair of white panties, perhaps thrown from a passing car. Murderous dissipation went with the music, inseparable, skin and bone. And always her luminous self-destruction.

She was fat the first time we saw her, large, brilliantly beautiful, fat. She seemed for this moment that never again returned to be almost a matron, someone real and sensible who carried money to the bank, signed papers, had curtains made to match, dresses hung and shoes in pairs, gold and silver, black and white, ready. What a strange, betraying apparition that was, madness, because never was any woman less a wife or mother, less attached; not even a daughter could she easily appear to be. Little called to mind the pitiful sweetness of a young girl. No, she was glittering, somber, and solitary, although of course never alone, never. Stately, sinister, and absolutely determined.

The creamy lips, the oily eyelids, the violent perfume—and in her voice the tropical l's and r's. Her presence, her singing created a large, swelling anxiety. Long red fingernails and the sound of electrified guitars. Here was woman who had never been a Christian.

To speak as part of the white audience of "knowing" this baroque and puzzling phantom is an immoderation; and yet there are many persons, discrete and reasonable, who have little splinters of memory that seem to have been personal. At times they have remembered an exchange of some sort. And always the lascivious gardenia, worn like a large, white, beautiful ear, the heavy laugh, marvelous teeth, and the splendid archaic head, dragged up from the Aegean. Sometimes she dyed her hair red and the curls lay flat against her skull, like dried blood.

Early in the week the clubs were dead, as they spoke of it. And the chill of failure inhabited the place, visible in the cold eyes of the owners. These men, always changing, were weary with futile calculations. They often held their ownership so briefly that one could scarcely believe the ink dry on the license. They started out with the embezzler's hope and moved swiftly to the bankrupt's torpor. The bartenders—thin, watchful, stubbornly crooked, resentful, silent thieves. Wandering soldiers, drunk and worried, musicians, and a few people, couples, hideously looking into each other's eyes, as if they were safe.

My friend and I, peculiar and tense, experienced during the quiet nights a tainted joy. Then, showing our fidelity, it seemed that a sort of motif would reveal itself, that under the glaze ancient patterns from a lost world were to be discovered. The mind strains to recover the blank spaces in history, and our pale, gray-green eyes looked into her swimming, dark, inconstant pools—and got back nothing.

In her presence on these tranquil nights it was possible to experience the depths of her disbelief, to feel sometimes the mean, horrible freedom of a thorough suspicion of destiny. And yet the heart always drew back from the power of her will and its engagement with disaster. An inclination bred upon punishing experiences compelled her to live gregariously and without affections. Her talents and the brilliance of her mind contended with the strength of the emptiness. Nothing should degrade this genuine nihilism; and so, in a sense, it is almost a dishonor to imagine that she lived in the lyrics of her songs.

Her message was otherwise. It was *style*. That was her meaning from the time she began at fifteen. It does not change the victory of her great effort, of the miraculous discovery or retrieval from darkness of pure style, to know that it was exercised on "I love my man, tell the world I do. . . ." How strange it was to me, almost unbalancing, to be sure that she did not love any man, or anyone. Also often one had the freezing perception that her own people, those around her, feared her. One thing she was ashamed of—or confused by, rather—that she was not sentimental.

In my youth, at home in Kentucky, there was a dance place just outside of town called Joyland Park. In the summer the great bands arrived, Ellington, Louis Armstrong, Chick Webb, sometimes for a Friday and Saturday or merely for one night. When I speak of the great bands it must not be taken to mean that we thought of them as such. No, they were part of the summer nights and the hot dog stands, the fetid swimming pool heavy with chlorine, the screaming roller coaster, the old rain-splintered picnic tables, the broken iron swings. And the bands were also part of Southern drunkenness, couples drinking coke and whisky, vomiting, being unfaithful, lovelorn, frantic. The black musicians, with their cumbersome instruments, their tuxedos, were simply there to beat out time for the stumbling, cuddling fox-trotting of the period.

The band busses, parked in the field, caravans in which they suffered the litter of cigarettes and bottles, the hot, streaking highways, all night, or resting for a few hours in the black quarters: the Via Dolorosa of show business. They arrived at last, nowhere, to audiences large or small, often with us depending upon the calendar of the Park, the other occasions from which the crowd would spill over into the dance hall. Ellington's band. And what were we doing, standing close, murmuring the lyrics?

At our high school dances in the winter, small, cheap, local events. We had our curls, red taffeta dresses, satin shoes with their new dye fading in the rain puddles; and most of all we were dressed in our ferocious hope for popularity. This was a stifling blanket, an airless tent; gasping, grinning, we stood anxious-eyed, next to the piano, hovering about Fats Waller who had come from Cincinnati for the occasion. Requests, perfidious glances, drunken teenagers, nodding teacher-chaperones: these we offered to the music, looking upon it, I suppose, as something inevitable, effortlessly pushing up from the common soil.

On 52nd Street: "Yeah, I remember your town," she said, without inflection.

And I remember her dog, Boxer. She was one of those women who admire large, overwhelming, impressive dogs and who give to them a care and courteous punctuality denied everything else. Several times we waited in panic for her in the bar of the Hotel Braddock in Harlem. (My friend, furious and tense with his new, hated work in "public relations," was now trying without success to get her name in Winchell's column. Today we were waiting to take her downtown to sit for the beautiful photographs Robin Carson took of her.) At the Braddock, the porters took plates of meat for the dog to her room. Soon, one of her friends, appearing almost like a child, so easily broken were others by the powerful, energetic horrors of her life, one of those young people would take the great dog to the street. These animals, asleep in dressing rooms, were like sculptured treasures, fit for the tomb of a queen.

The sheer enormity of her vices. The outrageousness of them. For the grand destruction one must be worthy. Her ruthless talent and the opulent devastation. Onto the heaviest addiction to heroin she piled up the rocks of her tomb with a prodigiousness of Scotch and brandy. She was never at any hour of the day or night free of these consumptions, never except when she was asleep. And there did not seem to be any pleading need to quit, to modify. With cold anger she spoke of various cures that had been forced upon her, and she would say, bearing down heavily, as sure of her rights as if she had been robbed, "And I paid for it myself." Out of a term at the Federal Women's Prison in West Virginia she stepped, puffy from a diet of potatoes, onto the stage of Town Hall to pick up some money and start up again the very day of release.

Still, even with her, authenticity was occasionally disrupted. An invitation for chili—improbable command. We went up to a street in Harlem just as the winter sun was turning black. Darkened windows with thin bands of watchful light above the sills. Inside the halls were dark and empty, filled only with the scent of dust. We, our faces bleached from the cold, in our thin coats, black gloves, had clinging to us the evangelical diffidence of hell-ringing members of a religious sect, a determination glacial, timid, and yet pedantic. Our frozen alarm and fascination carried us into the void of the dead tenement. The house was under a police ban and when we entered, whispering her name, the policeman stared at us with furious incredulity. She was hounded by the police, but for once the occasion was not hers. Somewhere, upstairs, behind another door there had been a catastrophe.

Her own records played over and over on the turntable; everything else was quiet. All of her living places were temporary in the purest meaning of the term. But she filled even a black hotel room with stinging, demonic weight. At the moment she was living with a trumpet player who was just becoming known and who soon after faded altogether. He was as thin as a stick and his lovely, round light face, with frightened, shiny, round eyes, looked like a sacrifice impaled upon the stalk of his neck. His younger brother came out of the bedroom. He stood before us, wavering between confusing possibilities. Tiny, thin, perhaps in his twenties, the young man was engrossed in a blur of functions. He was a sort of hectic Hermes, working in Hades, now buying cigarettes, now darting back to the bedroom, now almost inaudible on the phone, ordering or disposing of something in a light, shaking voice.

"Lady's a little behind. She's over-scheduled herself." Groans and coughs from the bedroom. In the peach shaded lights, the wan rosiness of a beaten sofa was visible. A shell, still flushed from the birth of some crustacean, was filled with cigarette ends. A stocking on the floor. And the record player, on and on, with the bright clarity of her songs. Smoke and perfume and somewhere a heart pounding.

One winter she wore a great lynx coat and in it she moved, menacing and handsome as a Cossack, pacing about in the trap of her vitality. Quarrelsome dreams sometimes rushed through her speech, and accounts of wounds she had inflicted with broken glass. And at the White Rose Bar, a thousand cigarettes punctuated her appearances, which, not only in their brilliance but in the fact of their taking place at all, had about them the aspect of magic. Waiting and waiting: that was what the pursuit of her was. One felt like an old carriage horse standing at the entrance, ready for the cold midnight race through the park. She was always behind a closed door—the fate of those addicted to whatever. And then at last she must come forward, emerge in powders and Vaseline, hair twisted with a curling iron, gloves of satin or silk jersey, flowers—the expensive martyrdom of the "entertainer."

At that time not so many of her records were in print and she was seldom heard on the radio because her voice did not accord with popular taste then. The appearances in night clubs were a necessity. It was a burden to be there night after night, although not a burden to sing, once she had started, her own way. She knew she could do it, that she had mastered it all, but why not ask the questions: Is this all there is? Her work took on, gradually, a destructive cast, as it so often does with the greatly gifted who are doomed to repeat endlessly their own heights of inspiration.

She was late for her mother's funeral. At last she arrived, ferociously appropriate in a black turban. A number of jazz musicians were there. The late morning light fell mercilessly on their unsteady, night faces. In the daytime these people, all except Billie, had a furtive, suburban aspect, like family men who work the night shift. The marks of a fractured domesticity, signals of a real life that is itself almost a secret existence for the performer, were drifting about the little church, adding to the awkward unreality.

Her mother, Sadie Holiday, was short and sentimental, bewildered to be the bearer of such news to the world. She made efforts to *sneak* into Billie's life, but there was no place and no need for her. She was set up from time to time in small restaurants which she ran without any talent and failed in quickly. She never achieved the aim of her life, the professional dream, which was to be "Billie's dresser." The two women bore no resemblance, neither of face nor of body. The daughter was profoundly intelligent and found the tragic use for it in the cunning of destruction. The mother seemed to face each day with the bald hopefulness of a baby and end each evening in a baffled little cry of disappointment. Sadie and Billie Holiday were a violation, a rift in the statistics of life. The great singer was one of those for whom the word *changeling* was invented. She shared the changeling's spectacular destiny and was acquainted with malevolent forces.

She lived to be forty-four; or should it better be said she died at forty-four. Of "enormous complications." Was it a long or a short life? The "highs" she sought with such concentration of course remained a mystery. "Ah, I fault Jimmy for all that," someone said once in a taxi, naming her first husband, Jimmy Monroe, a fabulous Harlem club owner* when she was young.

Once she came to see us in the Hotel Schuyler, accompanied by someone. We sat there in the neat squalor and there was nothing to do and nothing to say and she did not wish to eat. In the anxious gap, I felt the deepest melancholy in her black eyes, an abyss into which every question had fallen without an answer. She died in misery from the erosions and poisons of her fervent, felonious narcotism. The police were at the hospital bedside, vigilant lest she, in a coma, manage a last chemical inner migration.

Her whole life had taken place in the dark. The spotlight shone down on the black, hushed circle in a café; the moon slowly slid through the clouds. Night-working, smiling, in make-up, in long, silky dresses, singing over and over, again and again. The aim of it all is just to be drifting off to sleep when the first rays of the sun's brightness threaten the theatrical eyelids.

THE MAN WHO DANCED WITH BILLIE HOLIDAY
FRANCIS DAVIS

Jazz critic Francis Davis was intrigued by the novelists' view of Billie Holiday as an "apparition," and so he collected these fascinating excerpts from Alice Adams and Maya Angelou, to which he added his own essay and reportage.

Born in Philadelphia in 1946, Mr. Davis has written articles and reviews for the *Philadelphia Inquirer*, *Stereo Review*, and the *Village Voice*, and particularly at this time the *Atlantic Monthly*, where he is a contributing editor. His essays have been collected in books—*In the Moment* and *Outcats*. He wrote *The History of the Blues: The Roots, Music, and the People from Charley Patton to Robert Cray* to accompany a PBS series. In March 1996, his new collection, *Bebop and Nothingness*, was published by Schirmer Books. At work on a biography of John Coltrane, he also teaches a course on jazz blues in the folklore department at the University of Pennsylvania and had been awarded three fellowships in recent years, beginning with a Guggenheim in 1993, a Pew Fellowship in the Arts in 1994, and a Morroe Berger–Benny Carter Fellowship

*It was actually Jimmy's brother Clark who was the club owner [Editor].

from the Institute of Jazz Studies at Rutgers University, also in 1994. He is a member of the Jazz Journalists Association.

Since her death in 1959, Billie Holiday has achieved a sainted second existence in our national imagination. In death as in life, she is hailed as the greatest woman jazz singer of them all, but her legend transcends music, just as it transcended mortal bounds. Holiday is even more a pop icon today than during her lifetime—regrettably, less as a result of the reissues that have proliferated in recent years than as a side effect of *Lady Sings the Blues*, the 1972 Diana Ross star vehicle ostensibly based on the itself-none-too-reliable 1956 autobiography Holiday co-authored with William Dufty. In addition to her own colorful account, there have been at least two other Holiday biographies—Alexis DeVeaux's *Don't Explain* (1980), a shrill book-length prose poem that mother-milks the injustices Holiday suffered as a black woman for cheap pathos, and John Chilton's *Billie's Blues* (1975), a workmanlike sorting out of hard facts which limits itself to Holiday's twenty-five-year recording career.

But the Billie Holiday bibliography isn't limited to the books that inquire into her personal life or those that analyze her contributions to jazz. She is a recurring apparition in novels, poems, plays, and literary memoirs, including *The Autobiography of Malcolm X* (1965) and Frank O'Hara's "The Day Lady Died" (*Lunch Poems*, 1964). Her independence and the devastating costs, both real and psychological, that she paid for it make her a creature of premonitory fascination for women writers in particular.

Billie is late—of course, she is always late—but the crowd in this packed room is not resigned: people are restless, and tense. There is a lot of lighting of cigarets, looking at watches, loud orders for more drinks. And there are scattered rumors: she's sick, she's not coming, been in a wreck—she's just phoned to say she'll be here in ten minutes. And eerily, throughout all that waiting for Billie, on the huge and garish jukebox one of her records is playing; from out of all that poison-colored neon tubing Billie's beautiful, rich and lonely voice is singing, "I cover the waterfront, I'm watching the sea—"

And then suddenly she is there, and everybody knows, and they crane their heads backward to see her, since she has come in by the street entrance like anyone else. Or, not like anyone else at all: she is more beautiful, more shining, holding her face forward like a flower, bright-eyed and smiling, high cheekbones, white teeth and cream-white gardenia at her ear. . . .

With a wonderful gesture Billie throws her coat down on the stage, and for a moment she stands there in the spotlight, mouthing the words coming from the jukebox—"Will the one I love, be coming back to me?"—as everyone laughs and screams and applauds.

Somewhere in that audience, probably up near the front, is a very young and pretty small girl, who is not paying much attention to Billie. Eliza Hamilton, with long smooth blond hair that curls suddenly at the ends, and dark blue eyes. She has serious and obsessive problems of her own: is she pregnant? Her heavy breasts are heavier, and sore. And if she is pregnant, what should she do? Should she marry Evan Quarles, the paler blond and sad, Deep Southern young man at her right? He would like them to marry, and that is strange: Eliza knows that she is more in love than he is, but it is he who urges marriage. He is deeply disturbing, mysterious to her; she is both excited and obscurely alarmed by Evan—is that "in love"? . . . Now she looks at Evan with a mixture of enmity and curiosity: who is he?

Eliza is barely listening to Billie, who now, with her small combo in the background, is singing, "Once they called it jazztime, to a buck and wing—"

Singing, swinging it out.

But Eliza retained that scene of Billie's entrance, and Billie singing. (Singing what? What was she wearing?) She kept it somewhere in her mind; she brought it out and stared at it as she might a stone, something opalescent. At times she wondered how much of it she had imagined. . . .

Should she have an abortion? Who would know a doctor who would do it? Who would pay for it? . . .

But even in the midst of such frenzied speculation, Eliza is aware that this evening—these hours—are important; she *knows* she will remember. And she thinks of the following Monday, when she will be back in Connecticut, in school, and she will tell her friends about seeing Billie— how beautiful she was, her voice. How Evan Quarles, the interesting older man, took her to Fifty-second Street to hear Billie Holiday. She will not tell any friend that she might be pregnant.

Billie has stopped singing, left the stage, and Evan says, "I'd buy you a gardenia if I weren't allergic to them." . . .

Will he want to make love later? Will he take her back to his place, on Horatio Street, in the Village? Eliza can't be sure of anything with Evan. . . .

Eliza looks around at the other talking people, and she suddenly perceives, feels, that there is an extraordinary number of handsome young men, all strangers, all unexplored and possible. She looks at them intently . . . so *attractive* all of them. Aware of her own look, its intentness, she wonders what message she is delivering: is she somehow inviting them, or saying goodbye, as she would to other men if she should marry? And if she should not be pregnant, will she meet one of these new young men months later, and together will they remember hearing, seeing Billie? Will that happen?

Then Eliza notices that the young woman at the next table is heavily pregnant, so huge she must sit back in her chair. Eliza's spirits sink, her fantasy vanishes. She recognizes that young woman as an omen, a terrible sign: she, Eliza, *is* pregnant. . . .

Now Billie is walking back onto the stage; amid thundering applause, shouts, and whistles, she saunters into the smoke-beamed center of light; she stands there, one hip thrust forward. She scans the crowd as though she could see everyone there. Is she possibly seeing the men and feeling the urgent attraction Eliza felt a few minutes before? Her eyes are blank, and her smile says nothing.

"She looks bad," Evan whispers—too loudly, Eliza feels, even in this noisy room. "Drugs—she can't last long."

"Georgia, Georgia, no peace I find . . ." sings Billie, whose beautiful face has come alive, whose eyes say everything.

—*Alice Adams, Listening to Billie (1977)*

I had heard stories of Billie being beaten by men, cheated by drug pushers and hounded by narcotics agents, still I thought she was the most paranoid person I had ever met.

"Don't you have any friends? People you can trust?"

She jerked her body toward me. "Of course I have friends. Good friends. A person who don't have friends might as well be dead." She had relaxed, but my question put her abruptly on the defense again. I was wondering how to put her at ease. I heard Guy's footsteps on the stairs.

"My son is coming home."

"Oh. Shit. How old you say he is?"

"He's twelve and a very nice person" . . .

"Billie Holiday? Oh. Yes. I know about you. Good afternoon, Miss Holiday." He walked over and stuck out his hand. "I'm happy to know you. I read about you in a magazine. They said the police had been giving you a hard time. And that you've had a very hard life. Is that true? What did they do to you? Is there anything you can do back? I mean, sue them or anything?" . . .

Billie's face was a map of astonishment. After a moment, she looked at me. "Damn. He's something, ain't he? Smart. What's he want to be?"

"Sometimes a doctor, and sometimes a fireman. It depends on the day you ask him."

"Good. Don't let him go into show business. Black men in show business is bad news. When they can't get as far as they deserve, they start taking it out on their women. . . ."

. . . She stayed for dinner, saying that I could drop her off on my way to work. She talked to Guy while I cooked. Surprisingly, he sat quiet, listening as she spoke of Southern towns, police, agents, good musicians, and mean men she had known. She carefully avoided profanity and each time she slipped, she'd excuse herself to Guy, saying, "It's just another bad habit I got." After dinner, when the baby sitter arrived, Billie told Guy that she was going to sing him a good-night song.

They went into his room, and I followed. Guy sat on the side of his bed and Billie began, a cappella, "You're My Thrill," an old song heavy with sensuous meaning. She sang as if she was starved for sex and only the boy, looking at her out of bored young eyes, could give her satisfaction. . . .

For the next four days, Billie came to my house in the early mornings, talked all day long and sang a bedtime song to Guy, and stayed until I went to work. She said I was restful to be around because I was so goddam square. Although she continued to curse in Guy's absence, when he walked into the house her language not only changed, she made considerable effort to form her words with distinction.

On the night before she was leaving for New York, she told Guy she was going to sing "Strange Fruit" as her last song. We sat at the dining room table while Guy stood in the doorway.

Billie talked and sang in a hoarse, dry tone the well-known protest song. Her rasping voice and phrasing literally enchanted me. I saw the black bodies hanging from Southern trees. I saw the lynch victims' blood glide from the leaves down the trunks and onto the roots.

Guy interrupted, "How can there be blood at the root?" I made a hard face and warned him, "Shut up, Guy, just listen." Billie had continued under the interruption, her voice vibrating over harsh edges.

She painted a picture of a lovely land, pastoral and bucolic, then added eyes bulged and mouths twisted, onto the Southern landscape.

Guy broke into her song. "What's a pastoral scene, Miss Holiday?" Billie looked up suddenly and studied Guy for a second. Her face became cruel, and when she spoke her voice was scornful. "It means when the crackers are killing the niggers. It means when they take a little nigger like you and snatch off his nuts and shove them down his goddam throat. That's what it means."

The thrust of rage repelled Guy and stunned me.

Billie continued, "That's what they do. That's a goddam pastoral scene."

Guy gave us both a frozen look and said, "Excuse me, I'm going to bed." He turned and walked away.

I lied and said it was time for me to go to work. Billie didn't hear either statement.

I went to Guy's room and apologized to him for Billie's behavior. He smiled sarcastically as if I had been the one who had shouted at him, and he offered a cool cheek for my good night kiss.

—*Maya Angelou, The Heart of a Woman (1981)*

It isn't just in books that one encounters memories of and fantasies about Billie Holiday. Early one New Year's Eve, years ago, a tall, trim white man in his early sixties, who had visibly had many more than one too many, stumbled into the record store I was managing. A Billie Holiday record was playing—I don't remember which. He told me of another New Year's Eve, decades earlier, when as a sailor at liberty in New York, he had danced with Billie Holiday.

He was young then, he told me, and so was she. This supposedly was before she had recorded, before anyone knew who she was. She was performing unbilled in a Harlem nightclub where she and the other female performers were required to mingle with the male patrons and hustle drinks between sets. After hearing her sing, he decided he wanted to dance with her, even though he'd had so much to drink that it was an effort to stand—and even though he had never so much as spoken with a black woman before. At the urging of his shipmates, he found her alone at the bar and asked her to dance—an invitation she accepted silently, with no discernible enthusiasm, he thought.

As he struggled to keep his balance and she struggled to hold him up, he told her that she was the most beautiful woman he'd ever seen. She told him he was drunk. As they danced, he pressed a handful of bills into her palm; he made a point of shoving another handful down her cleavage. She said nothing, but once or twice he fancied that he felt her fingers trying to unlock his to engage them in a caress; once he thought he felt her hand brush against his groin. But he was so numb from the liquor that each time intimate contact was made—if it had been made—it was over before he could respond.

When the dance was over, his buddies cheered him loudly and helped him to his chair. He hollered for another round of drinks, on him, and, digging into his pocket to pay for them, discovered the six crumpled twenties that she had returned there. One hundred and twenty dollars, a good piece of change for the time.

He told me that he considered Billie Holiday's action (let's pretend for a moment that it was Billie Holiday) of rejecting both his money and his drunken advance an unquestionable and unsolicited kindness.

TURNING BACK THE CLOCK FOR LADY DAY
MELVIN MADDOCKS

Here is a philosophical essay rather than a review about the production, *Lady Day at Emerson's Bar and Grill*, a dramatic stage production with music that purported to be a biography of Lady. It inspired Melvin Maddocks to reminisce about Billie's impact as a performer, and he made a fascinating, unique observation about Billie's style: "She did so much with phrasing—as if something eager in her could not wait for the beat, or something sad in her lagged just behind it."

Lonette McKee also played Lady in the film *Round Midnight*, starring Dexter Gordon, who was nominated for an Academy Award.

An audience can accept an actor playing Mozart because the impersonator is required only to interpret the temperament of an odd little man, not compose a symphony. But an actress playing Billie Holiday—as Lonette McKee has been doing in Lanie Robertson's Off-Broadway musical biography, "Lady Day at Emerson's Bar and Grill," at the Vineyard Theater—must do more than portray a tormented woman. She has to deliver the goods—come out on stage and sing "Easy Living" and

"Don't Explain" and other show pieces of perhaps the greatest of all jazz vocalists.

It is an exorbitant demand, like asking an actor playing Ted Williams to step up to the plate and hit a 400-foot home run. No actress—no singer—can "do" Billie Holiday any more than an actor—or a singer or a trumpet player—could "do" Louis Armstrong.

Still, any reason is a good reason for returning our minds and hearts to the moving presence of the woman whom the saxophonist Lester Young named Lady Day.

Billie Holiday was a lot of different people at once. An actress would have plenty of problems interpreting her, even without singing.

There was the Billie with the magnolia in her hair and the silver blue mink coat and the pea-green Cadillac, living out the dreams of a wretched childhood.

And there was the appallingly lonely woman, cradling one dog after another in her lap, from the mongrel Rajah Ravoy to the chihuahua Pepi.

Billie put everything—the dreams and the nightmares—into her singing. She could take the most banal lyrics and fill them with a meaning that overflowed the words.

At her best, Billie sang with almost no mannerisms. She stood regally still, head slightly thrown back. She "held her arms," one musician noted, "in the position of a runner ready to sprint." Sometimes her fingers snapped, but lazily, disdainfully. Yet within this stillness, within this languor hid a pent-up power.

It was not the voice itself. Billie had about as small a range as even a pop singer could get away with. She produced a warm, burred one, husky to the point of a rasp as the years went by.

Billie had only two blues in her repertoire: "Fine and Mellow" and "Billie's Blues"—both her own compositions. She was too understated to be a blues shouter. But most of what she sang had a feeling of blues. She could melt the coldest heart with "Why Was I Born?"—simply by playing down despair to wistfulness. She did so much with phrasing—as if something eager in her could not wait for the beat, or something sad in her lagged just behind it.

She was a minimalist in technique with a volcano inside. Billie held onto certain notes, certain words like a child hugging a security blanket.

"Nobody sings the word 'hunger' like I do," she once said. "Or the word 'love.'"

Joy was another word she pronounced like nobody else, as if it were a sweet being savored on the tongue. Joy may have gone out of her life, but it survived in her singing, almost in spite of herself.

"The blues to me are like being very sad—and again, like going to church and being very happy," she explained to an interviewer toward the end of her life, as if she could not believe her own resilience.

This erratic but somehow holy elation in life she passed on to her listeners as no jazz singer since has done. No wonder everybody wants to bring her back any way possible—even as a theatrical clone.

KNOWING WHEN TO STOP
NED ROREM

In his autobiography, the critically acclaimed composer referred several times to the effect Billie's singing had on his own artistic development. And when he philosophized as a mature man, she assumed an important place, to his mind, in the cultural landscape of the world.

• • •

Upon first hearing her sing "Fine and Mellow," then "Strange Fruit" in 1938 on the original Commodore release, Rorem wrote: ". . . The effect of her performance would be as singular on my notion of what music was all about . . . Had anything remotely like it been heard before? . . . Billie's oxymoronic qualities—the studied freshness, the sorrowful pleasure, the tinny, velvet timbre—defined the music, even as they answered Yeats's question: 'How can we know the dancer from the dance?' . . . In bending a phrase, stretching a melody, delaying the beat so as to 'come in wrong' just right, she forever influenced my own approach to song writing . . ."

• • •

"Interesting, isn't it, how Billie Holiday, who is said to have spoken for her people more than any other black singer, spoke through white music? It lay in tone of voice. Not for years would she be a jukebox fixture, like the bright and younger Ella Fitzgerald, of whom Billie was the dark side. But if Ella had optimistic groupies, the tragedian Billie already had the cult mostly of the Caucasian intelligentsia, though she didn't know quite what to do with them."

• • •

One night, Rorem saw her in the audience at the Dizzy Club on 52nd Street. Her manner was warm, her perfume delightful. "She kept up a running commentary on 'Old Rocking Chair' being crooned by the pianist in the corner—*My dear old Aunt Harriett*—'Yeah, she was queer, too.'" Suddenly Billie began to sing "Night and Day." Rorem marveled that she could move so quickly from banter to high art.

. . .

"(Harpsichordist) Ralph (Kirkpatrick) loved Billie Holiday, even knew her a little (a little was all anyone knew her.) We visited the singer at the Onyx Club where I got drunk, and in adulation sank down to put my head 'neath her skirt, which smelled like a Catholic church. Bringing her back in the early hours to Ralph's small flat on Lexington Avenue, it became clear that Billie in all her uneducated glory could attend as astutely as any trained musicologue. She admired his harpsichord, its construction, its repertory . . ." Rorem and Ralph explained to her that the lyric of "Fine and Mellow" was written in "iambic pentameter." "Iambic pentameter," said Billie. "Yeah, that's it."

. . .

Rorem theorized, or philosophized, that "frivolity" is "a quality contained in all artists, since all art is made from the contrasts found by an ability to express relationships between the superb and the silly . . . the high camp, spiritually practical yet sad frivolity of say, Haydn, Voltaire, Gogol, Auden, Billie Holiday."

PART SIX

Heart and Soul:

Billie Holiday
Remembered

BILLIE HOLIDAY REMEMBERED
PRODUCED AND PUBLISHED BY THE NEW YORK JAZZ MUSEUM

Compiled and arranged by Linda Kuehl and Ellie Schocket and assisted by Dan Morgenstern, this booklet was produced by the New York Jazz Museum in 1973 as a collection of memoirs about Billie Holiday. It is entirely reproduced, including Frank O'Hara's poem, "The Day Lady Died," which appeared as the last word and crowning jewel.

Very few jazz musicians or singers could inspire this much adulation among their colleagues, critics, record and concert producers, and others involved in the jazz world. The last three sentences of Billy Taylor's commentary are the soul of pithiness and perhaps all that really needs to be said to introduce anyone to Billie's music. Others recognized her as a revolutionary jazz singer. John Hammond recalled his first impressions of her. Buck Clayton takes advantage of this opportunity to proclaim that the movie, *Lady Sings the Blues*, is a fairy tale. Barney Josephson, who hired Billie to sing in his secure, racially integrated club, Cafe Society, in Greenwich Village, gets a chance to remind people of "Strange Fruit," the song he gave her and asked her to sing. Roy Eldridge speaks of the other-worldliness of her effect on audiences.

The variety of viewpoints and fresh comments are still a joy to read, and perhaps they are even more touching now that many of them give us a chance to remember the spontaneity of the great and lovable musicians and others in the music and entertainment worlds who praised her and have also died.

Nothing was more perfect than what she was. Nor more willing to fail. (If we call failure something light can realize. Once you have seen it, or felt whatever thing she conjured growing in your flesh.)

At the point where what she did left singing, you were on your own. At the point where what she was was in her voice, you listen and make your own promises.

More than I have felt to say, she says always. More than she has ever felt is what we mean by fantasy. Emotion, is wherever you are. She stayed in the street.

The myth of blues is dragged from people. Though some others make categories no one understands. A man told me Billie Holiday wasn't singing the blues, and he knew. O.K., but what I ask myself is what had she seen to shape her singing so? What, in her life, proposed such tragedy, such final hopeless agony? Or flip the coin and she is singing, "Miss Brown To You." And none of you cats would dare cross her. One eye closed, and her arms held in such balance, as if all women were so aloof. Or could laugh so.

And even in the laughter, something other than brightness, completed the sound. A voice that grew from a singer's instrument to a woman's. And from that (those last records critics say are weak) to a black landscape of need, and perhaps, suffocated desire.

Sometimes you are afraid to listen to this lady.

—Imamu Amiri Baraka (LeRoi Jones)

Jo Jones: Billie introduced things. No innovator like her. Hasn't been one before, since and never will be. The innovations—they owe it all to Billie. Everybody's copying it.

Cozy Cole: The first time I heard Billie was when she was a young girl, at the Hot Cha in 1934. I knew she would make it big—and she did just that.

Mary Lou Williams: Billie Holiday was a pioneer and a genius. What she started nobody has ever been able to imitate. She was great because the suffering in her life developed into a true love that all heard who listened to her sing. Her singing reached people's hearts because it was a true thing. It's rare to find someone so beautiful who's a great artist at the same time.

Billy Taylor: Billie Holiday was a unique artist even though her roots were firmly planted in the traditional jazz she grew up with. She was an innovator of the finest order. Her sound was very personal and her conception of how to sing a song was more of a jazz conception than almost any other singer's of her period. Her charisma as a performer was unequaled. She was an extremely beautiful woman; the force of her personality and the depth of her talent enabled her to reach audiences on a level which transcended music. Though her personal life was tragic, her performances, both on record and in person, changed the direction of jazz singing. She was a superbly creative woman.

Duke Ellington: As an artist, as a person, to see or to hear, Lady Day was the *essence* of cool.

James P. Johnson: Her style revolutionized and advanced the art of singing.

Milt Gabler: She was the creator of a style which defies imitation. There are thousands of Holiday imitators, both male and female. And there have been queens before her. But there is only one Lady Day.

Rex Stewart: Miss Holiday is as essential to jazz as Miss Marian Anderson is to the classics.

Whitney Balliett: Billie Holiday and Bessie Smith, the two greatest jazz singers, attained with nothing more than their voices a majesty and wit and emotion that few instrumentalists have matched. Indeed, they suggested the direction in which jazz singing might go.

Leonard Feather: Every note of every lyric she sang proved her to be the complete, untrained, unadulterated, definitive jazz singer. It is impossible to describe Billie's voice: the tart, gritty timbre, the special way of bending a note downward, the capacity for reducing a melody to its bare bones or, when it seemed appropriate, for retaining all its original qualities. Billie Holiday's voice was the voice of living intensity, of soul in the true sense of that greatly abused word. As a human being she was sweet, sour, kind, mean, generous, profane, lovable, and impossible, and nobody who knew her expects to see anyone quite like her ever again.

Dan Morgenstern: Billie Holiday in person was an unforgettable experience. Fortunately, she is an artist who "comes through" on records with surprising presence (Louis Armstrong, Fats Waller and Bessie Smith are others). Her later work, with its sometimes nearly unbearable poignancy, is unique, but the Billie who means most to me is the young, vibrant Lady Day who, with Lester Young, Teddy Wilson and a host of the greatest jazzmen of the time, made music of imperishable loveliness and strength.

John Hammond: I first heard Billie in early 1933. She was 17, and she'd been scarred by life already. Her singing almost changed my musical taste and my musical life, because she was the first girl singer I'd come across who actually sang like an improvising jazz genius—an extension, almost, of a Louis Armstrong. The way she sang around a melody, her uncanny harmonic sense and her sense of lyric content were almost unbelievable in a girl of 17. And her time was something else.

Teddy Wilson: "What a Little Moonlight Can Do," "Miss Brown to You," all those tunes we did together in 1935 and '36, are known all over the world now. She influenced an awful lot of singers with those sides. I'd never heard a girl sing like Billie. She was so much a part of the groups on these records—everyone involved was a fan of the others, Billie included—and I don't think she ever surpassed her performances on those sessions.

Max Kaminsky: She really sang in those days. Her voice was the blues, but she could make you feel so happy, too. In her peak years, between 1935 and 1941, her stunning sense of phrasing and tempo were still completely unselfconscious and the unaffected sweet-sadness of her voice could make you ring with joy as well as sorrow. A large, fleshy, but beautifully boned woman with satin-smooth beige skin, she always possessed an air of hauteur, not only in her manner but in the arch of her brow, the pose of her head, and the dignity of her carriage. But her haughtiness hid a shyness so vast that she spoke in practically a whisper. And even in her most turbulent, tortured days later on, she was always basically what she had been then—an uncompromising, devastatingly honest kind of girl, and always, in the deepest sense, a lady. Her sobriquet, Lady Day, suited her exactly.

Barney Josephson: I never heard another singer begin to approach Billie's talent. She exerted tremendous influence on singing in this country. I listened to her sing "Strange Fruit" three times a night at Café Society and everytime she sang that song, it was unforgettable.

Count Basie: Billie sang the blues—sometimes, in her way—but she wasn't a blues singer. She was a stylist. She was the first girl singer we had. Playing for her was too much. I used to be just as thrilled to hear her as the audience was.

Buck Clayton: When she joined Count Basie, we had to rehearse because of the big band, mostly for the horns. Oh, we had places for her to come in, but that was all. She would follow Lester Young or me. All she needed to know was when to come in and when to quit. Aside from that, she'd sing the way she wanted to. Nobody would ever tell *her* how to sing. She sang the way she felt. It was a plaintive voice, with a lot of feeling. I haven't heard anyone sound like her since. (And as for that movie, *Lady Sings the Blues*, from the very first shot to the last, it was a complete fiction.)

Harry "Sweets" Edison: It would be most beautiful the whole trip because everybody loved Billie Holiday and everybody loved Pres. And everybody would wait for Pres to jump up and play because he had a sound plus a very unusual way of holding his horn. The audience would love to see it. And the way she would sing. He blew behind her all the time—all the time. No, there'll never be another Pres and there'll never be another Billie Holiday.

Roy Eldridge: To me, Billie Holiday must have come from another world because nobody had the effect on people she had. I saw it happen when we worked together for nine months at Kelly's Stables on 52nd Street. She seemed to have such rapport with the people. Billie could get to the people. I have seen her make people cry and make them happy. She was just out of sight.

Dizzy Gillespie: Billie Holiday was one of a kind for her generation.

Chris Albertson: About the only thing left that is truly Billie Holiday's and which no one dares tamper with are the records she made during the two-and-a-half decades of her turbulent career—records that preserve the nervous voice of a teenage girl making her debut among giants of instrumental jazz, the spirited poignancy of her voice at its peak of maturity, and the pathos of the latter-day Billie whose voice, like delicate china of another time, showed signs of wear but retained its indefinable beauty.

Miles Davis: I love the way Billie sings. She sings like Lester Young and Louis Armstrong play. What I like about Billie is that she sings it just the way she hears it and that's usually the way best suited for her. She sings way behind the beat and then she brings it up—hitting right on the beat. You can play behind the beat, but every once in a while you have to cut into the rhythm section on the beat and that keeps everybody together. Sinatra does it by accenting a word. A lot of singers try to sing like Billie, but just the act of playing behind the beat doesn't make it sound soulful. I'd rather hear her alone with Bobby Tucker, the pianist she used to have. She doesn't need any horns. She sounds like one anyway.

Bobby Tucker: I played for Lady Day for about two and a half years and I guess you'd call it quite an experience. I'll always remember the concert at Carnegie. It was one of the greatest thrills of my life. Lady was the easiest singer I ever played for. You know, with most singers you have to guide them and carry them along—they're either laying back or else running away from you. But not Billie Holiday. Man, it was a thrill to play for her. She had the greatest conception of a beat I ever heard. It just didn't matter what kind of a song she was singing. She could sing the fastest tune in the world or else something that was like a dirge, but you could take a metronome and she'd be right there. Hell! With Lady you could relax while you were playing for her. You could damn near forget the tune.

Milt Hinton: Billie Holiday was the first singer I ever recorded with, in '36 in New York City. Years later, I felt very honored that she asked me to do what turned out to be her last record date. She had a choice of bassists but she picked me—and of course I made it.

Billy Eckstine: Musicians? She idolized musicians—Lester Young, Roy Eldridge, Buck Clayton, Freddie Green, Basie, Jo Jones, Walter Page . . . The guys she loved, she loved.

Charlie Mingus: Oh, there's no way to describe how my boy felt when he was all tied up inside digging the mood conjured up by a lady in Philharmonic Hall singing to an audience that was with her every note and innuendo and someone called a tune that was great and Lady Soul who had already blessed the entire evening with her presence said, "You got it, Mingus, what's your 'Sophisticated Lady' like tonight?" Just pure music, no funny clothes or trick effects, 'cause that Lady has elegance in dress and manner and mind. She is the song and the people are pleased and showed it with their Bravos! and Encores!

Lionel Hampton: Boy, when she sang, she just kicked the band off, made the band just fly. She and Louis Armstrong both did that.

Mal Waldron: Billie was a great cook. She loved to entertain, to have people come to her house and have dinner. You had to eat everything and she kept piling food on your plate. Everytime I left her house I put on at least four pounds.

Sam Rivers: In the fall of 1956, I was on the verge of a nervous breakdown. I decided to go to Miami. Billie Holiday was there, Cab Calloway, King Cole, Dinah Washington, B. B. King, Ray Charles, Chet Baker . . . after work, everyone would go to the Sir John Motel to jam until 8 or 9 in the morning. I played next to Billie—she'd just done a chorus and I took my solo. She told her piano player, Carl Drinkard, that she liked the way I played. Then I had an attack, broke out in cold sweat, felt faint. Billie noticed and told me to go outside; she'd watch my horn. She said she'd watched Pres' horn for him when he had to go out. When I came back she was singing "Detour Ahead". I listened to the anguish in her voice and the lyrics seemed to be about my own problems. I started to cry.

Vernon Duke: Many a tune that seemed completely unexciting in cold print was turned into a near masterpiece by her ministrations. Can any composer ask for more?

Ned Rorem: With Billie Holiday it was not so much the song as her way with the song—she could make mediocrity seem masterful.

Sylvia Syms: I was one of those human beings (and there were many) who was greatly influenced by the Lady. More than anything, I wanted to sing. When I heard Billie that first night I walked in Kelly's Stable on 52nd Street, I knew this was the way I wanted to sing. So much so, I spent the first few professional years of my life imitating her . . . I have an album by one of the more recently popular ladies of jazz, a very talented one, I might add, who gives the identical performance of the song, "Yesterdays," that was one of Lady's great recordings. But this other singer gives the identical performance, even to include the same lyrical error—proving that the Lady still shows her influence on the jazz singers of today.

Frank Sinatra: It is Billie Holiday, whom I first heard in 52nd Street clubs in the thirties, who was and still remains the greatest single musical influence on me.

Ella Fitzgerald: Once, when we were playing at the Apollo, Billie was working a block away at the Harlem Opera House. Some of us went over between shows to catch her, and afterwards we went backstage. I did something then, and I still don't know if it was the right thing to do—I asked her for her autograph.

Tony Bennett: I was always a fan of hers. Each little song that she recorded was a production so that you got a Lester Young solo, some Teddy Wilson piano . . . No one seems to know that craft any more. She was a great teacher.

Lena Horne: Billie was not a tough woman. She was so vulnerable, she was like an open wound.

Clark Terry: I never know what to say about people like her because anything you say will sound trite compared to the way you feel. But I can say this—whenever I have the opportunity to coach young jazz singers. I tell them to study her style because her phrasing is a must for any jazz singer. I think they've missed the boat unless they've been enlightened to the style of Lady Day.

Stan Getz: I marveled at how strong she was for a person who had taken so many knocks from life, and at her honesty as an artist. When I had the opportunity to work with her, I found her to be nothing but sweet and gentle.

Carmen McRae: I'll say this about her—she sang the way she was. That's really Lady when you listen to her on a record. Whether it's a jump tune or a ballad, whatever you get out of a record of hers is really Lady. Only way she was happy was through a song. I don't think she expressed herself as she would want to when you met her in person. The only time she was at ease and at rest with herself was when she sang. She was my idol. She could do no wrong.

Annie Ross: You couldn't help but notice Lady with that incredible face and that presence. She really was a lady. She was my idol.

Pearl Bailey: She touched my life and I touched her life and I'm glad. She was one of a kind.

Joe Williams: Lady made you feel—really feel—whatever she was singing.

Leon Thomas: I think she was the heaviest singer since Bessie Smith. I can listen to "Lady in Satin" and break into tears.

James Brown: When I think of Billie Holiday I almost cry.

Martin Williams: It seems to me that the Billie Holiday of the Fifties was not only a great dramatic performer, but an even greater jazz singer because she became a greater musician. Her voice? It may well be that it deteriorated, but for me the disheveled edge of her sound comes from deeply suppressed tears, tears which she simply could not let go without the deeper self-pity she denied herself, suppressed tears upon which every emotion she undertook—from gaiety even to sadness—was imposed.

Barry Ulanov: The inner disturbance is dreadful, but the outer calm remains, and along with it perhaps the most brilliant and inspired singing in jazz.

Nat Hentoff: The most hurt and hurting style in jazz.

Norman Granz: Billie remains, as always, the greatest vocalist in jazz. (1946)

Bobby Colomby: My brother, Jules, had been involved in the jazz community while I was growing up. As a result, jazz was the music I was accustomed to hearing. Billie Holiday was an integral part of this music . . . When Blood, Sweat & Tears was selecting material for its second album, I suggested "God Bless the Child" because it is such a beautiful statement. The rest of the band agreed . . . Now that popular music has come to favor personal messages, I hope people start to look back and find out about Billie Holiday.

William Dufty: Billie heard Louis Armstrong singing when she was a child. He became her model. Later, he became her friend. In any listing of all-time jazz immortals, Louis is number one in his category, as Billie is in hers. Yet of this unlikely pair, Armstrong became a national monument, a traveling shrine. Billie was something else. Louis attained sainthood in his lifetime, Billie was the unrepentant sinner. Billie accepted this and understood it. It was her reverence for truth that made her a menace to what passes for art and culture . . . I always felt that a thousand years from now, as long as the language endures, people will still listen to her singing and be moved by it.

Cootie Williams: A truly creative jazz stylist.

Linda Keene: The world of jazz is eternally grateful to Billie Holiday.

George Simon: Billie has always projected a pulsating pliancy, a spontaneity and honesty of a truly great jazz artist. No wonder so many of us consider her a giant.

George Wein: People ask me who is my favorite musician or singer. I used to stop and think about all the people I know so well and whose music I love. Then I realized what the only honest reply could be. When I am home by myself, or with close friends, and not concerned with listening to records as a reviewer, or for academic purposes, but only to hear music that makes me feel good, I play Billie Holiday. She is my favorite. Lady Day will always be the queen.

Dickie Wells: Billie brought joy to song. Something like Pops. When she came into a room, it was joy there already.

Erroll Garner: She was like ice cream and cake, she was so lovely. But she was all soul, ALL soul.

Jimmy Rowles: I was in awe of her. All of us who worked with her were in constant awe. I loved her—oh, how I loved her!

Studs Terkel: She walked out onto the stage with a gardenia in her hair. She half closed her eyes and softly snapped her fingers. She swayed ever so gently—and she sang. She was The Lady.

The Day Lady Died
It is 12:20 in New York a Friday
three days after Bastille day, yes
It is 1959 and I go get a shoeshine
because I will get off the 4:19 in Easthampton
at 7:15 and then go straight to dinner
and I don't know the people who will feed me

I walk up the muggy street beginning to sun
and have a hamburger and a malted and buy
an ugly NEW WORLD WRITING to see what the poets
in Ghana are doing these days

I go on to the bank
and Miss Stillwagon (first name Linda I once Heard)
doesn't even look up my balance for once in her life
and in the GOLDEN GRIFFIN I get a little Verlaine
for Patsy with drawings by Bonnard although I do
think of Hesiod, trans. Richard Lattimore or
Brendan Behan's new play or Le Balcon or Les Negres
of Genet, but I don't, I stick with Verlaine
after practically going to sleep with quandariness

and for Mike I just stroll into the PARK LANE
Liquor Store and ask for a bottle of Strega and
then I go back where I came from the 6th Avenue
and the tobacconist in the Ziegfeld Theatre and
casually ask for a carton of Gauloises and a carton
of Picayunes, and a NEW YORK POST with her face on it

and I am sweating a lot by now and thinking of
leaning on the john door in the 5 SPOT
while she whispered a song along the keyboard
to Mal Waldron and everyone and I stopped breathing.

—Frank O'Hara, 1959

QUEEN OF THE BLUES IS DEAD AT 44
JAMES DONAHUE

Of the scores of obituaries I've read about Billie Holiday, the following one had, as Billie did in her singing, the most feeling. There are mistakes, as there were in many of the obituaries in even the most responsible publications. Billie was born in Philadelphia, not Baltimore. She made her first recording with Benny Goodman in November 1933, not 1935. She was not really Queen of the Blues; she sang all types of popular music. "Fine and Mellow" was probably a cowritten song, with Billie Holiday and record producer Milt Gabler as the primary participants, though Billie got the credit and collected the royalties. Her last appearance was at the Phoenix Theater in New York, not in the city Phoenix. And she was buried next to her mother in St. Raymond's Cemetery in the Bronx.

Eventually her widower, Louis McKay, who is now dead, put a marker on her grave.

Despite the mistakes, the obituary is a gem.

Every best effort has been made to locate James Donahue.

From Baltimore to New Orleans, from Kansas City to Chicago, wherever jazz holds reign, the blues rose and fell in a mournful wail yesterday.

Lady Day was dead.

Jazzdom's queen of queens, Billie Holiday, the girl with the tortured soul and the incomparable voice, would sing no more.

And the trumpets moaned, the trombones sighed, and the drums rolled out in disconsolation throughout the jazz world.

For with Billie, a magnificent part of that world died.

"A tragic, tragic loss," said Benny Goodman, with whom Billie cut her first record in 1935.

And his words were echoed in jazz chambers throughout the land as musicians who knew her, played with her, and best of all, heard her sing, fumbled for words to express themselves. Behind the unspoken words it was there for all to feel—the sense of irreplaceable loss.

For them, there was only this: there would never be another Lady Day.

For her passing—at 44—in the early hours yesterday at Metropolitan Hospital, was tragedy compounded on tragedy.

There were those that remembered her, not as the shriveled, tormented shadow of a woman whose fast life had finally caught up with her. They remembered her as she was—the very heart and soul of the blues, the woman who, above all, could capture and hold enthrallingly the spirit of all jazzdom.

But perhaps it was her life, one of sordidness, bitterness, ignominy and defeat, that made Billie great—that put the vibrance of suffering, the world of tortured feeling into the blues in which she drowned herself when she sang.

Perhaps it was all that that made her voice, in the very words of the song she herself wrote, "Fine and Mellow."

Billie was born in Baltimore on April 7, 1915, of a father who was a jazz musician and a mother who took in washing—and she later described her home as "just another one-night stand."

At 14 she was on marijuana, and it was heroin a few years later—a habit she never was able to shake and which, in the end, probably killed her, though kidney trouble and a faltering heart were given as the actual causes of the death.

At 15, she got her first job singing in a Harlem night spot, and from there on, musically speaking, it was all uphill—the record with Benny, later with Artie Shaw as the first Negro girl singer with a white band. She was with, and loved by, them all—Louis Armstrong, Count Basie, Jack Teagarden, the entire roll call of jazz.

But it was all downhill in other ways for Billie. Drink and dope were her twin consolations—and her destruction.

Arrested three times, she spent a year in prison—and was back on the dope almost as soon as she got out. The monkey remained on her back until the end. At Metropolitan Hospital, where she was taken after her collapsing May 31, police found heroin in her room and she admitted she had been "sniffing."* She was arrested in her hospital bed.

In her last public appearance, a benefit in Phoenix in May, Billie sang what turned out to be her curtain song, "T'ain't Nobody's Business If I Do."

That was the answer Lady Day always gave when friends remonstrated with her about the dope—it was nobody's business.

But she was wrong. It was their business, because it was their loss.

The jazz world today had, indeed, "The Right to Sing the Blues."

Miss Holiday will repose at a midtown funeral chapel until Tuesday morning. Then, after a funeral Mass at St. Paul the Apostle Roman Catholic Church on W. 59th St., she will be buried in Brooklyn.

MEMORIES
JIMMY ROWLES

It seemed fitting to me to end this book not with an obituary but with Jimmy Rowles's memories. One great raconteur deserves another; that is why Jimmy Rowles, who is not only a great jazz pianist but a gifted visual artist, gets the last word about Lady Day. Rowles's tales of Billie are bawdy, hilarious, profoundly perceptive, loving, and poignant. Donald Clarke saved Rowles's tape for the finale of his book, too.

In giving permission to use an excerpt of his memories originally published in *Wishing on the Moon,* Jimmy Rowles requested

---

*Editor's note: This is the only reference any place to Billie's admitting to sniffing heroin or using any other drugs, except for plain cigarettes, while she was in the hospital.

two deletions, and the compiler as editor has accommodated him. Rowles also wanted to add that Barney Kessel thought that Billie seemed to be a creature who lived in the moment, without a plan— "lost," Jimmy Rowles concluded. And Ben Webster commented, "Ooooh, that poor girl." Jimmy "felt very sorry for Lady Day sometimes; she was so lonesome," he said. Nevertheless, Mr. Rowles's monologue is upbeat, in part because he was mindful of the miracle of her musical superiority and success—the miracle of the distance she traveled.

Jimmy Rowles was born in Spokane, Washington, on August 19, 1918. After studying at the University of Washington, he moved to Los Angeles and played with Lester Young in 1942. Subsequently he played with Benny Goodman and Woody Herman. He was especially well-known for accompanying singers Peggy Lee, Billie Holiday, and Ella Fitzgerald. He worked in duos in New York City with saxophonist Zoot Sims, and bassists George Mraz and Buster Williams. He played and recorded a great deal with bassist Red Mitchell. One of Rowles's many fine compositions is "The Peacock." A sensitive player firmly rooted in the jazz tradition, he attracted other pianists to his gigs to study his style, and he had an exceptional ability to create a moody ambience. Jimmy Rowles died as this book was being prepared for publication.

One time my old lady fixed her hair a certain way and Lady liked it, so she fixed her hair that way too. They were tight. When Dorothy first met Lady was in '42, and all the bands would come in on Sunday afternoon, like Count Basie, Jimmie Lunceford, Duke, and I remember one Sunday, the first time I brought my old lady out, and Lady sat with us.

This was before the days of complexes, when somebody says "Hello" and somebody else says, "What did he mean by that?" It was very uncomplex, in those days, living. It had its own complexity, but there was nothing on the outside to fuck it up. It was just up to you to get to it, not like going through twelve doors first.

Anyway, Nat Cole was playing, and Buck Clayton was playing, and Lady starts screaming at him, "Go on, play it, you blue-eyed sonofabitch, you motherfucker, let 'em have it!" And Dorothy's hanging on to me and saying, "What's happening?" I had cautioned her out front, but she'd never heard it like that before. But she got used to it and started enjoying it. And Prez would be sitting over in the corner saying, "Isn't that nice. Isn't that nice." And he'd see a chick and he'd say, "Damn, I like that." And he'd empty his whisky glass and he'd get up there and start blowing and wipe 'em all out. It was really wild. Those that were there will remember. . . .

One time in New York I came out of the Roxy Theater and going into this Chinese joint across the street I see Lady coming along, and she has Pepe with her, and Pepe wants to get down and chew all the garbage, and she's cursing at Pepe, and everyone's stopping and saying, "Look at that terrible coloured girl," and the language is all coming out. And I'm standing behind her and she says, "What are you doing here?" I said, "I'm with Evelyn Knight at the Roxy." And she says, "That fuckin' bitch. She's doin' the Roxy for $10,000 a week and I'm still doin' the Apollo for $1,500. Fuck her. And fuck you." And I hadn't seen her for two years! I said, "Wait a minute. You're puttin' it all on *me*." And she says, "You motherfuckin' white ofay," and she goes through all of it, and Pepe goes into the garbage can and she's screamin' and the people are standing there and they're gettin' ready to call the police. Oh I loved her. Oh how I loved her.

Lady Day liked to have you tell her you loved her. Of course, I told her. Everybody used to tell her; you couldn't help it. She'd do something, and you'd have to say, "Jesus, how I love you!"

Another time she says to me, "Louis is out of town, so you've got to take me home." So I wait till she's ready. "You gotta feed me. I wanna go to a Chinese place." So all right; if she wants to go to Tokyo, we go.

So we go to a Chinese place a block away, and we sit down, and we order to go—because I want to take her home, she's going to have her food and I'm gonna go home. So we're sitting there and all of a sudden this coloured cat walked into the kitchen with a tray, and she flipped. She started throwing things, swearing, yelling, "Did you see that? There's not a Chinaman on earth who would let a black motherfucker in his kitchen or a white motherfucker either. This ain't no Chinese restaurant, this is a bunch of shit!" Then the owner comes over, and she chews his ass off, and finally the guy comes with the food, and we take the food, and I'm trying to drag her out, Come on Lady, I'm laughing and she's still screaming, "You fuckin' slant-eyed motherfucker, you Chinese can't, I bet this shit's gonna taste—"

I get her in the car, take her home, get her into her room, put her into bed, tuck her in with her food—"There's your shrimp, your foo young, you've got it all here. Now you're straight, now good night, you lovely bitch. (Kiss.) Talk to you tomorrow; now eat your goddam food, drink the rest of your gin." Then she'd get coy. She's in bed, and her titties are sticking out and all that shit. "Louis is out of town, you know." I know it. I wouldn't ball her, because I wouldn't spoil it for anything. . . .With Lady Day you thought permanent.

Selected Discography

Billie Holiday's recording career can be divided into three rough periods: her first recordings for Brunswick (now Columbia) from during the '30s; her Decca recordings from the mid-'40s through 1951; and the Verve years through the late-'50s. She returned to Columbia for a final swan song, *Lady in Satin*, in 1959. There were also other recordings for smaller labels, notably for Milt Gabler's Commodore label in the late '30s, that show up in various places. This material has been issued in both "complete" (and expensive) sets as well as in various anthologies and selections, first on LP, then on cassette and CD. The following is a list of some of the highlights of the currently available catalog for both first-time and more experienced listeners.

Complete Sets

The Quintessential Billie Holiday, Vols. 1–9. Columbia Jazz Masterpieces 40646/40790/44048/44252/44423/45449/46180/47030/47031
    Nine CDs containing all her original recordings for Brunswick and related labels, including Roy Eldridge, Benny Carter, Lester Young, Teddy Wilson, et al., in the backing groups.

Lady's Decca Days, Vols. 1 and 2. MCA 31321/31322.
    Her more pop-oriented recordings for Decca cut between 1944 and 1950. Also issued as *The Complete Decca Recordings* (Decca Jazz 2-601).

The Complete Billie Holiday on Verve, 1945–1959. Verve 10-314-517658-2.
    A 10-CD set of everything Holiday recorded for Verve and related labels, plus a 220-page booklet by Phil Schaap.

The Legacy, 1933–1959. Columbia Legacy 3-47724.

Just her Columbia-owned recordings, so this is fairly good on the early recordings and includes some of her very last, but has nothing in between. Three CDs.

16 Most Requested Songs. Columbia Legacy 53776.

One CD of her "biggest hits."

From the Original Decca Masters. MCA 5766.

Selections from the two-CD set.

Billie Holiday. Verve 831371-2.

History of the Real Billie Holiday. Verve 823233-4.

The Billie Holiday Songbook. Verve 823246-2.

Nice single-CD selection of Holiday singing jazz standards with accompanists Harry "Sweets" Edison, Coleman Hawkins, Buck Clayton, Oscar Peterson, and other '50s jazz luminaries.

Lady in Autumn: The Best of the Verve Years. Verve 2-849434-2.

Two-CD set of Verve recordings.

Later Recordings

Lady in Satin. Columbia Jazz Masterpieces 40247.

Reissue of controversial last issued album, featuring string arrangements accompanying a vocally limited Holiday.

The Last Recordings. Verve 846470-2.

More Ray Ellis string arrangements on this (unissued at the time) last album.

Permissions

In order of their appearance in the book; titles are as they originally appeared on each work (some titles were changed for the sake of identification in this anthology).

"Lady Day" by Whitney Balliett, from the *New Yorker*, Nov. 4, 1991. Reprinted by permission; © Whitney Balliett. Originally in the *New Yorker*. All rights reserved.

"Lady Day" by Leonard Feather, from the book *From Satchmo to Miles*, Da Capo Press, Inc., New York, 1972, reprinted 1984. Used with permission of Jane Feather, copyright © Leonard Feather.

Foreword by Buck Clayton for *Billie's Blues: The Billie Holiday Story, 1933–1959*, a biography by John Chilton. Used with permission of Candi Clayton Bryson.

"A Crucial Engagement," by Bud Kliment, from his biography for young adults, *Billie Holiday*, by Chelsea House Publishers. Used with permission from Chelsea House Publishers, copyright Bud Kliment © 1990.

"Billie Holiday" by Max Jones, from his book, *Talking Jazz*. Used with permission, W. W. Norton & Company, Inc., copyright © 1987 Max Jones.

Excerpt from *Billie's Blues* by John Chilton.

"Billie Holiday: Storyville, Boston," a review by Dom Cerulli, *Down Beat* magazine, Nov. 30, 1955.

"Billie Holiday—Jazz Singing Pure and Simple," by John S. Wilson from *The New York Times*, July 6, 1958. Copyright © 1958 by The New York Times Company. Reprinted by permission.

Index

About the Editor

Leslie Gourse was born in Providence, Rhode Island, on January 1, 1939, and raised in Fall River, Massachusetts. After graduating from Columbia University's School of General Studies with a BS in creative writing in 1960, she published a novel, *With Gall and Honey*, with Doubleday in 1961, for which she had won an undergraduate award in 1959.

She pursued a career as a reporter, writing a news analysis show, "The Morning Report," for CBS Network News from 1966 to 1968, and social trends stories as a stringer for the national desk of *The New York Times* from 1970 to 1974. During those years, she contributed articles on jazz and Latin music to periodicals including *New York Magazine* and *The New York Times* Arts and Leisure section. In the mid-1970s, she concentrated more on jazz articles and in 1984 published a book, *Louis's Children*, about the history of jazz singing. A contributor to many music magazines, she received a Deems Taylor–ASCAP award for a series of articles on women jazz musicians. Among her ten published books about jazz are *Every Day: The Story of Joe Williams*, *Unforgettable: The Life and Mystique of Nat King Cole*, *Sassy: The Life of Sarah Vaughan*, *Madame Jazz: Contemporary Women Instrumentalists*, and, for young adults, *Dizzy Gillespie and the Birth of Bebop*, *Aretha Franklin, Lady Soul*, *The Tragedy and Triumph of Billie Holiday*, and *Mahalia Jackson: Queen of Gospel Song*.

In 1997 Franklin Watts will begin to publish a series of six books on jazz history by instrument written by Ms. Gourse for young adults. She is writing a biography of Thelonious Monk and compiling an *Ella Fitzgerald Companion* for Schirmer Books.